A Plain Language Handbook for Legal Writers

Christine Mowat, B.A. (HONS.), M.A.

CARSWELL

A THOMSON COMPANY

Canadian Cataloguing in Publication Data

Mowat, Christine
    A plain language handbook for legal writers

    Includes bibliographical references.
    ISBN 0-459-23907-4

    1. Legal composition.   I. Title.

KE265.M68 1998   808'.06634   C98-932650-0
KF250.M68 1998

The paper used in this publication meets the minimum requirements of the American National Standard for Information Sciences — Permanence of Paper for Printed Library Materials, ANSI Z39.48-1984.

Front cover illustration © The British Museum. Reprinted with permission of the British Museum.

About the front cover illustration
An octagonal cylinder with inscriptions in Assyrian, recording the campaigns, hunting expeditions and building activities of Tiglathpileser I , King of Assyria (1114-1076 BC). In 1857, The Royal Asiatic Society used this text (then still unknown) to test the validity of the decipherment of the cuneiform script. (British Museum; Department of Western Asiatic Antiquities; 911003)

 CARSWELL

A THOMSON COMPANY

One Corporate Plaza, 2075 Kennedy Road, Toronto, Ontario M1T 3V4
Customer Service:
Toronto 1-416-609-3800
Elsewhere in Canada/U.S. 1-800-387-5164
Fax 1-416-298-5094

To my children,
Carol, Alex, and Vicki

Acknowledgements

This book is essentially a collaboration. I am grateful, first, for my own education from authors in the international plain language community. I thank my business partner of years ago, Lorri Neilson, who helped ignite my passion for plain language writing.

Special thanks go next to the chapter consultants who generously shared ideas, time and materials. Thank you to my long-time friend Peg James, the consultant on the wills chapter, who has encouraged me over many years. Her initiation into the plain language world was co-instructing Wordsmith's legal writing workshops with me. Thanks to Mavis Nathoo, the municipal bylaw chapter consultant, for her tenacity and gusto as a plain language crusader at the City of Edmonton. Thanks to David Elliott—his moniker is Mr. Plain Language in Edmonton—who gently steered me through the legal landmines in the legislation chapter. Thank you to Jane Bergman, who consulted on the family law chapter twice, because in the interim the Divorce Act had changed! Thanks to Peggy Kobly who ably contributed to the collective agreements chapter in the midst of a busy law practice. Thank you to Cassandra Haraba, the release forms chapter consultant, who, as a new young lawyer, is dedicated to plain language. Finally, thank you to Susan Barylo, the Public Forms chapter consultant, for her conscientious plain language forms project with the Alberta government. All these consultants are what I call "plain language champions" in their respective fields. I am indebted to them for their generous sharing of knowledge and legal skills. The collaborations were satisfying and great fun!

A thank you to Susan Jackel, who provided valuable counsel on several chapters.

I also wish to thank my editor, Jane McDonald, who patiently believed in this book over many years, and Ottilie Sanderson, whose ingenious artistic eye translated my concept for the book into the fine cover design.

Thank you to Ross Campbell, and to Daltry Rose, Jozel, and Riel, for lovingly sharing my life through this process.

Finally, I am deeply grateful to Leanne Kisilevich for her painstaking and creative assistance in designing and implementing the form and specifications for this *Handbook*. Her humour and diligence are honoured here.

Whatever mistakes or weaknesses remain are mine alone.

Preface

This *Handbook* is designed to fill a gap in published writings about plain language for legal writers. Its intention is practical—to provide a workshop-in-a-book approach for lawyers, law faculty, and law students who wish to learn how to write legal documents in a clear and straightforward style. Though there is no specific chapter on judgment writing, judges may also find the book's plain language principles useful.

In 1978, Robert Dick described the state of legal writing as "word smog". Two decades later, there *has* been improvement, but the bulk of legal writing remains enshrouded in cant and verbosity. Law precedents are poorly written and designed, and, in general, legal writing still overwhelms the public. Few, if any, law firms in Canada use plain language strategies to improve their services or to market themselves. Few law students graduate with an informed vision of the usefulness and power of plain language for legal documents. The book sets out to overcome these obstacles.

The fact that the examples are *befores* and *afters* suggests that all plain language writing is derivative, but this is clearly not the case. However, much legal writing is based on precedent, and on cutting, pasting, and tailoring, and for that reason, comparisons are instructive.

In the *Handbook*, you will find theory, practice, models and resources. The first five chapters establish **A Context for Plain Language** for the rest of the book:

Chapter 1 compares definitions of plain language by leading thinkers in the field, includes a proposal to re-examine plain language from an interdisciplinary perspective, and suggests a *Handbook* definition for the plain language process the book teaches.

Chapter 2, using the paradigm of the *Communication Triad*, establishes a theoretical framework for readers to develop plain language documents. The theory comes alive through a prototypal analysis of the process of transforming a tired, traditional school consent form into a succinct and practical new design—one which parents will immediately understand and sign.

Chapter 3 investigates the ethical foundations of plain language and finds linkages between it and the just and democratic society.

Chapter 4 examines sexist language in legal writing and makes inclusive language part of a plain language approach.

Chapter 5 documents various methods of evaluating and field testing plain language documents.

The second section of the book, **Plain Language at Work**, applies plain language to key representative documents:

Chapter 6 examines wills projects undertaken by legal organizations.

Chapter 7 reviews one municipality's plain language initiatives with bylaws.

Chapter 8 tracks international developments with legislation.

Chapter 9 explores the benefits plain language brings to collective agreements.

Chapter 10 looks at *befores* and *afters* of two family law documents.

Chapter 11 tells the story of how a traditional garbled release form could be transformed into a clear document.

Chapter 12 researches various aspects of plain language forms including cost savings.

Finally, **Chapter 13** looks at key issues affecting the future of plain language.

The *Before* and *After* **Samples** section provides numerous real examples, either segments or completed plain language documents, to illustrate a range of excellent models.

The Plain Language Toolbox is a comprehensive 120-page set of practice exercises designed to help the legal writer self-diagnose strengths and weaknesses in writing, and overcome the problems. The book includes answers for all exercises. The exercises consist of *CLARITY* exercises, which teach the seven principles of plain language, and *Legal Wordskills* exercises, which cover everything from ancient language and substitutes to visual layout skills to the most common grammatical problems found in legal writing.

I am interested in your comments, criticisms, ideas, and plain language experiences. Please send them to me through the publisher at: Carswell Thomson Publishing, Suite 1200, 311 - 6th Avenue S.W., Calgary, AB T2P 3H2.

Table of Contents

A Context for
Plain Language

Chapter 1
Defining Plain Language

What this chapter does

This chapter:
1   describes the terms *plain English* and *plain language*
2   presents definitions of plain language from *Mellinkoff's Dictionary of American Legal Usage*, the Legal Writing Institute, Robert D. Eagleson (Australia), Richard Wydick (U.S.A.) Robert Dick (Canada), Michele Asprey (Australia), the Canadian Bar Association and Canadian Bankers' Association, Bryan Garner's *A Dictionary of Modern Legal Usage*, and from an interdisciplinary perspective, and this *Handbook's* perspective

> In an effort to clear up confusion (or ignorance) about the meaning of a word, does anyone ask, What is *a* definition of this word? Just about always, the way of putting the question is, What is *the* definition of a word?
>
> (Neil Postman: *The End of Education*, 1995)

This chapter examines perspectives and definitions about plain legal language to (i) familiarize students and legal writers with the history of plain language as an evolving discipline, and (ii) provide knowledge for its practice. As Neil Postman argues, our learning deepens when we know whose definitions are chosen, why they were created, and what alternative definitions may serve equally well.

Though much early writing about plain language uses the terminology *plain English*, the term *plain language* is less restrictive as it refers to other languages as well. The plain language movement began primarily in several English-speaking nations—the United States, Britain, Australia, New Zealand and Canada—but western European countries, Denmark and Finland, south-east Asian countries, India, China, Japan, Singapore, South Africa, and French-speaking Quebec[1] are participants in *plain language* initiatives as well.

Robert Dick's 1995 edition of his legal drafting text is now retitled, *Legal Drafting in Plain Language*. In 1992, *Mellinkoff's Dictionary of American Legal Usage* took 10 lines to define *plain language*, and only notes "See plain language" in his entry for *plain English*. Five years earlier, the only entry in Bryan A. Garner's *A Dictionary of Modern Legal Usage* had been *Plain English*. Joseph Kimble's *Plain English: A Charter for Clear*

---

[1] In The Canadian Bar Association and The Canadian Bankers' Association Joint Committee Report, *The Decline and Fall of Gobbledygook: Report on Plain Language Documentation* (Ottawa: 1990), pp. 32-36, the authors report that Quebec is already involved in plain legal language because (i) the Civil Code of Lower Canada and its amendments are written in a plain language style and (ii) Quebec legal writers have studiously avoided the grandiloquent style from France.

Writing[2] sets out the elements of a resolution later submitted to the Legal Writing Institute to support *plain English*. In July, 1992, members of the Institute changed the wording to *plain language*.[3] Interestingly, the wording of part of the resolution (see #2 in footnote 3 below) draws on the language of an early precursor of plain language texts, the 1963 *The Language of the Law*[4] by David Mellinkoff.

This chapter provides ten definitions or characterizations of plain language from internationally recognized experts. The final definition introduces the methodology for this book.

Definition I

plain language: an imprecise expression of hope for improvement in the language of the law. Criteria of plainness are not standard: e.g., "plain", "clear and coherent," "common and everyday meanings," "easily readable," "understandable", "understandable without the assistance of a professional"; patterns of typography; limits on syllables per word, words per sentence, and words per paragraph; and a host of specific do's and don'ts. In some jurisdictions, regulations and *plain language laws* require some sort of *plain language* in a variety of legal writings, e.g., consumer contracts, loan agreements, insurance policies, pleadings, regulations, statutes. *Plain language* is also referred to *as plain English*.[5]

I like this definition, and its emphasis. The difficulty of pinning plain language against exact measurements is widely acknowledged. Because the audiences, purposes, contexts, and histories of documents are unique, criteria for evaluating success are also variable. At the beginning of his dictionary, a fine reference for plain language legal writers, Professor Mellinkoff notes that American law dictionaries date back to 1839. His dictionary, he says, is new and different: most of it is written in ordinary English.

Definition II

In his charter on plain language,[6] Joseph Kimble cautions that if the idea of "definition" seems too strong or limiting, we should consider his elements as guidelines. Here they are:

---

[2] Joseph Kimble, "Plain English: A Charter for Clear Writing" in *Thomas M. Cooley Law Review*, Vol. 9 No. 1, 1992.

[3] The adopted resolution said: 1) The way lawyers write has been a source of complaint about lawyers for more than four centuries. 2) The language used by lawyers should agree with the common speech, unless there are reasons for a difference. 3) Legalese is unnecessary and no more precise than plain language. 4) Plain language is an important part of good legal writing. 5) Plain language means language that is clear and readily understandable to the intended readers. 6) To encourage the use of plain language, the Legal Writing Institute should try to identify members who would be willing to work with their bar associations to establish plain language committees like those in Michigan and Texas.

[4] David Mellinkoff, *The Language of the Law* (Toronto: Little, Brown and Company, 1963).

[5] David Mellinkoff, *Mellinkoff's Dictionary of American Legal Usage* (St. Paul, MN: West Publishing Co., 1992).

[6] As above, footnote 2.

The Elements of Plain English[7]

A. **In General**
1. As the starting point and at every point, design and write the document in a way that best serves the reader. Your main goal is to convey your ideas with the greatest possible clarity.
2. Make a table of contents for long documents.
3. Use examples as needed to help explain the text.
4. Whenever possible, test consumer documents on a small group of typical users.

B. **Design**
1. Use at least 8- to 10-point type for text,[8] and a readable typeface.
2. Try to use between 50 and 70 characters a line.
3. Use ample white space in margins, between sections and around headings and other special items.
4. Use highlighting techniques such as boldface, underlining[9], and bullet dots. But don't overuse them, and be consistent throughout the document.
5. Avoid using all capital letters, except possibly for main headings.
6. Use diagrams, tables, and charts as needed to help explain the text.

C. **Organization**
1. Divide the document into sections, and into smaller parts as needed.
2. Put related material together.
3. Order the parts in a logical sequence. Usually, put the more important before the less important, the general before the specific, and the ordinary before the extraordinary.
4. Omit unnecessary detail. Try to boil down the information to what your reader needs to know.
5. Use informative headings for the main divisions and subdivisions.

(The next four items apply to analytical documents, such as briefs and memorandums, and to most informational documents.)

6. Try to begin the document and main divisions with a paragraph that introduces and summarizes what follows, and states your conclusion.
7. Use a topic sentence to summarize the main idea of each paragraph, or a series of paragraphs on the same topic.
8. Make sure each paragraph develops the main idea through a logical sequence of sentences.
9. Use transitions to link your ideas and to introduce new ideas.

D. **Sentences**
1. Prefer short- and medium-length sentences. As a guideline, keep the average length under 25 words.
2. In most sentences, put the subject near the beginning; keep it short and concrete; make it something the reader already knows about; and make it the agent of the action in the verb.

---

[7] As above, note 2.

[8] With many typefaces, a 12-point is best. The *Handbook* is in 11-point Palatino and the quotations are in 10-point. Palatino is a relatively open font, however, which makes it easier to read in a somewhat smaller font.

[9] Note that underlining is now considered by computer specialists to be merely a typing device. See Robin Williams' *The PC is not a Typewriter* (Berkeley, CA: Peachpit Press, 1992), p. 25.

The Elements of Plain English (cont'd)

D.   **Sentences (cont'd)**
      3.   Put the central action in short verbs, not in abstract nouns. ("If the seller delivers the goods late, the buyer may cancel the contract. Not: Late delivery of the goods may result in cancellation of the contract.")
      4.   Keep the subject near the verb, and the verb near the object (or complement). Avoid intrusive phrases.
      5.   Put your strongest point, your most important information at the end.
      6.   Prefer the active voice. Use the passive voice if the agent is unknown or unimportant. Or use it if, for continuity, you want to focus attention on the object of the action instead of the agent. ("No more legalese. It has been ridiculed long enough.")
      7.   Connect modifying words to what they modify.
      8.   Use parallel structure for parallel ideas. Consider using a list or tabulation if the items are at all complicated, as when you have multiple conditions or rules.

E.   **Words**
      1.   Prefer familiar words—usually the shorter ones.
      2.   Avoid legal jargon: stuffy old formalisms (*Now comes; In witness whereof*); *here-*, *there-*, and *where-* words (*hereby, therein*); unnecessary Latin (*arguendo, inter alia*); and all the rest (*and/or, provided that, pursuant to, the instant case*).
      3.   Avoid doublets and triplets (*any and all; give, devise and bequeath*).
      4.   In consumer documents, explain technical terms that you cannot avoid using.
      5.   Omit unnecessary words.
      6   Replace wordy phrases (*prior to, with regard to, in the event that*).
      7.   In consumer documents, consider making the consumer "you."
      8.   Avoid multiple negatives.
      9.   Be consistent; use the same term for the same thing, without guilt.

                                                                            Joseph Kimble

---

Joseph Kimble has summarized a great deal of information in a useful manner in this charter.

Definition III

Robert Eagleson, linguist and founding member of the Australian plain language movement, traces the first contemporary plain language documents to 1975 in the United States and 1976 in Australia. Yet he earmarks the 1986 *Plain English and the Law* report published by the Law Reform Commission of Victoria (Australia) as giving plain legal writing a new lease of life. "In it," he says, "we established that legislation could be written in plain language and demonstrated that even highly complex laws could yield to plain expression. The one bastion of legalese that previously had stood outside the thrust for plain language was conquered."[10]

---

[10] Robert Eagleson, "Lawyers' Skills and the Success of Plain Language", paper given to the Legal Writing Institute, Tacoma, Washington, 1992 (in author's collection).

Definition IV

The next plain language definition reflects the advice of a New York lawyer who told young associates that ". . . good legal writing does not sound as though it had been written by a lawyer."[11] Richard Wydick's definition, the first part taken from David Mellinkoff's *The Language of the Law* (1963), is succinct: "[G]ood legal writing should not differ, without good reason, from ordinary well-written English. . . In short, good legal writing is plain English."[12]

Tautologous though it is, the definition points out that all the features of good writing must be observed to produce excellent plain language text. That is why Wydick devotes 25% of his book to punctuation. His other chapter headings represent practice skills for plain language writers:

> Omit surplus words
> Use base verbs, not nominalizations
> Prefer the active voice
> Use short sentences
> Arrange your words with care
> Use familiar, concrete words
> Avoid language quirks
> (e.g., sexist language, cosmic detachment, or elegant variation)

Definition V

In the third edition of his legal drafting text, Robert Dick declares that plain language principles and techniques apply equally to business writing and legislation. He continues:

Plain language advocates point out that plain language is not a restriction or debasement of the language. It should not be likened to "simple" or "simplified" language. Plain language uses the entire resources of the language and is the normal language in daily use.[13]

Dick considers the following design elements as integral to plain language drafting:

page layout	boxing or enclosing words
type fonts	use of bullets to enumerate
spacing	ragged right versus justified
underlining (for cautions, exceptions)[14]	right-hand margins
line lengths	appropriate use of colours
highlighting	perhaps two column formats

Definition VI

In 1991, Australian Michele Asprey added new dimensions to the international discussions on plain language:

---

[11] Richard C.Wydick, *Plain English for Lawyers*, 2nd ed. (Durham, NC: Carolina Academic Press, 1985), p. 4.

[12] Richard C. Wydick, *Plain English for Lawyers*, 3rd ed. (Durham, NC: Carolina Academic Press, 1994), p. 3.

[13] Robert C. Dick, *Legal Drafting in Plain Language*, 3rd ed. (Toronto: Carswell, 1995), p.1.

[14] In *The PC is not a typewriter*, as above, note 8, p. 25, Robin Williams says underlining is for typewriters; italics are for professional text.

Some people think that because plain language is simple, it must be simplistic—a kind of baby-talk. That is also wrong. Simple in this sense doesn't mean simplistic. It means straightforward, clear, precise. It can be elegant and dramatic. It can even be beautiful.[15]

Beautiful! Asprey opens the door to discussions of styles of plain language and the skills required to produce it:

In fact, we show our skill more keenly, more sharply, when we write in plain words. The frills, the frippery, the bells and the whistles are stripped away and what remains is pure and clear.[16]

At the end of her book, Asprey gives lawyers new support for plain language. She examines interpretation acts and rules to see if they are a bar to plain language and concludes:

. . . it is clear that the rules of interpretation do not create a context in which plain language drafting is dangerous. None of these rules says "words will be construed according to what they meant the last time they were used" or "traditional or technical words are to be preferred over new or simple words". On the contrary, all the rules are designed to operate only if what the parties have written is confused, contradictory, unclear, or does not reflect what they must have intended to write. If what is written is clear, the rules and maxims of interpretation simply do not apply.[17]

Definition VII

When the Canadian Bar Association and Canadian Bankers' Association published their report on plain language (1990), some of the features of plain language they emphasized came from research on the composing process:

Plain language drafting is a form of writing that focuses on the needs of the reader. This style of drafting proceeds from the premise that, in written communication, it is the duty of the writer to make the effort to convey meaning to the reader. The reader should not be required, because of the writer's laziness, to struggle with the meaning of the text.

Plain language drafting is a deceptively simple task that requires considerable intellectual effort in order to be done well. . . . It also involves a thinking and writing process that calls for discipline and time commitment on the part of the writer.[18]

Other features of plain language were drawn from reading research:

More than 100 factors contributing to reading difficulty have been identified in [reading] research. Vocabulary difficulty and sentence length are the best known of these factors. Other key factors are (1) the background knowledge of the reader, (2) whether the text is cohesively linked, and (3) how the text is organized.[19]

---

[15] Michele M. Asprey, *Plain Language for Lawyers* (Annandale, Australia: The Federation Press, 1991), p. 10.
[16] As above, pp. 4-5.
[17] As above, p. 169.
[18] As above, note 1, p. 1.
[19] As above, p. 7.

This attention to research in writing and reading brings into focus the first elements of an interdisciplinary approach to the study of plain language.

Definition VIII

Bryan Garner's *A Dictionary of Modern Legal Usage* is an invaluable resource for plain language writers. The book is equally helpful to American or British English users. Garner sees his dictionary as an instrument of reform which presents standards to enhance rather than destroy valuable nuances. He examines usages by lawyers and judges which are imprecise, ambiguous or incorrect, yet seeks to preserve "the rich differentiation in our legal vocabulary". He describes his approach as encompassing an *informed* conservatism. The book seeks to make legal writers "sensitive to the aesthetic possibilities of their prose, to goad them into thinking more acutely about what works in a given context, and what does not."[20] Under his entry on plain English, Garner refers readers to selected plain language texts for general drafting and for jury instructions.

Definition IX: plain language as an interdisciplinary study

Plain language writers draw resources and techniques from a broad set of knowledge contexts. For example, research in linguistics and psychology gives us information on how average readers read.[21] A comprehensive and scholarly analysis of relevant reading research is found in "The End of Legalese: The Game is Over".[22]

Plain language legal writers (either authors of text about plain language writing or writers who produce plain language documents, or both) integrate knowledge from numerous areas: rhetoric and composition theory, reading theory, forms design, writing-across-the-curriculum studies, communications theory, psycholinguistics, computer desktopping, business and government writing, legal drafting, the law as literature, legal ethics and substantive law. To think of plain language writing as an interdisciplinary study is a new idea, but one with strong foundations and exciting possibilities. Figure 1 on page 10 presents a diagrammatic of the rich contexts which nurture the plain language movement.

Writing has long been regarded as the mere handmaid of literature in university English departments; seldom is it seen as a separate discipline, even when classified under Rhetoric and Composition. In law faculties, the role of legal drafting is similarly undervalued. Substantive law takes centre stage, and legal writing training (or legal drafting as it is often called) is most often shunted to the margins of law programs.[23]

---

[20] Bryan A. Garner, *A Dictionary of Modern Legal Usage* (New York: Oxford University Press, 1987), p. xii.

[21] Veda R. Charrow and Myra K. Erhardt, *Clear and Effective Legal Writing* (Toronto: Little Brown and Company, 1986), p. 96.

[22] Robert W. Benson, "The End of Legalese: The Game is Over", *New York University Review of Law and Social Change*, Vol. XIII, No. 3, 1984-85.

[23] A survey of 13 law schools in Canada about approaches to teaching legal drafting showed that ". . . plain language drafting is not receiving much attention from legal educators." As above, note 1, p. 20.

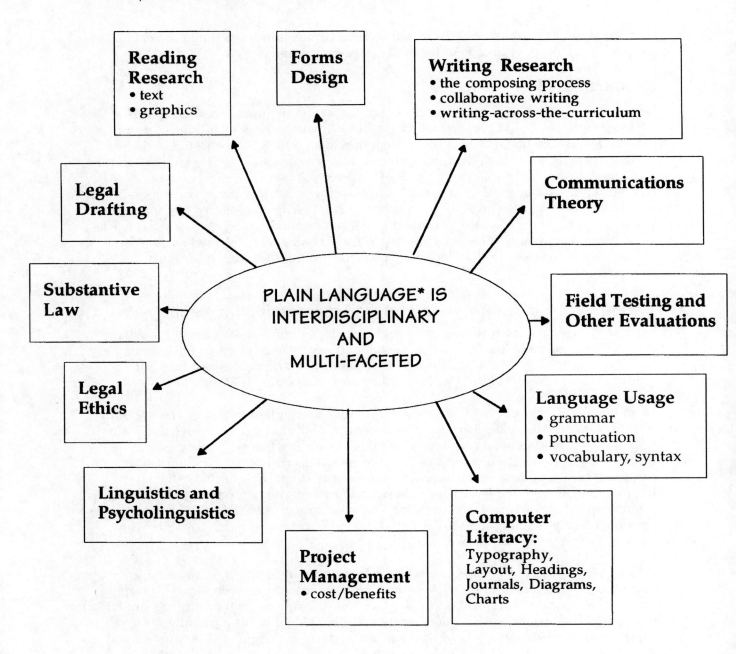

Figure 1: Diagrammatic of plain language and its contexts

*Plain language is both a method for writing and producing legal text and a descriptor for excellent reader-focused legal writing.

As long as writing in the universities is seen merely as supportive, and its value as a distinct field of study largely unproven, we seem to have a shaky beginning for exploring the interdisciplinary[24] aspects of plain language. Researchers in interdisciplinarity (I know—a very unplain word!) refer to the *de-colonizing* of disciplines and the emergence of new fields: American, Australian, and Canadian Studies; movements with transdisciplinary goals, the general science movement, general systems theory, and structuralism; and new scholarship movements such as Women's Studies and Afro-American Studies. The interdisciplinary character of these innovative studies may involve a political mission or a broad holistic impulse, or be problem-driven.

In time, plain language legal writing may take its place as a recognized interdisciplinary study. The evolution of the plain language movement reflects the character of our times, and is a response to the demands of consumers. It makes little sense to talk about plain language as though it were an entity separate from a growing human and community rights issue. Plain language has emerged from political, historical and global contexts. Acknowledging the interdisciplinary character of the plain language impetus may help to persuade more legal writers of its value. The goals of plain language reflect values that answer to all readers of legal documents, not merely to privileged, or exclusively legal, groups.

Neither philistine nor simplistic, plain language forms a nexus among several disciplines. Included in a later chapter are conclusions from reading research which are particularly relevant to producing plain legal writing. Though beyond the scope of this book, study of the composing process is a final strand in the interdisciplinary paradigm for plain language.

Definition X: The Handbook's perspective on plain language

The learning paradigm in this Handbook represents a final definition. It offers a method for studying and practising plain language and incorporates both theory and practice.

An analogy may help set the stage. The contrast between plain language documents and traditional legal writing reminds me of the difference between viewing an IMAX film and watching an ordinary one. In regular movies, there is always a frame and a smaller perspective to remind you, as spectator, that you are watching a picture that is not real. IMAX viewers, however, feel as though they are participants in the action. They are immediately part of the experience, and no obvious frame separates them from the reality of the action. Legalese frames and separates, too. The document stuffed with legalese and clogged with other features of an unplain style talks at, or down to, the reader, or cuts the reader out with elitist language. Instead, plain language involves and draws in its participants. Plain language is a kind of IMAX partnering with readers. The *Handbook's* theoretical context is based on the *Communications Triad*, explained and illustrated in the next chapter. Two sets of practical techniques from the Toolbox at the end of the book, CLARITY[25] and *Legal*

---

[24] Julie Thompson Klein's *Interdisciplinarity: History, Theory and Practice* (Detroit: Wayne State University Press, 1990) is a seminal book on the subject and a possible resource for creators of integrated plain language studies.
[25] See CLARITY guidelines on p. 52 and exercises on pp. 261-83.

Wordskills[26], provide guidelines and exercises. CLARITY (see table of contents) is an acronym that describes precepts for producing plain language documents. If plain language democratizes legal language for those who read and use it, then CLARITY shines light into the process of producing clear documents. Twenty-seven *Legal Wordskills* practice exercises and answers allow writers to identify their own weak areas and strengthen them.

---

[26] See table of contents for Legal Wordskills on p. x.

Chapter 2
The Communication Triad

What this chapter does

This chapter:
1   explores the foundations of plain language: interrelationships between the audience, purpose and message
2   reviews the shortcomings of a traditional release and indemnity form in light of the communication triad
3   provides an *Audience Questionnaire* to use before producing plain language documents
4   comprehensively analyses all the purposes for the release and indemnity form
5   includes an *Audience-sensitive Factors Checklist* for writing the message
6   discusses how the rewritten release message meets the audience and purpose requirements
7   may be used to introduce the plain language writing and thinking process to legal writers

---

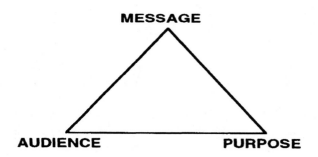

Figure 1: The Communication Triad

Lawyers unfamiliar with the complexity and interdisciplinary aspects of plain language may fasten on measurable surface matters such as short words or sentences. Yet legal writers need to understand the social function of language and to learn a range of communications skills. Plain language requires new educational initiatives informed by a theoretical context.

However, unlike reform movements in schools, with a back-to-basics emphasis on teaching school essays—a form students will almost never again use in the real world—the international plain language movement is immensely practical. It transforms real legal documents in a world of real human transactions.

Three components frame every act of writing. The communication triad (see Figure 1 above) consists of the **audience** (or more usually, audiences) *who* reads and regularly re-reads the document, the **purpose(s)**, *why* the document is written, and the **message**, *what* the content is and how it is presented. A legal writer's knowledge of the audiences (and the contexts) for a document should shape its purposes, and both audiences and purposes significantly influence the message—its shape and physical presentation, tone, length, kind and amount of detail, vocabulary and organization.

The invisible audiences join the writing process

Much legal writing is produced with only lawyers or the courts in mind. One result is that the parties to the document become almost irrelevant, ignored as outsiders or tourists. With plain language writing, a new focus on audience enables clients, consumers or the public to read documents as active and knowledgeable participants— or at least to have the option to do so.

"Who are you writing for?" is the first question plain language writers must ask themselves. It is easy to identify the audience for a letter describing the steps a client will take to participate in a legal action—one reader whom you have already met and talked to. But many legal documents have primary, secondary, and even tertiary readerships, readers their authors never know. As writers, however, we can make educated guesses about the categories of readers for their documents. We are familiar with the biases of joint venture partners, the needs of second language speakers, the vulnerabilities of single parents, and the range of reading abilities of the various publics legal documents serve. Unlike many historical legal documents, plain language documents do not exclude non-legal readers.

Share authorship with your readers

Once you have identified the readers for a document, you will need to "revision" or read your writing with your readers' eyes. Michele Asprey wryly directs lawyers to consider that audiences for their legal texts are most often "non-Roman non-lawyers".[1]

The following example, an Alberta school release form, is a document written for its primary non-legal audience. Parents were requested to sign the form before their children could participate in a weekend trip with the school choir. A rewrite of the form later in the chapter shows the dramatic difference that paying attention to user needs makes.

---

[1] Michele M. Asprey, *Plain Language for Lawyers* (Annandale, Australia: The Federation Press, 1991), p. 119.

FORM - *Before*

Release and Indemnity

Ensemble   Mountain Prairie School Youth Choir

Event   Crowsnest Pass Consolidated High School
                                       Friday, March 20 - Saturday March 21, 1998

Name of Ensemble
Member   _____

In consideration of the above named Ensemble Youth Choir Member being allowed to participate in the Event described above, I/we being the undersigned, being the parents(s) or guardian(s) of the Youth Choir Member, recognizing that there may be an element of risk of injury arising from participation in the Event, and arrangements related thereto, do hereby release the Ensemble, as hereinafter defined, Mountain Prairie School, and the Timbuctu School Board, from any and all actions, suits, claims and demands whatsoever, unless such loss or damages are due to gross negligence of the Ensemble or any of its supervisors.

In the event it becomes necessary in the judgement and discretion of the Ensemble or the Ensemble Member to receive medical or surgical treatment or attention, the Ensemble and supervisors of the trip may authorize the rendering of medical or surgical treatment or attention by or as recommended or directed by a duly recognized physician. In such event, I/we hereby release the Ensemble, as hereinafter defined, and the Mountain Prairie School and the Timbuctu School Board, from any and all actions, suits, claims and demands whatsoever, which may arise as a result of the said treatment or attention and further indemnify and save harmless the Ensemble and the School and School Board from all claims, demands, suits, actions or claims which may be brought as a result of such treatment or attention.

The expression "Ensemble" used in this document shall include the Mountain Prairie School Youth Choir, Mountain Prairie School, Timbuctu School Board, and any of their supervising teachers.

DATED at the City of Timbuctu, this _____ day of _____ 1998.

_____   _____

WITNESS   ENSEMBLE MEMBER

_____

PARENT/GUARDIAN

Literate societies are not always benign

Chronologically, the probable readers of this release would be a School Board representative, the principal, the teachers supervising the activity, students, and most importantly, the parents or guardians who have English as a first or second language, and a wide range of educational backgrounds and reading skills. Secondary audiences would be lawyers and the courts.

As is so often the case, this legal document has been written mainly for the secondary audiences.

Our literate society is not always benign: legal documents may reveal cultural and linguistic insensitivity, and subject readers to circuitous and legalese-laden prose, both of which present barriers to understanding.

Many of the release form's primary readers would have difficulty reading this form. For example, *release and indemnity, actions, suits, claims, and demands, in consideration of, thereto, hereby, hereinafter, said,* and *indemnify and save harmless* all belong to a dialect with which most parents are unfamiliar.

In fact, a weekend trip to the mountains with the choir *does* sound like a release—both for the parents and the child! How easy it is to misunderstand.

Such legal forms are not uncommon. Actually, the self-referential nature of any discipline may produce unplain language. In *Drafting Legal Writing: Practices and Principles* (1992), Barbara Child advises legal writers about the significance of audience sensitivity in the plain language drafting of an affidavit:

> You may want to change style and diction somewhat depending on the level of sophistication of the affiant [the primary reader], to the extent that you know it. Consider the ramifications of having an affiant sign an affidavit drafted in language that is incomprehensible to that person. Explaining it orally may help, but it does not prevent potential problems. *Moreover, plain language does not itself convey any lack of sophistication and may help to convey the authenticity of the statement.*[2] [author's emphasis]

Note that the authors of the release form overlooked most of the answers to the following audience questionnaire. The questionnaire focuses on readers' needs, interests, biases, contexts, and reading skills. The audience analysis is an important tool for plain language writers.

---

[2] Barbara Child, *Drafting Legal Documents: Principles and Practices* (St. Paul, MN: West Publishing Co., 1992), p. 78.

Audience Questionnaire for Plain Language Writers

Audiences may cover a wide ranges of readers: experts, technical specialists, professionals, lay readers, members of special publics or ethnic communities, the general public, and corporate, international, business, or industry professionals.

Identification

1. Who is (are) your primary audience(s)?

2. Who is (are) your secondary audience(s)?

3. Are there other possible audiences?

Note: Audiences may include a prime decision-maker who will read the document only rarely, and other readers who work extensively with the document. It may be difficult to delineate only one of these audiences as primary. Each audience brings different concerns and interests. Consider the rest of this questionnaire as referring to either an individual, more than one, groups, or all of these.

Role-related characteristics

4. What is the reader's role in relation to the document's content?

5. What are the reader's concerns and attitudes?

6. What role-related knowledge will the reader have about the subject?

7. How will your document affect the individual's family, staff, department, company, etc., and their roles?

Personal characteristics

8. What is the reader's relationship to the writer?

9. How prepared is the reader for the communication?

10. What is the individual reader's knowledge of the subject?

11. What are the reader's probable feelings or biases about the subject?

Language

12. Is English or French (or other language) a first or second language of the primary, secondary, or other audiences?

Reading Skills

13. Assess the reading skills of your readers according to the categories of uniformly high, uniformly low, or variable:

	Primary readers	Secondary readers	Other readers
Uniformly high	_____	_____	_____
Uniformly low	_____	_____	_____
Variable	_____	_____	_____

Background

14. What is the expected range of education, experience, and specific language background which might impede or help readers understand your text?

Needs

15. What background or contextual information do your readers need in the document?

16. What are your readers' purposes in reading the document?

17. Do they need a glossary of terms, or certain words or phrases translated?

18. Should you include the benefits (or detriments) of the program, policy or agreement?

19. Will your readers know the eligibility criteria?

20. Are deadlines spelled out?

21. What examples, explanations or visual aids do readers need to understand the text?

22. Are readers familiar with the format?

(Questions 15-22 are illustrative only. You will need to pose relevant questions about your own documents.)

Plain language makes purposes plain

Examining the purposes of the Alberta school release form shows how inadequate the drafter's audience analysis was. The School Board's lawyer clearly wished to protect the Ensemble Youth Choir, the School Board and the school from possible financial and legal risks. Legal protection became the main purpose for the form. Yet there are several other purposes:

1.   to gain the parents' understanding of the release and obtain their written permission for their child to take part in the weekend choir trip. Two key points are:

    •   to ensure that the parents have considered and appreciate the risks to which the child will be exposed by participating.

    •   to clarify that, in agreeing to their child's participation in the school trip, the parents are also agreeing not to take legal action against the school, School Board, or teachers if anything happened to their child on the trip.

2.   to give the teachers the authority to act on behalf of the parents in the case of a need for emergency medical treatment, and to have necessary information about the child to make medical action easy if required.

3.   to specify that the permission-giver has the authority to consent for the child.

4.   to create a document which will be understood, signed, dated, and witnessed.

5.   to convey all required information in a language and format which is easily accessible to parents with a wide range of reading skills and with English as either a first or second language.

Identifying a document's purposes and audiences helps determine the context and conditions for writing and leads to sound decisions about the message.

Note that several of the purposes for the trip release form have been overlooked.

The medium *and* the message are the message

The message is far more than mere content, as the old McLuhan saying "the medium is the message" helps to explain. Shaping an audience-sensitive message requires attending to many factors. A checklist follows.

Audience-sensitive Factors Checklist for Writing the Message

1. subject matter
2. level of complexity
3. amount of detail
4. voice and tone
5. format
6. point of view
7. length
8. vocabulary and diction

9. organization: order, openers, and closers
10. argumentative strategy or other rhetorical strategies
11. layout and design
12. graphics
13. editing and correctness issues
14. distributorship
15. document use

The text we read is linear, yet the composing process is not. Much of the writer's attention to these factors is unconsciously accomplished in cyclical, overlapping, and integrative patterns which are irreducible to recipe-like lists. You could use the list *after* writing a couple of drafts, or you could use the list items as prompts to create questions related to audience and purpose.

Now we can ask these questions about the school release form:

1. Does it clearly cover all matters necessary to achieve the many purposes of the parties involved?

2. Are the tone and language appropriate for the non-legal primary readers?

3. Is the organization and layout the most efficient for both the school who retains the forms and the parents who must read and sign them? etc.

The following rewritten trip release form is one attempt to respond to such questions. Notes after the rewrite explain how the relevant factors influenced message choices. The brief covering letter below provides an orientation for parents:

Dear Parent (or Guardian):

We need your written permission for your son's or daughter's participation in the event described on the attached form. The consent form is an important legal document. Please read it carefully, sign and return to us by _____.

FORM - After

Parent or Guardian's Consent Form[3]
(This form is to be filled out by one parent or by one guardian.)

(To be filled in by the school)

Event _____ Event Dates_____

School _____ Class_____

Student's Name _____

Address _____

Parent/Guardian's Name _____

Phone (home) _____ (work) _____

Child's Alberta Health Care Number _____

Event description and my permission
(School Name) has organized **(description of event)** to **(location)** from **(date)** to **(date)**. My daughter/son/ward, **(name)**, has my permission to participate in this event. I am aware that school teachers, **(names)**, will be responsible for the supervision, care and control of the students on the trip. I have read the **(number of)** information sheets sent by the school, and have noted the trip schedule.

I acknowledge risks
I recognize that when a student goes on a school-sponsored trip, there may be an element of risk of personal injury, death, or property damage, or loss.

My release of School Board and employees from responsibility for accidents
If anything happens to my child or my child's property on this trip, I agree not to hold the teachers supervising the trip, the school principal, or the School Board responsible, unless the injury, loss or damage is due to gross negligence[4] of **(name of school)** or its teacher supervisors. I am responsible for insuring my child and my child's property.

I authorize school supervision and permission of emergency medical treatment
In an emergency, my child may need medical or surgical treatment. If an emergency occurs, representatives of **(the school)** must make every reasonable effort to contact me. If I cannot be reached, or if the emergency demands immediate action, I give permission for one of the trip's supervising teachers to consent to emergency treatment of my child. Supervising teachers may also make other decisions necessary for the care, control, and protection of my child during the trip.

1 of 2

---

[3] The rewritten form draws on the work of the Alberta Law Reform Institute's Plain Language Demonstration Project #5.

[4] The Alberta Law Reform Institute's draft said "I will not hold them responsible even if they have been negligent." A drafter may wish to insist on this wording and a parent might reasonably object.

FORM - After (p.2)

MEDICAL CONDITION OF MY CHILD
I have checked one of the following:

As far as I know, my child is physically fit and able to travel to ❏
(location) for this school trip. My child has no special medical needs.

My child is not suffering from any medical condition that might ❏
prevent travelling to **(location)** for this school trip. I have described
my child's special medical needs in the space provided below.

_____
_____
_____
_____

Signatures

_____   _____
Date   Signature of witness

_____   _____
Signature of parent or   Printed name of witness
guardian with custody of child

SPECIAL ARRANGEMENTS CONSENT
**Complete this section only if your child will join or leave the group in
an unusual way**
The arrangements under which my child will join [ ] or separate [ ] from
the group during the trip are as follows:

_____
_____
_____

Signature of parent _____ Date _____
or guardian

2 of 2

Changes to the Parent or Guardian's Consent Form

Content
No permission was given by the parents in the original, so focused was the form on protection. In the rewrite, parents specifically give permission to the supervisors to deal with emergencies or supervision.

Layout
The desktopped rewrite with its reader-friendly layout incorporates audience perspectives and changed subject matter. Format segmentation allows quick topic selection.

Headings
The main heading or title, *Parent or Guardian's Consent form*, has changed to reflect the main purpose of the document in non-legal language. Other headings represent the primary reader's perspective by consistently using "*I*" or "*my*".

Headings are specific "storylines" which both conceptually and visually make comprehension easier. The type point size is increased to allow readers quicker and more selective reading.

The first heading provides a context for the document, and the next two headings stress parental acknowledgement of risk and consent to release the school from liability if anything unexpected happens. The last heading authorizes school supervision of emergency medical treatment.

Boxes of content
The shaded box (top page 1) responds to the school's need to quickly identify key information on trip participants. This solution allows easier filing for the school, and anticipates the practical steps in the case of an emergency—thus the inclusion of the child's Alberta Health Care Number.

The box on "Medical condition of my child" (page 2) makes the information on each child immediately accessible. If a child is on medication, that fact is noted here. The box also allows parents to detail even minor past or present medical conditions of concern. Such sensitivity to parent audience needs is absent in the original.

The final shaded box (page 2) anticipates variations in travel arrangements, and ensures that unusual arrangements are endorsed by parents.

Complexity, detail, length
Though the rewrite is longer than the original, the form's focus on parent-readers simplifies both style and substance, without sacrificing the required legal protection. The message is clarified with segmentation, elimination of repetition, and more accessible language.

Voice and tone
From a didactic voice replete with legalese in the original, the voice has become more personal and helpful in the rewrite. The tone suggests a collaborative approach

between parents and school. The personal pronouns and active voice help parents focus on their obligations and promises.

Points of view

There are two points of view: the first is the pervasive "I" perspective; at the same time, the school as a diligent caretaker is reflected in the three information collection boxes.

Vocabulary and diction

Plain language vocabulary replaces legalese. Sentences are significantly shorter: the two main paragraphs in the original contain one sentence each, the first with 99 words, and the second with 133. The average length of sentences in the rewrite is 22 words; paragraphs have two to four sentences.

Thus the readability level has changed from a grade 17+ level to a grade 10 level using Fry's readability formula (see chapter 5 for a discussion on readability in plain language). Verbs in both versions are in active voice.

Distributorship and use

The majority of students about whom the form is written will now be able to understand the trip release form. Even more important, the parents and guardians as signers will understand what they are agreeing to. Teachers will have a better understanding of their rights and obligations as trip supervisors, and principals and school boards will have a clearer policy protection for their teachers and students. Finally, school office staff will process paper work more efficiently.

Underlying every rewrite in the *Handbook* is an analysis based on the communication triad. You can extrapolate the underpinnings of this chapter to any plain language writing project. Apply the principles of audience and purpose to your plain language task, and create objectives based on the *Audience-sensitive Factors Checklist* (p. 20).

Chapter 3
Ethical Foundations
of Plain Language

What this chapter does

This chapter:

1 looks at historical and ethical roots of plain language
2 links the plain language movement to consumer needs
3 examines plain language as an open-door policy for the law
4 shows how poor legal writing affects relationships with the public
5 questions whether some legal writing is fraudulent
6 looks to signs of change
7 discusses possible sources of authority for plain language

In 1604, Robert Cawdry wrote the first English dictionary to explain foreign-derived words in "plaine English wordes, gathered for the benefit and helpe of Ladies, Gentlewomen, or any other unskilfull perfons".[1] Cawdry's motivation was to translate the classical legacy for those who had no opportunity to study it. His publication was an early plain language text. But not the earliest.

Tom McArthur, the writer who uncovered that fascinating bit of plain language lore, also put a bit of mid-14th century Chaucer into plain language for attendees at the National Plain English Conference held in Cambridge, England in 1990. Here is the poet Chaucer's host speaking to the academic, the Clerke of Oxenforde, and McArthur's rewrite:

BEFORE

Telle us som mery thing of aventures;—
Your termes, your colours, and your figures,
Kepe hem in stoor till so be ye endyte
Heigh style, as whan that men to kinges write.
Speketh so pleyn at this time, I yow preye,
That we may understonde what ye seye.

(Geoffrey Chaucer, *The Canterbury Tales*)

AFTER

Tell us something amusing and adventurous,
And keep back your special words and
flourishes,
And your figures of speech, for when you write
In the high style that men use to write to kings.
I beg you, here and now, to speak so plain
That we can understand just what you say.

(Tom McArthur)

---

[1] Described by Tom McArthur, "The pedigree of plain English" in *English Today: The International Review of the English Language*, Vol. 7, No. 3, July 1991, p. 15.

What the plain language movement today is advocating is similar: language which is professional and clear, and which uses natural, common words, more like those we hear in everyday speech. The "special words and flourishes" of traditional legalese isolate people from their rights and obligations. Plain language provides equitable access to the law.

Plain language reflects an empathy for readers. Its proponents believe it is desirable to be courteously clear to their audiences. Their function is not unlike that of Chaucer's host, making sure everyone is comfortably in-the-know. Plain language respects differing knowledge frames of non-legal readers; it overturns assumptions about what is "improper" or "unnecessary" for lay readers to understand. Plain language writers bring all the ingenuities of their language resources to bear on the production of documents.

Plain language is linked to consumer needs

In 1989, a fascinating international study which examined a large number of reports from Western European governments and universities was published. Its authors discovered that many citizens who have a right to social security benefits receive little or nothing of what they are entitled to. For example, in the Netherlands, 55% of those entitled to rent rebates do not receive the full amount; in Great Britain, 49% do not receive the family income supplements they are entitled to.[2]

Among the obstacles to social security entitlements the study identifies are a lack of knowledge of rights and difficulties with claim forms, both of which involve reading official or legal text.

In 1995, when a proposed *Canadian Endangered Species Protection Act* had been written, a member of parliament released an 18-page summary of the legislation so the public would be able to tell the government what they thought. This was necessary so the public could understand the law. It is a great irony of our Canadian democracy that we need English (or French) translations of our English (or French) laws to take part in our own societies.

The plain language movement is rooted in the consumer demand to democratize legal language. Criticism against legalese and poorly drafted legal text are often arguments which strike against the privatization of public knowledge—or at the least, privatizing knowledge which should be shared with relevant parties.

Plain language as an open-door policy for the law

Awareness that print is central to our justice system is making legal writers think about the importance of the literacy levels of their clients. Laird Hunter, former Chair of the Task Force on Legal Literacy for the Canadian Bar Association, writes:

> The dual nature of legal literacy must be understood. The connections between
> the ability to read and the ability to derive meanings from a legal context must
> be better appreciated. In coming to understand these relationships, the alliance

---

[2] Carel Jansen and Michaël Steehouder, "Forms as a Source of Communication Problems," *Journal of Technical Writing and Communication*, Vol. 22(2), 1992, pp. 179-180.

> between lawyer and client must be more effective. . . . Lawyers have a
> responsibility to recognize and deal with limited literacy as a problem of
> justice.[3]

Do not misunderstand. We cannot, nor should we, reduce all legal writing to a grade 4 or 5 readability level. But we can write most materials at a grade 8, 10, or 12 level, and we can provide client "translations" for lower-level readers.

Empathy for readers and its related access to the law form the ethical core of plain language.

The former British Columbia Plain Language Institute published a useful booklet on writing for adults who are new English speakers. Its authors argued that writers can make society more fair by adjusting texts to special backgrounds, abilities, and needs.[4]

How poor legal writing affects relationships with the public

A study on the readability of collective bargaining agreements from a wide range of unions in both the public and private sectors found that 95% of contracts analysed were either difficult or very difficult to read. The authors of the study suggest that the levels of obfuscation and evasiveness found in the documents could contribute to distrust between workers and management, and to an adversarial relationship. Further, they say:

> An unclear contract ultimately forces workers into a psychologically unsettling
> parent-child relationship with management and even with their union. Stripped
> of autonomy, workers must depend on management and the union to explain
> what they can do, what they can be punished for and what are their job rights.[5]

When a legal document is made understandable, and designed in a manner that allows ease of access to key information, the "voice" of the document is made human. The voice of the law then casts a more pervasive—and persuasive—net of meaning. Parties to agreements are more likely to trust each other and understand the implications of their promises. Clients, involved parties, and the public now share the keys to meaning with legal drafters.

We know that the lay public is often cowed by legal documents. Those used to legal language inadvertently impose it on others. As one writer has said of administrators of legal forms, and it applies equally to many legal writers:

---

[3] Laird Hunter, "A Lawyerly Reading — Please", *Law Now*, Vol. 17, No. 6, March 1993, p. 26.

[4] Plain Language Notes, *Plain Language and Literacy Series*, The Plain Language Institute (British Columbia), September, 1992. Their guidelines included:
1. When writing for First Nations groups, consult closely and hire them to do the writing or editing.
2. Consider translating into the group's first language.
3. Be sensitive to cultural backgrounds.
4. Accommodate different views.
5. Relate the visual image of the document to the cultural background of readers.
6. Avoid idioms, metaphors and words with multiple meanings.

[5] James Suchan and Clyde Scott, "Unclear Contract Language and its Effect on Corporate Culture", *Business Horizons*, Jan/Feb 1986, p. 24.

> The difficulty . . . is that they came from cultures that automatically place them at the centre of things: they are dominated by a lay tradition of imperialist ways of thinking which, irrespective of the ideological framework, creates the illusion that they are able, as if by natural right to impose their way of thinking on the world.[6]

When lawyers say, "I don't have time to rewrite a precedent for my client" ("sign it and trust me"), they disempower the client.

The use of plain legal language and a collaborative process is essentially about the way we as writers treat and think about others. An understandable document is humane. It can enhance or preserve relationships between parties. Being forthright or "plain" encourages dialogue and establishes trust.

Signs of change

Recently, one of Canada's most senior judges, Justice Frank Iacobucci of the Supreme Court of Canada, has criticized the legal profession for its growing preoccupation with making money.[7] He points to the focus on the bottom line and the business of law as major contributions to the poor public image of lawyers. Justice Iacobucci's suggestions include: (i) rethinking the concept of a "successful" legal career to be more humane and (ii) restating lawyers' values and goals as a profession to emphasize their role in the service of clients and society. Writing legal documents in plain language is an important step in achieving these objectives.

A Canadian Bar Association task force has recommended that the entire Canadian civil system needs to become more "user-friendly". They believe clients should know their options and understand the process right down to "seeing plainer language in all court forms and documents".[8]

In a move to humanize the courtroom, and as a consequence of the wrongful conviction of Guy-Paul Morin on a murder charge, the Ontario Ministry of the Attorney General has told prosecutors to address defendants by their proper names rather than as "the accused". Criminal lawyers have praised the change because "too often a jury or judge can lose sight of the presumption of innocence. . .". Another lawyer referred to the poisonous effect of having his client virtually nameless and ensconced in what is known as *the prisoner's box*.[9] In our rewritten Minutes of Settlement (see pp. 108-114) we have replaced the inappropriate *wife* or *husband* with names.

Are some kinds of legal writing fraudulent?

In law, as in ordinary English, fraud means gaining an advantage by deceiving someone. It is consistent with plain language principles to argue that legal language which is unintelligible to its readers may be a species of fraud. Some poorly written legal documents are evasive or clandestine or purposely garbled. The bulk of poor legal writing, however, is merely inept, hackneyed, and poorly organized. The

---

[6] David Sless, *A Matter of Position*, 1987 Presidential Address, Australian Communication Association, Canberra, Australia.

[7] "Justice vs. the Billable Hour", *Edmonton Journal*, March 30, 1998.

[8] From a presentation by task force member David Tavender, at a Canadian Bar Association meeting in Vancouver, August 1996, in reference to the Civil Justice Task Force Report.

[9] "Use Defendants' Names, Lawyers Told", *The Globe and Mail*, May 16, 1998.

deception from incomprehensible text is most often due to haste, carelessness, and habit.

Law firms develop and redraft precedents to save their lawyers' time. Yet most precedents in computer systems are not in plain language nor context-specific. There is a tendency for one-size-fits-all legal drafting and a subtext that assumes the public need not understand the intricacies of the law. For its part, the public often regards commonly-used precedents as necessarily complex and technical. Even the use of legalese is often accepted as beyond the grasp of most and only enforceable when encased in specialist language. Poor legal writing preys on this mythology. The best legal writing reflects an ethical assumption: that access to justice means accepting the public's right to understand.

From where is the authority for plain language derived?

Many have written about the threads that early plain language thinkers have woven over the centuries—from the 1380 John Wyclif translation of the Bible from Latin into English to Jeremy Bentham to President Carter's early seventies' plain language initiatives.[10] From the seventies on, it seems as though spontaneous plain language combustions have occurred in dozens of countries and thousands of organizations.

Nothing comes from nothing. As we move to the end of the millennium, social and political changes have spawned environments conducive to plain language. The fall of the Berlin Wall, the globalization of commercial transactions, the ending of apartheid and the growth of English as the international language of business have all expanded opportunities for the growth of plain language.

Lawyers' codes of conduct, the need for clearly communicating with clients, access to information legislation, plain language re-drafting of legislation and regulations, plain language projects related to literacy and access to justice, and government, non-profit and corporate plain language initiatives—all bear on the intent to make the law more understandable to the non-legal community it serves.

One could even argue that our *Canadian Charter of Rights and Freedoms* gives support to plain language law:

> 15. (1) Every individual is equal before and under the law and has *the right to the equal protection and equal benefit of the law without discrimination* and, in particular, without discrimination based on race, natural or ethnic origin, colour, religion, sex, age, or mental or physical disability. [my emphasis]

I believe the plain language conference in British Columbia, Canada, hit the nail on the head with its name: it was called "Just Language", a synonym for plain language.

---

[10] I am painfully aware of tromping ungenerously over others' detailed documentations of plain language history and developments. One of the best is Tom McArthur's "The Pedigree of Plain English", *English Today: The International Review of the English Language*, Vol. 7, No. 3, July 1991, pp. 13-19.

Chapter 4
Language, Gender, and the Law

What this chapter does
This chapter:
1 provides a rationale for inclusive language for plain language legal drafting
2 gives common examples of sexist language and simple alternatives, and examples of effective inclusive language
3 looks at why the masculine model has been perpetuated
4 reports on the singular *they* question
5 presents guidelines for using gender-neutral language

> The woman's search for self-identity has been seriously hampered by a legal system which designates her a "he" . . . Like institutionalized racism, institutionalized sexism is difficult to root out, especially if the language of sexism is perpetuated by the judicial and legislative institutions in our society.[1]

Inclusive language for plain language drafting

Politically correct is now a phrase with pejorative connotations. The labelling of a word or phrase as *politically correct* now implies there is no merit in its use. Political correctness is not the issue when promoting gender-neutral language—equitable treatment is. The issue is fundamentally a social and ethical one.

Research on the effects of sexist language is voluminous. The main tenets are:

1. Language is fundamental to our lives and to the ways we think and interact with each other. It is a key element in social evolution.

2. Language creates reality. Male-dominated language marginalizes and trivializes women, or makes them invisible.

3. Legal speakers and writers are seen as authoritative. Inevitably, they serve as models or set standards for others. Sexist legal language creates, reflects, and promulgates sexist culture.

4. Still entrenched in much legal writing, the linguistic habit of using masculine words to refer to both sexes reinscribes the view that women are secondary to men. Research concludes that the generic masculine is a false generic. It does not equally communicate the two genders.

5. For plain language drafters who write in an audience-sensitive manner, it is essential to update their vocabulary with inclusive language.

---

[1] Haig Bosmajian, "Sexism in the Language of Legislatures and Courts", *Sexism and Language* (Urbana, IL: National Council of Teachers of English, 1977), p. 104.

How common is sexist language?

Society regularly provides examples of violations of the now widely-accepted principle of non-sexist language. The reasons are complex: historical vestiges of the dominant masculine vocabulary in English, inadvertent use of sexist language, and habitual sexist precedents. Some fear that rewrites will be gracelessly unfamiliar.

The ghost of the false generic is a persistent and pernicious problem in business and legal writing. Generics are nouns and pronouns intended to be used for both men and women. Linguistically, however, some false generics are also male-specific, creating ambiguity and excluding women. Their continued use is incompatible with a gender-neutral language policy.

In legislation

It took the drafters of the *Alberta Individual's Protection Act* only 25 lines before they fell into the trap of the false generic—ironically, in the very clause that promised protection of equality before the law. In clause 3, we read:

> 3. No person, directly or indirectly, alone or with another, **by himself or by the interposition of another**, shall
>
> > (a) deny to any person or class of persons any accommodation, services or facilities customarily available to the public, or
> >
> > (b) discriminate against any person or class of persons with respect to any accommodation, services or facilities customarily available to the public, because of the race, religious beliefs, colour, **gender**, physical disability, mental disability, ancestry or place of origin . . . [my emphasis]

A simple substitute for **by himself or by the interposition of another** would be **as an individual, or as represented by another**.

In papal law

In his encyclical on the defence of life, Pope John Paul branded abortion as an evil "**no man** can justify" (*Edmonton Journal*, March 31, 1995). This example doubly denies the moral authority of women. **No one can justify** solves the problem, at least at the linguistic level.

In newspapers

A caption under a May, 1993 *Calgary Herald* photograph of the abortion crusader, Dr. Henry Morgentaler, proclaimed that he "believes in the **dignity of man** and that it is everyone's responsibility to create a better society." He "believes in **human dignity**" is just as clear and more appropriate.

In several following examples, the bolded version in parenthesis is a suggested gender-neutral alternative.

In the investment industry

Let us take the example of someone looking to run a business as an investment. **His investment considerations** (Gender-neutral: **Investment considerations**) are different. **He** (Gender-neutral: **The person**) compares the business with other options such as term deposits, GICs, T-bills, etc. . .

Some buyers would be prepared to pay for goodwill based on this formula: Take the net income on the vendor's income statement and multiply it by two or three. This means **he** (Gender-neutral: **the buyer**) will pay for two or three years of surplus income as goodwill. But is the vendor's income as shown on **his** (Gender-neutral: **a**) business income statement truly representative of what a purchaser would realize after the purchase of that business?

("The Real Value of a Business", *The Calgary Herald*, February 10, 1992)

In corporations

But restructurings are intended to be permanent; **a terminated worker is** (Gender-neutral: **terminated workers are**) told **he** (Gender-neutral: **they**) will never come back to his job (Gender-neutral: **their jobs**).

("Downsizing now as clean as expected", *The Calgary Herald*, March 10, 1992)

In the church

In 1990, an American Roman Catholic bishop's document, which took nearly nine years to prepare, referred to sexism in the Church as a sin and said women should be "equal as persons" in the church. In 1988, the Pope had said women could not become priests because Christ chose only men as his Apostles. The document also called for inclusive, or non-sexist, language in the liturgy. In a wonderful theological pun, the bishops write, "the church . . . does not consider **herself** (Gender-neutral: **itself**) authorized to admit women to priestly ordination."

("Pope Calls Meeting on 'Sin of Sexism'", The Calgary Herald)

How common is sexist language? Very. Yet, there are now many institutions and organizations with carefully drafted policies and guidelines exhorting writers to use equitable language. Two examples of public even-handedness follow.

From the Banff Centre for Management

An advertisement for a Vice President and Director for the Centre for Arts says:

The incumbent reports directly to the President of The Banff Centre . . . **He or she** is responsible for . . . The successful candidate will have a passion for the arts . . . **She or he** will have a strong sense of vision . . .".

(Personnel advertisement, *The Calgary Herald*, February 8, 1992)

From the Canadian Banking Association

The Chair and Chief Executive Officer's text to the annual shareholder's meeting included this:

> Dr. Tuchman notes that very early in **humankind's** long march of folly, the Trojans hauled the wooden horse inside their walls, even though they were warned it was a trick by the Greeks . . ."

From the Alberta Law Society

In 1991 the Alberta Law Society changed the sexist language of its oath for admittance to the provincial bar. Instead of swearing "not to destroy any **man's** property", lawyers now swear "not to destroy **anyone's** property". As the *Herald* editorial stated, with this newly worded oath, the Alberta Law Society has "relieved the province of a particularly hoary example of male exclusiveness and greatly advanced the cause of gender equality".

Why the masculine model has been perpetuated

Although Martin Cutts acknowledges the need for a review of sexist language in laws, he outlines the difficulties he had in writing his *Clearer Timeshare Act*:

> I cannot imagine that men would be happy if the dominant pronoun were *she* but there is no acceptable gender-neutral range of pronouns. As the *Clearer Timeshare Act* defines *customers* as private individuals, who cannot be corporate or unincorporate bodies, I have used an individual's title (e.g., *customer*) as the first choice term, then *he or she* in appropriate places. Elsewhere I have stuck with *person* and *he* as in the original Act.[2]

Here are some of the "he" examples with suggested changes:

Before	After
If an authorized officer of an enforcement authority has reasonable grounds for suspecting an offence has been committed under section 2, **he** may . . .	. . . under section 2, **that officer** may . . .
Before a seller enters into a timeshare agreement, **he** must give the customer . . .	Before entering into a timeshare agreement, **a seller** must . . . or Before **sellers** enter into a timeshare agreement, **they** must . . .
A certificate signed by or on behalf of the prosecutor, and stating when **he** discovered the offence is conclusive proof of that fact, unless the contrary is proved.	A certificate signed by or on behalf of the prosecutor, and stating **he or she** discovered the offence, is conclusive proof of that fact, unless the contrary is proved.

[2] Martin Cutts, *Lucid Law* (Stockport, UK: Spectrum Press, 1994), p. 15.

At times, it *is* difficult to refer to both genders together and requires careful and creative reshaping of syntax. Less acceptable is the view that gender-neutral language is unimportant. The need to draft documents to fit a changing society, our audience, is compelling. Michele Asprey writes:

> It seems pointless to try to resist the trend to gender-neutral language. Who can tell whether readers will be male or female? Why should we write assuming that the world is male when we risk offence by doing so? It is not always *easy* to make your writing gender-neutral, but is always *possible*.[3]

Can *they* be singular?

In 1985, the Ontario government instigated its gender-neutral language policy for all official publications, including bills and regulations. In 1988, the task of revising all statutes and regulations began. Since in law *person* refers to both individuals and corporations, the gender-neutral replacement would be *he, she or it*, a clumsy structure to say the least.

To merely replace the masculine singular pronouns, the Ontario drafters chose *he or she*. However, if a corporation were also involved, they decided to avoid the cumbersome word strings. Research showed that *they, their*, and *them* have a long history of use as singulars. The Ontario government decided to use these pronouns in this singular sense. Surprisingly, the proponents of this approach leapt one step further, a seemingly radical move that has happily produced no sound and fury. They write:

> Reflexive verbs remained a problem. Our research indicated virtually no commentary on whether or not *themself* was an acceptable replacement for *himself, herself*, or *itself*. After considerable debate in our office, we decided that this usage was a logical extension of the use of the other third person "plural" pronouns as singulars.

Shocking though this may seem (and it has taken me a few years to come around to accepting *themself*), the Chief Legislative Counsel for Ontario, Donald Revell, and his co-authors claim that there has been no adverse reaction to their efforts or to the government policy.[4]

The article ends with insightful conclusions:

> In adopting the new style we noticed two things. The first is that one must develop the self-discipline to use it. The second is that some clients must be educated to the fact that the *Interpretation Act* does not require us to use "he" for "she". We note that there have been no negative comments from the House, the press or the public with respect to the Ontario "non-sexist" style. Indeed, there have been almost no comments at all, which confirms our view that "he or she" is plain English and is taken for granted by users of our legislation.
>
> In our opinion, the use of a non-sexist style in English results in better drafting. The restructuring that becomes necessary to avoid repetitive

---

[3] Michele M. Asprey, *Plain Language for Lawyers* (Annandale, Australia: The Federation Press, 1991), p. 112.
[4] Donald L. Revell, Cornelia Schuh, and Michel Moisan, "Themself and Nonsexist Style in Canadian Legislative Drafting", *English Today: The International Review of the English Language*, January, 1994, pp. 10-11.

language or unnecessary pronouns often yields clearer, more concise sentences.[5]

Here is what the changed language looks like in law:

Tobacco Tax Act

1. In this Act,

"consumer" means any **person** who,

    (a) in Ontario, purchases or receives delivery of tobacco, or

    (b) in the case of a person ordinarily resident in Ontario or carrying on business in Ontario, brings into Ontario tobacco acquired outside Ontario,

for **their** own use or consumption or for the use or consumption by others at **their** expense, or on behalf of, or as the agent for, a principal who desires to acquire the tobacco for use or consumption by **themself** or other persons at **their** expense;[6]

(my emphasis)

Rules for gender-neutral language

1. *Drop **he** or **his** when the reference to both women and men is possible. Instead, use articles (a, the) or plurals.*

Before
Between a lawyer and *his* client, a physician and *his* patient, and a clergyman and *his* parishioner develop a relationship of trust and expectation.

After
Between a lawyer and client, a physician and patient, and a member of the clergy and parishioner develops a relationship of trust and expectation.

(or use plurals)

---

[5] As above, p. 17.
[6] *Tobacco Tax Act*, R.S.O. 1990, c. T. 10.

2. *Use gender-neutral substitutes if the job title could refer to both men and women.*

   Before
   It's the great secret of *doctors*, known only to their *wives*, that most illnesses get better by themselves.

   After
   It's the great secret of *doctors*, known only to their *spouses*, that most illnesses get better by themselves.

3. *Choose genderless vocabulary for job designations, descriptions of people, or legal principles.*

Before	**After**
manpower	personnel
workmen's compensation	workers' compensation
male nurse	nurse
female lawyer	lawyer
the doctrine of the reasonable man	the doctrine of the reasonable person
the prudent man	the prudent person
the average working man	the average worker
chairman	*chair, chairman*, or *chairwoman*, or *chairperson* as appropriate[7]
juryman	juror
statesmanlike	diplomatic, or tactful
landman	land manager
the man in the street	the average person
policewoman	police officer
mankind	humans, people
Dear Sir or Madam	Dear Householder, Resident, Coordinator of X, John Douglas or Eileen Hall
policemen manning an airport metal detector	police officers working at an airport metal detector
ombudsman	ombuds (example from a *Globe and Mail* ad, March 1998. The ad also used *ombuds* as an adjective as in *Ombuds Services*.

---

[7] Robertson Cochrane's "The Apotheosis of the Human Chair" in *The Globe and Mail*, October 22, 1994, documents how the metaphorical use of chair for the position dates back to 1658. We need no longer be cowed by those who claim that people cannot be pieces of furniture.

4. *Do not use this sexist boilerplate, sadly still seen in many legal documents:*

   Before
   . . . and the masculine shall be construed as meaning the feminine or a body corporate as the sex or context requires.

   After[8]
   In most cases, you can use the appropriate gender instead of relying on this artifical rule of construction. If not, try this:

   "*Person* includes a corporation."

   or

   "Words indicating male persons include female persons and words indicating female persons include male persons. Words indicating either sex include corporations."

5. *Use the plural form when appropriate.*

   Before
   A researcher must have the resources to continue *his* critical work.

   After
   Researchers must have the resources to continue their critical work.

6. *Avoid ambiguous plurals, however.*

   Before
   A person with a handicap may file an affidavit to support *his* application for exemption.

   After (Ambiguous plurals)
   Persons with handicaps may file affidavits to support applications for exemption.

   The pluralized version suggests a person must have more than one handicap.

   Better
   Handicapped persons may file affidavits to support their applications for exemption.

As Mellinkoff notes, centuries of male-dominated society have pervasively affected the language of the law. Some old-form usage is so standard that its sexist consequences are forgotten, ignored, or denied.[9]

The final word on the issue of gender and legal language goes to the newsletter of the Centre for Plain Legal Language:

> Today it is commonly understood that sexist language is offensive. But sexist language is also inefficient. It threatens to alleviate at least half (but usually

---

[8] David Elliott, "Writing Wills in Plain Language", a paper presented to the Canadian Bar Association (Alberta Branch) Wills and Trusts Section, Edmonton, June, 1990, p. 16-17.

[9] David Mellinkoff, *Mellinkoff's Dictionary of American Legal Usage* (St. Paul, MN: West Publishing Co., 1992), p. 600.

more) of a document's intended audience. In legal terms, sexist language is imprecise and leads to uncertainty.

Sexist language says something about the writer of the document. A sexist document usually means that its writer has given it little thought. The most common justifications given by lawyers for using sexist language are habit and convenience. This also tells us the writer is lazy. [10]

Scrupulous attention to rewriting sexist legal language creates language which is more accurate, and ultimately, more just.

---

[10] Arthur Spyrou, "Avoid Sexist Language", *Explain, Newsletter of the Centre for Plain Legal Language*, Sydney (Australia), December 1995, p. 2.

Chapter 5
Testing & Evaluation

What this chapter does
The chapter:
1 discusses why testing matters in the plain language context
2 charts ten tests for plain language documents
3 describes decision steps for testing
4 briefly looks at individual tests, group tests, questionnaires, and pretesting
5 examines readability formulas
6 compares advantages and disadvantages of comprehension tests
7 realistically faces the "no test" syndrome
8 provides a CLARITY checklist for use in testing precedents or documents in your organization

Testing of legal writing matters

Perhaps more than ever, financial accountability governs corporate and government decisions today. Plain language advocates and specialists, too, are often asked to test their products before sending them out into the world. Decision-makers insist on documents that make a difference, are more useful to clients, or more readily accepted by specialist audiences or the public. They may ask for "proof" that documents save money and time or present a new, more striking image for their organizations.

Apart from fiscal matters, there is an emerging awareness in the legal community of the need for ethical accountability. Members of the public need to understand judges and lawyers. For example, references later in this chapter on the urgency for plain language jury instructions came about only as a result of careful testing.

Interest in diagnostic techniques is now reflected in computer software which allows users to quickly obtain word counts, identify passive verbs, and find a limited number of grammatical problems. Important as these are, focusing merely on countable issues may blind writers to the need for a more comprehensive assessment of plain language features. Rhythm, grace, clarity, organization, tone, format and audience sensitivity are less easily digitized and programmable. These factors require descriptive tests which are more subjective. Some techniques described below require the intuition and heightened sensibility to language use which comes from skilled and experienced readers. Yet the choice of methods and the details offered should enhance any legal writer's ability to assess the success of a document.

Charting test options

Testing is only one of many words we could use for assessing plain language projects. Plain language audits, evaluations, usability testing or field testing are all ways to describe similar processes. Tests reassure us that readers understand (or they're confused), that key information is easy to find (or it's not), or that we do have to hire extra staff to answer telephone and personal inquiries (or we don't).

The chart below maps a range of testing choices:

Ten Tests of Plain Language Documents

(any of these may vary from formal to informal, brief to extensive, and inexpensive to costly)

1. *One-on-one* feedback (could be by a plain language specialist, a subject specialist, or an intender reader, or all)

2. *Before* and *After* data collection on whether fewer phone calls or questions. You could also document positive and negative responses.

3. *Talk-aloud protocols with potential readers* who describe the materials in their own words

4. *Reactions or written comments from in-the-know readers* (possibly colleagues, too)

5. *Structured discussion group* with document's potential readers

6. *Questionnaires* to selected focus groups

7. *Site testing* with targeted audiences

8. *Before* and *After* analysis (if project involves a rewrite)

9. *Computer tools and readability formulas,* computer counts of passive voice, etc.

10. *CLARITY Checklist* (may be used in tandem with other methods. This *Checklist* appears on p. 52.

Decisions for testing

1. **Decide what sort of reader(s) to test the document on**
   Clarify the relevant characteristics of your readers—their educational range, language spoken, gender, age, economic status, knowledge of the relevant law, family status and special needs. If there are two parties to an agreement, management and union readers, for example, you will need representatives from both groups. Think about whether a small or large number is best.

2. **Establish the time and budget constraints for the testing**
   Whether you obtain one-on-one feedback from one client or colleague or a wider assessment from a large focus group is governed by the tester's time and budget. Think about how you might enhance the credibility of the document by the scope and type of your test.

3. **Design the test**
   Whether designing guide questions for a one-to-one or structured group discussion or for a questionnaire, you need to establish what type of feedback you want. Think about questions related to content, organization, tone,

appearance, layout and visuals, and language. Consider open-ended questions on additions, deletions, or style issues.

4.   Identify actual participants for the testing

One field testing guide on plain language projects[1] notes the difficulty in finding people willing to participate in the testing. The authors suggest contacting community groups, church groups, service organizations, self-help or advocacy groups, literacy groups or ESL classes. To those, I would add colleagues, law students or faculty, bar associations, legal aid societies and other relevant professional organizations. Goldsmith et al suggest that it is easier to find participants for testing if they have been involved in the early stages of the document. For example, if you asked parents for their input on an original parent consent form, you will have their buy-in to contribute to later testing. You may entice people or organizations to participate in testing by offering them resources or a service, a talk, or an article on a legal topic.

5.   Tell the participants[2]

- you are testing your materials, not the participants
- there are no wrong answers
- they are the experts
- their contribution is wholly voluntary
- their feedback will make the document better or establish that it is already sound
- exactly how much time the test will take
- what type of test it will be (if it will not skew your results)
- if they need to read the material beforehand
- you may ask for personal information to prepare a participant profile
- if necessary, that their feedback will remain confidential (you could use a code identifier for each person)
- they can highlight on their copy of the document parts they don't understand, language which slows them down, or parts they particularly like

Individual Tests

The Goldsmith field testing guide provides three ways to test a document with individuals:

(1) using fictional scenarios which describe a problem the tested person imagines he or she is experiencing

(2) if relatively brief, asking a person to summarize what the material says, or

(3) asking readers questions to assess their levels of understanding

---

[1] Penny Goldsmith, Gayla Reid, and Sidney Sawyer, *Reaching your readers: a field testing guide for community groups* (Vancouver: Legal Services Society of B.C., 1993), p. 7.
[2] Most of these suggestions are made by Goldsmith et al.

Group Tests

A skilled, neutral facilitator will help ensure a test's success. Beware of the effect that strong individuals may have on others if the test is an oral discussion. You can have someone else tape the discussion or record comments. If the group is large, break it into smaller discussion groups which report back. You may wish to have hard copies of questions for all participants.

The following shows the changes resulting from group testing a welfare rights booklet:[3]

Original cover   Revised cover

Figure 1: Welfare Rights Booklet

FIELD TESTING PARTICIPANTS SAID:
- cover should say that the publication is free
- title should stress "rights" not "information"
- maybe a picture on the cover would make it friendlier-looking

Questionnaires

The traditional methods for designing questionnaires include:

- open-ended questions. (Ask for personal views. Descriptive data may be valuable but hard to quantify)
- closed questions (*yes/no*, for example)
- scaled evaluations (*too difficult, just right, too easy*, etc.)

---

[3] The Welfare Rights and GAIN *before* and *afters* are reproduced with the permission of The Legal Services Society (B.C.) and contained in *Reaching your readers: a field testing guide for community groups* by Penny Goldsmith et al.

- multiple choice (time consuming to construct as they need carefully thought out detractors. However, they allow discriminating questions on content. They may be too "school oriented" for some.)

Pre-testing

You may need to pre-test the test! The answers may not provide the type of help you need. Or the test itself could be poor.

Readability formulas

Readability formula testing is the best known test for plain language. When Canada's Charlottetown Accord was soundly defeated, I assessed the readability of the document that was presented to the Canadian public to vote on. The complexity of presenting so many key national issues was exacerbated by the grade 17+ readability level.

Readability formulas have existed for over 75 years and nearly 40 formulas were published between 1928 and 1959.[4] Presently, there are about 100 recognized readability tests.[5] Nearly all are based on at least these factors: syllables or letters per word, sentence length and sentence type. The anomaly among readability methods is the *cloze procedure*. In close testing, you usually delete every fifth word but leave standard-sized blanks. Then readers fill in the blanks by guessing what was deleted. The higher the number of correct guesses, the higher the comprehension. *The Handbook of Reading Research* contains nearly 300 references to research on readability.

Below I reproduce one readability formula because:

1. It is the easiest to use.
2. Its author, Dr. Edward Fry, expressly encourages its publication.

As you will see, the test is a simple matter of tabulating the average number of syllables and the average number of sentences in three 100-word passages, then plotting the grade level from a graph. If the passage is less than 300 words, Dr. Fry provides another method.[6]

---

[4] Richard L. Venezky, "The History of Reading Research" in *Handbook of Reading Research*, ed. P. David Pearson (New York: Longman, 1984), p. 25.
[5] Carl Felsenfield and Alan Siegel, *Writing Contracts in Plain English* (St. Paul, MN: West Publishing Co., 1981), p. 224.
[6] Presented in "A readability formula for short passages", *The Journal of Reading*, Vol. 33, No. 8, May 1990, p. 595.

GRAPH FOR ESTIMATING READABILITY —EXTENDED

by Edward Fry, Rutgers University Reading Center, New Brunswick, N.J. 08904

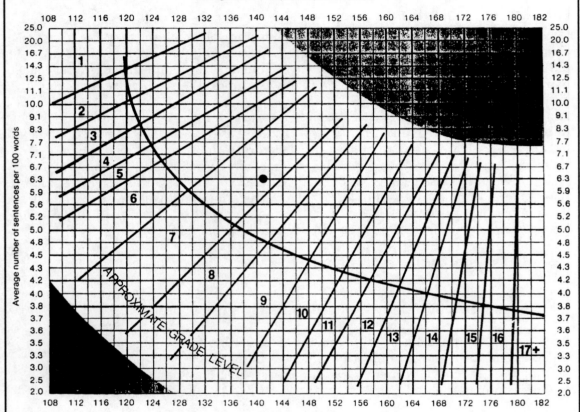

Average number of syllables per 100 words

DIRECTIONS: Randomly select 3 one hundred word passages from a book or an article. Plot average number of syllables and average number of sentences per 100 words on graph to determine the grade level of the material. Choose more passages per book if great variability is observed and conclude that the book has uneven readability. Few books will fall in gray area but when they do grade level scores are invalid.

Count proper nouns, numerals and initializations as words. Count a syllable for each symbol. For example, "1945" is 1 word and 4 syllables and "IRA" is 1 word and 3 syllables.

EXAMPLE:

	SYLLABLES	SENTENCES
1st Hundred Words	124	6.6
2nd Hundred Words	141	5.5
3rd Hundred Words	158	6.8
AVERAGE	141	6.3

READABILITY 7th GRADE (see dot plotted on graph)

For further information and validity data see the Journal of Reading December, 1977.

RUTGERS
THE STATE UNIVERSITY
OF NEW JERSEY

READING CENTER

GRADUATE SCHOOL OF EDUCATION • 10 SEMINARY PLACE • NEW BRUNSWICK • NEW JERSEY 08903

EXPANDED DIRECTIONS FOR WORKING READABILITY GRAPH

1. Randomly select three (3) sample passages and count out exactly 100 words beginning with the beginning of a sentence. Do count proper nouns, initializations, and numerals.

2. Count the number of sentences in the hundred words estimating length of the fraction of the last sentence to the nearest 1/10th.

3. Count the total number of syllables in the 100-word passage. If you don't have a hand counter available, an easy way is to simply put a mark above every syllable over one in each word, then when you get to the end of the passage, count the number of marks and add 100. Small calculators can also be used as counters by pushing numeral "1", then push the "+" sign for each word or syllable when counting.

4. Enter graph with average sentence length and average number of syllables; plot dot where the two lines intersect. Area where dot is plotted will give you the approximate grade level.

5. If a great deal of variability is found in syllable count or sentence count, putting more samples into the average is desirable.

6. A word is defined as a group of symbols with a space on either side; thus, "Joe," "IRA," "1945," and "&" are each one word.

7. A syllable is defined as a phonetic syllable. Generally, there are as many syllables as vowel sounds. For example, "stopped" is one syllable and "wanted" is two syllables. When counting syllables for numerals and initializations, count one syllable for each symbol. For example, "1945" is 4 syllables and "IRA" is 3 syllables, and "&" is 1 syllable.

FOOTNOTE: This "extended graph" does not outmode or render the earlier (1968) version inoperative or inaccurate; it is an extension.

In *Writing Contracts in Plain English*, Carl Felsenfield and Alan Siegel document the widespread use of Flesch's readability formula in early plain English laws in the late 70s and 80s in the U.S.A. These were a direct outgrowth of legislation proposed by life insurance agencies. The Flesch formula is also one of the best known.

In their analysis, Felsenfield and Siegal refer to mathematical reading formulas as objective standards. However, they acknowledge the weaknesses of readability tests—they tell us nothing about content, logic, organization, interest level, grammar, whether the ideas or vocabulary is familiar to readers or whether the content makes sense at all. To show how restrictive the readability formula is, I give my workshop participants a telling example. The famous Cartesian dictum, "I think; therefore, I am" is at grade one readability level. Yet these are, historically, two of the most complex thoughts penned in conjunction with one another.

Readability measurement has been used most by educators for text selection, by school librarians, by College Entrance testing, and by literacy organizations. Edward B. Fry documents uses of readability formulas in business (insurance, health, and banking industries), in court cases, in government, and the publishing industry.[7]

Readability formulas that translate readily to grade levels help us quickly establish whether documents are too difficult for specialized publics, for example.[8] Whatever faults readability formulas have, they are firmly ensconced in the educational and plain language contexts. They provide one quick type of benchmark to justify changing our documents.

---

[7] Edward B. Fry, "The varied uses of readability measurement today", *Journal of Reading*, January 1987, Vol. 30, No. 4, pp. 338-343.

[8] The notion that newspapers were written at a grade 8 readability level was bandied about for years. We now know that the readability levels vary widely, and appropriately so. Skill in reading is based on more than educational levels — among the factors are interest, prior knowledge and motivation. Documents produced at too low a readability level may ironically be difficult to process because of their segmented, choppy style.

Comparing comprehension test results

The following table briefly describes the advantages and disadvantages of some tests on comprehension:

	Advantages	Disadvantages
Multiple choice tests	• easy to score • allows quick content testing	• difficult to create valid questions • time-consuming to create distractors
Oral questioning (paraphrase or "tell in own words")	• effective in obtaining a mirror of a reader's understanding • individual testing comes close to a real situation • easy to set up: just need one or more people to review the material from a user's perspective	• answers dependent on the structure of the question • examiner's bias may subtly influence the respondent through body language or intonation • respondents have diverse abilities in expressing what they have understood • time-consuming • may be too dependent on examiner's view of the "right" answer
Cloze procedure[9]	• easy to apply • tests only the materials, not the questions or the examiner's bias	• because good readers make better use of contextual information, they are more successful on close tasks • younger and poorer readers are less efficient in using context as predictors

Because close procedure simply gives raw numbers, not a level of difficulty, it must be correlated to some other scale of difficulty. Robert Benson shows that extensive research variations in administering close procedures demonstrate that results of close testing have highly significant and positive correlation coefficients with scores on both multiple choice comprehension tests and oral reading tests.[10]

When Benson wrote his now famous article, there was no research using close testing on legal materials. Therefore, he set up two large-scale tests with 90 law students and 100 non-lawyers. Included in the test passages were standard and plain language jury instructions, a statute and a consent-to-surgery form widely used in American hospitals.

---

[9] *Cloze procedure* is based on the Gestalt psychology principle that there is a human tendency to mentally "close" a gap in a picture of an incomplete circle to make it conform to the conventional whole circle. Similarly, we "close" gaps in language to conform to familiar meanings if words are deleted. This explains why proofreading is different from reading for meaning.

[10] Robert W. Benson, "The End of Legalese: The Game is Over", *New York University Review of Law and Social Change*, Vol. XIII, No. 3, 1984-1985, pp. 538-540.

The results of Benson's experiment were:

• 100 non-lawyers (highly educated) could understand only the plain language jury instructions. Their results correlated to an A on a traditional test. Benson concluded that complex legal ideas can indeed be written clearly. Also, tests may be administered to demonstrate that.

• the non-lawyer respondents showed poor comprehension of the old jury instructions and the hospital consent form and dropped to frustration level with the statute.

• the law students, as Benson expected, understood all passages well.

Benson gives other examples of the results of testing readers' comprehension of jury instructions and concludes, "They all point to the same sobering conclusion reached by the Loyola close test of jury instructions: extremely high percentages of jurors do not understand jury instructions".[11] The research also showed that oral jury instructions can be improved if delivered in plain language, but still comprehension is low enough to cause grave concern. Yet readers understood, almost fully, plain language written instructions.

Can you forget about testing?

Many do because of constraints on time, and money, and interest. After training in plain language techniques, the Alberta Association of Registered Nurses sent out 25,000 new legal registration forms[12] without field testing at all. They report that they have had only positive feedback and that people keep phoning to say how much they like the new form. The registrar says that the registration form allows better data collection and is easier to administer. After all, to most of us, the benefits of plain language are intuitive.

But tests provide evidence for the plain language case. Joe Kimble, a plain language legal writing professor, has summarized 25 studies on the benefits of plain language. The summaries, he says, show conclusively that plain language works.

Here are five examples of his summaries of test results of plain language projects:

(1) **One form letter × thousands**
The savings on one rewritten form letter in the U.S. Department of Veteran Affairs (VA) was $40,000. (And the VA sends out thousands of different letters.)

(2) **U.K. Forms Simplification Project Tests**
This was probably the most extensive forms project ever by the British Government. Between 1983 and 1985, the government had scrapped 15,700 types of forms, improved another 21,300 and reviewed 46,900. Estimated cost savings to departments was 9 million pounds. For example, a legalistic "Notice Claiming the Right to Buy" had its error rate to one London borough reduced from 60% to 5%.

---

[11] Robert W. Benson, as above, p. 545.
[12] The previous registration form was a two-sided 8½ by 11" form pock-marked with tiny typeface, a mishmash of boxes, and packed with long sentences and unnecessary legalese.

(3)   The classic American test of lawyers and judges themselves: what do they prefer?

Joe Kimble and Joseph A. Prokop Jr. tested 425 Michigan judges and lawyers on preferences between two versions of six different paragraphs from various legal documents. (Neither the word "legalese" nor "plain language" appeared in the survey or the covering letter.) The test was replicated in Florida, Louisiana, and Texas, with only judges in the latter two States. The results were startling. In all four states, " . . . [lawyers and judges] preferred the plain language versions by margins running from 80% to 86%. A slam dunk."[13]

(4)   Apellate documents

This was a test on two versions of two paragraphs from appellate documents by California Court of Appeal judges and research attorneys. By statistically significant margins, readers rated the passages in legalese as substantively weaker and less persuasive than the plain language versions.

(5)   Court rules

In April 1998, the U.S. Supreme Court gave final approval to "a remarkably progressive set of court rules", the Federal Rules of Appellate Procedure, revised as a possible first set toward redrafting all the federal court rules.[14] Rather than formal testing, committees of judges and lawyers reviewed the drafts and suggested improvements.

These examples are just a few of the thousands of international results of carefully designed and tested or evaluated projects. Of course you may ignore the last "test" stage. But such final "proof" cumulatively persuades others of the value of plain language.

CLARITY Checklist

The Handbook's CLARITY Checklist follows. You may use it to assess old documents, as a progress check in the early draft stages or as a final audit or the hoped-for last draft. Law students may even use it for academic papers.

---

[13] Joseph Kimble, "Writing for Dollars, Writing to Please", *The Scribes Journal of Legal Writing*, Vol. 6, 1996-1997, pp. 19-20.

[14] As above, p. 23.

CLARITY Checklist
A plain language checklist for legal writers

C Conciseness
1. Keep sentences brief when possible. A good rule of thumb is to keep sentences between 15-30 words.
2. Segment long sentences reflecting complex relationships between ideas: colons and semicolons partition ideas well.
3. Prune out deadwood language; reduce phrases to one word.
4. Head documents of four or more pages with summaries (5 -10% of length).
5. Provide succinct numbered action statements and recommendations.

L Lean and Lively Language
1. Create maps for your readers with subject headings and tables of contents that tell your story.
2. Purge your language of legalese (including the "unholy" doublets and triplets), gobbledegook, office jargon, inappropriate technical jargon, and redundancies.
3. Use language which is familiar yet used in a fresh and interesting manner.

A Active Voice
1. Use active voice verbs for directness, whenever possible. Passive verbs can be ambiguous and distancing.

R Regular and Reasonable
1. Review your document for any non-standard usages; use the Legal WORDSKILLS to help identify problems.
2. Consistently refer to a comprehensive and up-to-date dictionary (not more than three or four years old).
3. When in doubt, check style and grammar issues in a modern usage manual.
4. Ensure your document is written in complete sentences and properly punctuated.
5. Develop the habit of peer editing with a colleague whose judgement you trust.

I Image-evoking, Concrete, and Specific
1. Replace abstractions with specifics — costs, names, numbers, places, qualities, methods, timelines, reasons, and steps when appropriate.
2. Create reader-friendly pages with clear headings systems, visual aids that are independent of the text, short paragraphs, lists, or matrices, and pleasing type style and layout.
3. When appropriate, choose language that mirrors images; it is easier to process and remember.
4. Use verbs, not their noun forms (*modify* not *modification*) when possible.

T Tight Organization
1. Check for STAR (subject focus) ➤ CHAIN (logical links in thought) ➤ HOOK (a link to the next action).
2. Decide whether an indirect or direct pattern of presentation is best. Most readers prefer the main ideas at the beginning. Leave general, or consequential items to the end of an agreement.
3. Use parallelism whenever describing comparable items. This page uses a parallel format.
4. Organize material to allow for selective reading if parts only apply to one set of readers. Headings which "tell the story" help readers judge what to omit.

Y You and Your Audience
1. Tailor the message to the audience(s) — a summary to decision makers, technical discussion to colleagues. Aim different parts of a document at differing audiences.
2. Review appropriateness of tone and language for sending up, down, laterally, or out. Assess amount of detail, background information, and language level for diverse audiences. Read with the reader's eyes. Avoid the trap of writing primarily for lawyers and the courts.
3. Edit and proofread scrupulously. Appearance and correctness count. You and your organization are judged by your written presentation. Your writing reflects your thinking, efficiency, care over subject knowledge, and productivity. Your writing represents you and your organization's image.

Plain Language
at Work

Chapter 6
Wills

Chapter Consultant: Peg James, B.Ed., LL.B.

What this chapter does

The chapter:
1 explores the potential character of wills from the willmaker's perspective
2 identifies purposes and audiences for wills
3 reviews the work of two organizations who have worked on plain language wills
4 presents *before* and *after* segments from wills including ways to present *per stirpes*
5 provides a short case history from a client's perspective on getting her B.C. lawyer to prepare a plain language will
6 suggests compiling glossaries on technical wills language for clients

Complete *before* and *after* samples of a will are on pages 157 to 170.

Wills are personal in intent but traditionally impersonal

Wills, perhaps the best known legal document to the public, are among the most personal we write. Yet they are everywhere clothed in standard and depersonalized legal prose. Wills can be written memorials reflecting the spirit and key relationships of our lives. Legal drafters of wills in effect become legal speech-writers for their clients.

Wills have the potential to (and sometimes do) express their owners' personalities and life missions.[1] George Washington ordered the freedom of all his slaves after his death and the death of his wife. Harry Houdini specified the embalming and entombing procedures to allow his return from the dead! Alfred Hitchcock's will, however, illustrates the paradox underlying most wills: "Compared to the richness of his cinematic imagery, Hitchcock's twenty-five page will is rather dry. Despite the lengthy legal verbiage, there is little of Hitchcock's personality showing through."[2] Pity.

The third edition to Robert Dick's classic legal drafting text has a new name: *Legal Drafting in Plain Language*. In its wills chapter, Dick states that wills need to be drafted in plainer language. He writes, "Most seem to ramble on without much thought for the reader and clients must take it on faith that their wishes are being carried out."[3] A 1981 paper presented to the Tennessee Bar Association Will Drafting Seminar, "Writing a Clearer Will", claimed that a will does not have to look or sound like a traditional will

---

[1] When I wrote my first will in the early nineties, a holograph will, I included humour and a "write-to-my-beneficiaries" perspective. I wanted to make my loved ones laugh heartily at my words and the memories they evoked. Later when my lawyer drafted a plain language will for me, an initial 20-page draft was produced. Together we whittled it down to four pages. I regret to say it's no longer very funny. I intend to remedy that.
[2] Herbert E. Nass. Esq., *Wills of the Rich and Famous* (New York: Warner Books, Inc., 1991).
[3] Robert C. Dick, *Legal Drafting in Plain Language* (Toronto: Carswell, 1995), p. 217.

in order to be legally valid. The author further argued that ambiguous wills are more susceptible to litigation which, in turn, may prompt actions for legal malpractice.[4]

In British Columbia, 7 out of every 10 adults die without a will. If that statistic represents the population without wills across North America, it suggests an ample market for enterprising plain language wills drafters. An American writer suggests the reason most people put off making their wills is "the turgid, redundant legal prose [of] wills" and he quips, "after the hereins, hithertos and heretofores, the hereafter will be a breeze."[5]

Audiences and purposes of wills

Traditionally, wills have been written for readers at the probate court or the tax department. In reality, the audiences for wills begin with the signer of the will, and expand to include family members, beneficiaries, executors, trustees, other fiduciaries, guardians, lawyers, judges, accountants, creditors, and other interested parties. The style of standard wills often says to the client, "Leave this matter to your lawyer; you don't need to understand the complexities of your will."

A will sets up a relationship between willmakers and the people who will carry out their personal and business wishes. A will (i) documents the specific directives for giving away property after death (ii) ensures that only the people whom willmakers want to receive their money and possessions will do so (iii) ensures that the government does not get an inappropriate amount of one's property, and (iv) when written plainly, allows all readers to understand their rights and obligations.

The following describes the work of two organizations who mounted projects to rewrite wills in plain language.

The synopses of two organizations' plain language wills projects

(1)   **Continuing Legal Education (CLE) Society of British Columbia's Plain Language Project**
In 1993, a team of lawyers from the Canadian Bar Association Wills Section worked with Peg James, Director of CLE Plain Language Project, over a six-month period on a lawyer-drafted will. They rewrote, revised and tested their plain language version of the will. After the testing, they made further improvements.

The analysis of the conversion process is most interesting. I have summarized salient points below:

* Team members acknowledged that, although some plain language advocates may argue that further changes are necessary, the lawyers who helped CLE would not simplify the will further.

* They cautioned that every will must be drafted to suit the individual client. Many of the clauses in the plain language will would be

---

[4] Veda R. Charrow, "Writing a Clearer Will", presented at the Tennessee Bar Association Will Drafting Seminar, 1981

[5] David Holah, *My Last Will and Testament*, column from an unknown Connecticut newspaper.

inappropriate in other circumstances. Additional provisions might be necessary.

- CLE used a *cloze procedure*[6] on the original precedent to establish the reading comprehension level. Subjects, who included seniors, other adults, and ESL college students, all failed: the highest score was 20%.

- CLE tested the first final draft on 15 adults, none of whom were lawyers and nine of whom had post-secondary education. The project report states:

  > This group felt the will was well organized and with concentration they could understand all of the concepts in it. Only three people rated the will as still quite difficult to read. . . Our testing resulted in a few further changes, including shortening a detailed table of contents and adding definitions for *codicil* and *testamentary disposition*.[7]

- The CLE plain language drafters questioned how well traditional style wills are understood after they received comments from a test group on the content. The group was surprised at the Trustee's wide powers. They did not like the fact that, if a testator's child died, the spouse of the testator's child would receive nothing. Only the child's descendants would be beneficiaries. Some wanted to limit the gift over to grandchildren or to friends. (Author's note: It is the responsibility of the drafter to ensure that willmakers understand the consequences of their "own" directives.)

The report concludes:

> With greater acceptance of plain language precedents in the legal community and more feedback from readers of wills, we expect an even plainer version will emerge. In the meantime, we hope that lawyers can adapt this plainer will to use in their practice . . .[8]

(2)   The Alberta Law Reform Institute's Plain Language Initiative (ALRI)

ALRI's objectives for its 1992 Plain Language Initiative was to promote plain language legal writing by showing lawyers the advantages of drafting legal documents in a plain English style. They produced six[9] commonly used legal documents in plain language, among them a will. The writing teams were made up of a writer, a legal expert, and an Institute counsel. At the time of distributing the packages of the model forms, the documents had not been tested.

---

[6] See chapter on readability and reading comprehension tests, p. 45 for an explanation of *cloze procedure*.

[7] "Plain Language Will: phase 2", CLE Plain Language Project, 1993, p. 5.

[8] As above. Complete texts of the original and plain language wills are included in the *Before and After* section of this book, pp. 157 to 170.

[9] The documents were a minutes of settlement, a restraining order, a parental consent form, a will, a guarantee, and an enduring power of attorney. The projects were drafts, and the Institute plans forms testing before completing the projects for its website.

Authors for the Plain Language Initiative emphasized that the exercise was much more than a rewording exercise. The process involved closely examining implicit legal concepts, reorganizing, and reformatting. As well, team members found themselves debating policy issues.

To produce a precedent which typifies a usual will, the team focused on a shorter document. They deliberately excluded gifts of personal property or legacies, remote contingencies such as a grandchild dying before receiving his or her entire share, and a family demise clause. Rather than a definitions section, drafters defined a word or phrase where it was used (e.g. *executor*) or left the definition to the general law (e.g. *children* which now includes illegitimate children). There was no interpretation section: this was left to *The Interpretation Act*.

The preliminary notes to the Institute's plain language will include excellent explanations and diagrams. In the next section, I have included key parts of these notes as part of the *per stirpes* discussion. The *before* and *after* sections below compare (1) openings (2) *per stirpes* and (3) endings.

Before *and* After *Segments of* Wills
(1)   Openings

Sample A - Opening - BEFORE	Sample B - Opening - AFTER	Sample C - Opening - AFTER
Continuing Legal Education of British Columbia Original Will	Continuing Legal Education of British Columbia Plain Language Will	Alberta Law Reform Institute's Plain Language Will
THIS IS THE LAST WILL AND TESTAMENT of me, PETER JOSEPH JONES, of 555 West Water Street, Vancouver in the Province of British Columbia, V0J 7Z1 1. I HEREBY revoke all Wills and Testamentary Dispositions heretofore made by me and DECLARE this to be my Last Will and Testament.	**WILL OF PETER JOSEPH JONES** **Last Will** 1. This is my last Will. I am Peter Joseph Jones of 555 West Water Street, Vancouver, British Columbia. 2. I cancel all my former wills and codicils. (A codicil is a legal addition or change to a Will.)	**WILL OF DOREEN SMITH** This is my last Will, which disposes of all my property. **PART I** **1. Revocation** I revoke all earlier Wills and codicils.
(48 words)	(37 words)	(19 words)

Sample A represents several idiosyncrasies of legal language: arbitrary and unhelpful capitalization, ancient syntax (the last will . . . of me), and unfamiliar language (*testament, revoke, testamentary dispositions, heretofore*). Samples B and C eliminate these unhelpful characteristics. Sample B has substituted *cancel* for *revoke* and removes all capitals. Mellinkoff describes *last will and testament* as "an historical relic still often used to mean *will* (n) in its usual sense. *Will* (Old English) and *testament* (Latin) are coupled synonyms. Today their linkage adds no legal substance to the forthright simplicity of *will*."[10] As for the word last, as in *last will and testament* or in *last will*, he says " . . . *last* in these usages is worthless or worse." He suggests that last will in a codicil may refer not to last in time but to the last reference to a particular topic. Mellinkoff admonishes drafters to drop *last* and prefer a date.

Both plain language versions include a reference to codicils, supplements to a will. In the same way that a reference to an Act includes its amendments, so reference to a will includes its supplements. The shortest opening might be:

> I make this will on March 20, 1998. I cancel all former wills.

This opening would follow a title page with the will maker's name and address and a table of contents, which is the model the Continuing Legal Education Plain Language project used. Interestingly, an American lawyer, Thomas S. Word, has argued that the whole revocation clause is surplus. He says that " . . . a complete will revokes all prior ones by operation of law."[11] If you put the date on the title page with the name, for example, **Elma Palmer's February 23, 1998 Will**, you could begin: This is my will.

(2)   *Per Stirpes* Clauses

For their plain language will, the Alberta Law Reform Institute devised an ingenious set of notes[12] and a diagram[13] to explain the complexities of *per stirpes* distribution of property within a certain family. They first diagrammed the family as below:

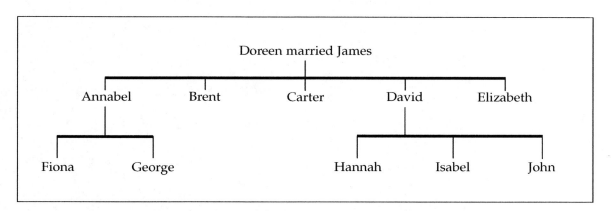

Figure 1: Per Stirpes Distribution Diagram

---

[10] David Mellinkoff, *Mellinkoff's Dictionary of American Legal Usage* (St. Paul, MN: West Publishing Co., 1992), p. 687.

[11] Thomas S. Word, "A Brief for Plain English Wills and Trusts", *University of Richmond Law Review*, Vol. 14, No. 472, 1980.

[12] With permission of Alberta Law Reform Institute, Demonstration project #4: Will (Edmonton: 1992), pp. 2-3.

[13] As above, p. 1.

The notes are reproduced in full below:

Notes[14]

The most difficult section of the will to write was the *per stirpes* section—clause 6.2. To help practitioners explain the operation of this clause, we have prepared the following description which sets out five permutations provided for in clause 6.2.

It is also quite common for practitioners to draw the testator's family tree and then explain *per stirpes* through diagrams. We considered including a diagram in the will itself. However this idea met with resistance as going "too far" in plain language!

Operation of Clause 6.2

Assume that Carter and David died before Doreen.

a. Divide the estate into:

3 living shares:	Annabel	1/4
	Brent	1/4
	Elizabeth	1/4
1 deceased share:	David	1/4

b. Divide the deceased share equally among David's children:

	Hannah	$1/4 \times 1/3$
	Isabel	$1/4 \times 1/3$
	John	$1/4 \times 1/3$

c. Give no share to Carter as he predeceased Doreen and has no children.

d. If Annabel dies after Doreen and before she is 25, divide her remaining undistributed share (X) equally between her children:

	Fiona	$X \times 1/2$
	George	$X \times 1/2$

e. Or if Brent then dies after Doreen and before he is 25, divide his remaining undistributed share (Y) into:

2 living shares:	Annabel	$Y \times 1/3$
	Elizabeth	$Y \times 1/3$
1 deceased share:	David	$Y \times 1/3$

---

[14] As above, note 12, pp. 2-3.

The diagram and notes make the choices clear to a lay reader and could helpfully be appended to the will. The following boxes allow you to compare the original and plain language *per stirpes* clauses in the Continuing Legal Education Project wills:

Sample A - *Per stirpes* clauses only - BEFORE
Continuing Legal Education Society of British Columbia Original Will[15]

2. . . . and I GIVE to my Trustee all my estate upon the following trusts:

    (d)   If my wife shall die before me, to divide the residue of my estate into as many equal shares as there shall be children of mine alive at my death, PROVIDED that if any child of mine shall then be dead and if any ISSUE of such deceased child shall be living such deceased child of mine shall be considered alive for the purposes of such division.

       My Trustee shall set aside one of such equal shares for each child of mine who shall be living at my death and shall keep such share invested and pay the net income derived from such share to or for such child until he or she attains the age of TWENTY-FIVE (25) years when ONE-HALF (1/2) of such share shall be paid or transferred to him or her and thereafter the net income from the remainder of such share shall be paid to or for such child until he or she attains the age of THIRTY (30) years when the remainder of such share shall be paid or transferred to him or her. If such child should die before becoming entitled to receive the whole of his or her share in my estate, such share or the amount thereof remaining shall be held by my Trustee, in trust, for the children of such child who survive him or her in equal shares. If such child should leave no child of him or her surviving, such share or the amount thereof remaining shall be held by my Trustee, in trust, for my issue alive at the death of such child in equal shares *per stirpes*.

       My Trustee shall set aside one of such equal shares for the issues of each child of mine who shall have predeceased me but shall have issue alive at my death and shall divide such share among the issue of such deceased child then alive in equal shares *per stirpes*.

---

[15] With permission of Plain Language Project, The Continuing Legal Education Society of British Columbia (Vancouver: 1991).

Sample B - *Per stirpes* clauses only - AFTER
Continuing Legal Education Society of British Columbia Plain Language Will[16]

9. I direct my Trustee to distribute the remainder of my Estate as follows:

    (b) If Genie does not survive me for 30 days, to hold the reminder of my Estate in trust in equal shares, one share for each child of mine who is alive at my death, and one share for each child of mine who died before me but who left descendants alive at my death. If a child of mine died before me but left descendants alive at my death, the descendants will take that child's share of the reminder of my Estate in equal shares *per stirpes*. (For the meaning of *per stirpes*, see paragraph 14.)

12. If any child of mine dies after me but before he or she is 25, I direct my Trustee to hold the rest of that child's share on these terms:

    (a) If a child dies before he or she is 25 but leaves surviving descendants, I direct my Trustee to hold the rest of that child's share in trust for those descendants in equal shares *per stirpes*. (For the meaning of *per stirpes*, see paragraph 14.)

    (b) If a child dies before he or she is 25 and leaves no descendants, I direct my Trustee to hold the rest of that child's share in trust in equal shares *per stirpes* for my descendants who survive that child. (For the meaning of *per stirpes*, see paragraph 14.)

    (c) If any child of mine is under 25 and becomes entitled to some or all of the share of a deceased child of mine, I direct my Trustee to add my living child's part of the deceased child's share to the share my Trustee already holds for that living child and on the same terms.

14. Where I have directed my Trustee to distribute some part of my estate in equal shares *per stirpes*, I mean that my Trustee should do the following:

    (a) Note the person the potential beneficiaries must be descendant from. In paragraphs 9 (b) and 12 (a), they must be descendant from a child of mine. In paragraph 12 (b), they must be descendant from me.

    (b) For the noted person, determine which is that person's nearest generation of descendants with living members.

    (c) Divide the share into as many equal shares as there are living members of that generation plus deceased members of that generation who leave descendants then living.

    (d) Give each living member of that nearest generation one share.

    (e) Divide the share of each deceased member of that nearest generation among his or her descendants in the same manner.

---

[16] As above, note 15.

Sample A (p. 7) is a good example of how will writers carelessly use the word *shall* to mean either the present tense of the verb, other tenses, *must, may,* or some other meaning. A sampling follows:

If my wife shall die before me	*dies*
as there shall be children	*are*
if any child of mine shall then be dead	*is then*
such deceased child of mine shall be considered	*is considered*
my trustee shall set aside	*must set*
each child of mine who shall have predeceased me	*has*

The average word count for 4 sentences in Sample A is 80, well beyond grade 17 readability level and the paragraph lengths are correspondingly intimidating. The average number of words per sentence with 18 sentences in Sample B is 40.

Article 14 in Sample B provides trustees with a precise set of instructions to track *per stirpes* distribution. This makes the will administration much less difficult than solving a Hitchcock mystery!

The Continuing Legal Education Society Plain Language Project suggests three ways to explain *per stirpes* in plain language in their wills drafting course: definitions, scenarios, and diagrams. Their *per stirpes* distribution diagram[17] follows:

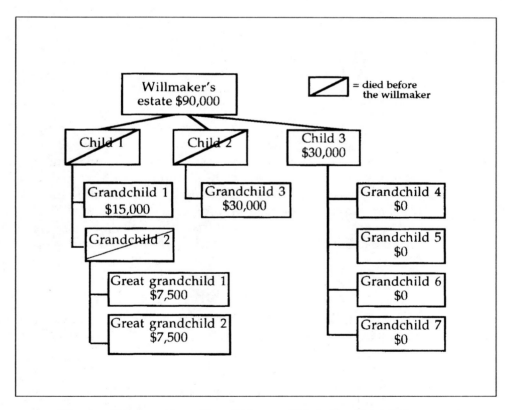

Figure 2: Another Per Stirpes Distribution Diagram

---

[17] As above, note 15, p. 7.

The last set of comparisons looks at the final section of a will, the signing and witnessing.

(3)   **Will Endings**

Sample A - Ending - BEFORE Continuing Legal Education of British Columbia Original Will	Sample B - Ending - AFTER Continuing Legal Education of British Columbia Plain Language Will	Sample C - Ending - AFTER Alberta Law Reform Institute's Plain Language Will
In witness whereof I have hereunto set my hand this first day of September, 1992. SIGNED, PUBLISHED AND DECLARED by the above-named Testator, PETER JOSEPH JONES, as and for his Last Will and Testament, in the presence of us, both present at the same time who, at his request, in his presence and in the presence of each other, have hereunto subscribed our names as witnesses: (66 words)	Signed by Peter Joseph Jones as his last will on September 1, 1992. At the request of Peter Joseph Jones, we were both present when he signed this will. Then in his presence and in the presence of each other, we signed as witnesses. (39 words)	ON 9 OCTOBER 1992 I SIGNED MY WILL AND INITIALLED THE PREVIOUS 4 PAGES IN THE PRESENCE OF TWO WITNESSES, WHO SIGNED IN THE PRESENCE OF ME AND OF EACH OTHER. (31 words)

Sample A represents antiquated will language. You no longer need to use the unholy triplet of "signed, published, and declared" as it represents outdated requirements[18] and "subscribed" is easily changed to "signed". Mellinkoff describes "in witness whereof" as a "flourish of a style long dead, an encumbrance" insisting on its "liquidation".[19] The plain language rewrites in samples B and C meet all these requirements. I am unclear why the Law Reform Institute capitalized its signing and witnessing segment. Lower-cased text is easier to read. The two sentences in sample B are also easier to read.

Case History: Shopping for a plain language will

I love real stories about plain language. The short story below was kindly written by a colleague, Nancy Carlman, who has been promoting and teaching clear writing for many years.

---

[18] As above, note 3, p. 220.
[19] As above, note 10, pp. 253-4.

Case History: Shopping for a Plain Language Will[20]

My husband, Stephen, and I went to a lawyer, whom I will call Jim Marshall, to ask him to draw up our wills. Jim is a middle-aged lawyer who has been a partner in two large Vancouver law firms but is now in a new, two-partner law firm. We had arranged the appointment ahead of time and were both seated across the desk from the lawyer late one afternoon in 1993.

Jim took details of our names, addresses, and ages and then decided to start with my will. He began to take notes about how I wanted my estate to be handled. I explained that I wanted to leave most of my estate to my husband but that I wanted to leave something to my nephews. We discussed the advantages and disadvantages of leaving a percentage or fixed sum to the two nephews and decided on fixed sums. It took only about ten minutes to answer his questions and tell him what I wanted done.

He said he would draft the will and let me look at it before I "executed" it.

At this point, I asked him if he would be willing to draft my will in plain English. As I asked him, I handed him a pamphlet about plain language wills published by the Continuing Legal Education Society of B.C.

He immediately said, "No. I don't favour plain English"—but he started to thumb through the pamphlet.

Neither my husband nor I said anything as Jim read through the pamphlet, talking as he read. Although I did not take notes, his comments went something like this:

"Wills have been written the same way for years; I don't see what's wrong with them."

"I don't see anything wrong with the word *bequeath*. Of course, you can use *give*, but it's so plain; it loses the poetry."

"That's the trouble with education these days; no one knows all those marvelous references to the Bible and Shakespeare. And the traditional language of wills and other legal documents goes right back to the time of King James. We're losing our history, the history of the language."

"I realize that *null* and *void* are unnecessary, but the language of wills is a tradition; it's stood the test of time."

He continued in this vein for about fifteen minutes, during which time Stephen and I said nothing, though we looked at each other with small smiles.

By the time he had finished reading the pamphlet (and it was clear he was reading it), he said, "Alright, I'll try it, if that's what you want; but we'll be losing the poetry."

---

[20] With permission of Dr. Nancy Carlman, private collection.

Case History: Shopping for a Plain Language Will (cont'd)

At this point I thought, but my husband said, "Jim, this is a will, not a poem."

Jim then took the information about Stephen's will and said he'd draft the wills and send them to us to look over before we executed them. (I did not say anything about "execute".)

We heard the next week from Jim's partner that Jim had spent an afternoon in the Law Foundation Library looking up plain English wills, that ours were the first ones he had drafted and that he was taking our request seriously even though he really didn't like the idea. Here is a copy of the draft of my plain English will:

THIS IS THE LAST WILL of me, NANCY CARLMAN, of 923 East 13th Avenue, Vancouver, British Columbia.

1. I CANCEL all my former Wills.

2. I GIVE the sum of $5,000 to my nephew KEVIN BURT RICHARDSON if he survives me.

3. I GIVE the sum of $5,000 to my nephew JAMES PALMER RICHARDSON if he survives me.

4. IF my husband, STEPHEN CARLMAN, survives me for a period of 30 days, I GIVE the remainder of my estate, to my husband STEPHEN CARLMAN, and I appoint my said husband to be my Trustee.

5. IF my husband, STEPHEN CARLMAN, dies before me or dies within 30 days of my death, I DIRECT that the following clauses of my Will shall take effect, but that otherwise such clauses shall be of no effect whatsoever.

6. I APPOINT my nephew, KEVIN BURT RICHARDSON, to be my Trustee.

7. I GIVE my remainder of my Estate to my two nephews, KEVIN BURT RICHARDSON and JAMES PALMER RICHARDSON or to the survivor of them if one has died before me.

I have signed my name to this Will on _____.

SIGNED BY NANCY CARLMAN as her)	
Last Will in the presence of us,)	_____
both present at the same time. We have)	NANCY CARLMAN
signed our names as witnesses to this Will)	
at the request of NANCY CARLMAN)	
and in her presence, and in the presence)	
of each other.)	

(witnesses' names, addresses and occupations blocks omitted)

You will probably be thinking of a few more improvements to Nancy Carlman's will:

(1) changing all the capitalized words and phrases to lower case including *estate* and *will* (2) changing the opening to **This is my will. I am . . .** (3) deleting the comma after *estate* in point 4 and deleting *said* (4) changing the wording in point 5 to **I direct that the following clauses of my will apply** (5) in point 7, deleting *of them* (6) deleting *as her Last Will* and changing the wording to *in our presence*.[21]

Glossaries for clients
The law of wills includes many terms which are unfamiliar to your client. As in any area of law, it would be helpful to compile a glossary with translations for clients. These could be handouts your firm or organization has available in its office. Some troublesome words from wills for lay readers are:

codicil	*give, devise, and bequeath*	testamentary
beneficiaries	goods and chattels	testamentary guardian
executor	*last will and testament*	*per stirpes*
fiduciary	testator	*rest, residue and remainder*

The Australian Centre for Plain Language's *Law Words: 30 Essays on Legal Words and Phrases*[22] presents meticulous research on commonly overused terms including the four italicized phrases above. As other plain language writers have suggested in this chapter, the Centre's authors suggest alternatives to these phrases.

---

[21] Peg James and I agree that, as long as a heading such as **Carol Jean Douglas's March 20, 1998 Will** appears at the top of page 1 of a will, you could begin the will with appointments.
[22] *Law Words: 30 Essays on Legal Words and Phrases*, eds. Mark Duckworth and Arthur Spyrou (Sydney, Australia: Centre for Plain Legal Language, 1995).

Chapter 7
Municipal Bylaws
Chapter Consultant: Mavis Nathoo, LL.B.

What this chapter does
This chapter:
1. presents a case history of how one municipality began the process of using plain language to produce bylaws
2. reviews the genesis and plain language features of the "catalyst" bylaw, the *Procedures and Committees Bylaw*
3. compares Before and After segments of that bylaw
4. discusses how to transform stereotypical clauses
5. demonstrates changes in form and substance

No. 9999: The little bylaw that could

Legislation should not present information in the form of a jigsaw puzzle.[1]

It is strange that free societies should thus arrive at a situation where their members are governed from cradle to grave by texts they cannot comprehend.[2]

In 1988, an Edmonton lawyer, and consultant to this chapter, Mavis Nathoo, attended a two-day *Improving Legal Writing* workshop on plain language. Subsequently, she was hired by the City of Edmonton as legal researcher for the Office of the City Clerk. Initially hired to work with a Council Committee, the Procedures Review Committee, she was enthusiastic about the opportunity to apply plain language principles to municipal bylaw writing. In effect, over several years, she became a champion of plain language for the City.

The mandate of the committee was to oversee the rewriting of a bylaw on procedures and governance for the City. The plan was to consolidate and update information from several bylaws, and to write the new bylaw in plain language.

To set the stage, Mavis wrote a detailed report about the plain language project and made recommendations which Council passed. The report brought Council on side. It established an anticipatory framework for administration and gained interest in plain language among City personnel.

By now, the City Clerk, a lawyer herself, had become interested in plain language, and decided to educate her staff through two plain language workshops. Included in the workshops were also a couple of lawyers from the Office of the City Solicitor. Though

---

[1] Victoria Law Reform Commission (Australia), *Access to the Law: The Structure and Format of Legislation, Report No. 33*, May 1990, p.8.
[2] Francis Bennion, *Statute Law*, 2nd ed. (London: Oyezlongman, 1983), p. 8.

the focus of these workshops was to modernize the Council Minutes' writing, knowledge gained about plain language techniques meant the staff would be more accepting of a less bureaucratic style of writing.

By fall of 1991, after innumerable drafts, some hesitancy on the part of some new to plain language, and much good will and negotiation, Bylaw 9999, *The Procedures and Committees Bylaw*, was passed.

The 36 pages of old bylaws had blossomed into a well-organized, clearly written 46-page bylaw. Although no formal testing of the document was done, an employee who had worked for the City of Edmonton for 40 years proclaimed it the clearest bylaw he'd ever read. Mavis wrote an article for *Cityline*, the City of Edmonton's employee newsletter, to describe the new bylaw features.

As so often happens in plain language conversions, the changes were dramatic. In this case, the whole political process had been transformed from a reporting system with all policy committees reporting first to a strong central committee, and then to Council. The new bylaw created three equal policy committees reporting directly to Council. The combination of substance change and a first plain language bylaw attracted attention to plain language.

By 1993, Mavis had written four bylaws in plain language. A Legislative Skills Counselling group of 7 or 8 lawyers was set up to work on setting standards for writing bylaws and agreements. In December, 1993, the City showed its commitment to plain language by putting its 22 lawyers, including the City Solicitor, through Wordsmith's *Improving Legal Writing* workshop. The workshop focused on group rewriting of participants' work-in-progress. We applied plain language principles to rewriting bylaws, and other documents the lawyers were working on. Knowledge of plain language strategies resulted in a new project—creating a manual of plain language guidelines for drafting bylaws.

The City's first plain language bylaw had acted as a catalyst, the little-engine-that-could. It had changed in appearance, format, substance, layout, vocabulary, style, and tone. The rest of this chapter provides *Before* and *After* illustrations of these changes, based on reconceptualizing the bylaw's audiences and purposes.

Appearance

Bylaw 9999, the key to governance in the City, was by its nature destined to be used by more people than other bylaws. The original bylaw was a stapled document with no title page. The drafters ensured the reader friendliness of the new document by incorporating new visual and organizational aids:

- *coloured card covers* (may not continue)
- *title page* for ease of identification
- *cerlox-binding* for easier handling (may not continue)
- *table of contents* organized by page number, not section or clause (a reading protocol the public is unfamiliar with)
- *index* for quick access to subjects (important in long bylaws)
- *typography with ragged right* and justified left (This choice eliminates the "rivers of space" or uneven spacing when both edges are justified. Research on reading has shown that this slows down the reading.)

- *columnar layout* of text with marginal headings and good use of space
- *more logical and specific organization* of subject headings
- *more white space and improved layout*

Titles

The historic custom of creating two titles, a long and a short, is antithetical to plain language drafting. Short titles to bylaws make references easier and eliminate the practice of inserting long purpose statements into the title. As well, there is no need to include a section in the bylaw saying "this bylaw may be cited as _____". Nor do you even need to write "The" as part of the title, even though the City did so. The streamlined versions follow:

Before	After
Being a Bylaw to Deal with Procedure and the Transacting of Business of the Municipal Council of the City of Edmonton	The Procedures and Committees Bylaw
Bylaw to Provide for Municipal Elections in the City of Edmonton	The Elections Bylaw
A Bylaw to Appoint a City Auditor General for the City of Edmonton	The Auditor General Bylaw

Preambles and enacting words

According to one writer in the Middle Ages, preambles were originally included in bylaws for the same reason as in Acts of Parliament, namely, "to shewe the cause why the statute was made and what was the mischief at the common law". Indeed, much mischief and consternation have preambles caused for many a century since.

My chief objection to preambles, as well as to many recitals, is their overbearing length and tautologous natures. If a title is well crafted to synthesize its subject matter, brief enacting and purpose statements will substitute for the historically circuitous preambles.

Although usually unnecessary, there may be a particular reason for stating the legislative authority for the bylaw. A brief section headed "Legislative Authority" may suffice. As well, you need only refer to "the Act" not "the Act as amended" or "as amended from time to time".[3] Unless legislation clearly requires a bylaw to have a preamble, try to eliminate it. If you cannot avoid a preamble, don't use the archaic *whereas* syntax. Instead, try something like: "The reasons for this bylaw are: (1) . . ."

Compare the following ancient and plain language versions:

---

[3] This is because the *Interpretation Act* says that an Act includes its amendments.

Before (93 words)	After (27 words)
WHEREAS the Municipal Government Act prescribes certain requirements and makes certain provisions with respect to meetings of City Council, and further provides that Council may make rules and regulations with respect to its meetings and proceedings, the conduct of its members, the appointment of committees and the transaction of its business; AND WHEREAS the Council has been conducting its procedure in accordance with Bylaw No. 6295, as amended, and it is deemed desirable to enact a new bylaw; NOW THEREFORE the Municipal Council of the City of Edmonton duly assembled enacts as follows:	The Council of the City of Edmonton enacts the following:[4] 1. The purpose of this bylaw is to establish rules to follow in governing the City of Edmonton.

Definitions

The three often overlooked plain language considerations for defined terms are layout, location, and identifiers. To eliminate the repetition inherent in "A means, B means, C means and so on . . .", the City of Edmonton decided to streamline the layout and present definitions in a tabular format:

Definitions	2. The following words and phrases mean:
(1) Administrative Inquiry	an inquiry made at a meeting by a Councillor relating to the business of the City;
(2) Chair	the person who has been given the authority to direct the conduct of a meeting including the appointed head of a Committee;
(3) Challenge	an appeal of a ruling of the Chair;[5]

For those who insist on *the word means* in each definition, and who are willing to use a bolded identifier for defined terms instead of capitals, an alternative tabular layout could look like this:

---

[4] This short enacting segment was reduced to "Edmonton City Council enacts" in their next bylaw.

[5] This section could be further refined by eliminating the semicolons (unnecessary and even ungainly, in this tabular format). Since definitions mean "meanings", and it is patently obvious the definitions are for this bylaw, I also suggest deleting "The following words and phrases mean". Also, it is quicker to find a term in an alphabetical list if the terms are not preceded by numbers.

DEFINITIONS

Administrative inquiry	means an inquiry made at a meeting by a **councillor** relating to the business of the **City**
Chair	means the person who has been given authority to direct the conduct of a meeting including the appointed head of a **committee**
Challenge	means an appeal of a ruling of the **chair**

Text improvements

The drafters of Bylaw 9999 focused on text clarity. The *After* examples below illustrate various plain language features—succinctness, new detailed content, better organization, positive wording, shorter sentences, elimination of legalese and passive verb forms, new headings, parallelism, and itemized formats:

Before	After
1. From the date of the passing of this bylaw the following rules and regulations only shall be observed for the order and dispatch of business in Council and all committees thereof, and all motions, rules or regulations existing which are inconsistent with this bylaw are hereby repealed. (47 words)	**PARAMOUNT RULES** 7. If the provisions in any other bylaw conflict with the rules in this Bylaw, this Bylaw will prevail. (20 words)

Before	After
2. This bylaw shall not be repealed, amended or suspended, except so far as the terms hereof permit, unless it is repealed, amended or suspended: a) by a bylaw unanimously passed at a regular or special meeting of the Council at which all the members thereof are present, or b) by a bylaw passed at a regular meeting of Council pursuant to a notice of motion in writing given and openly announced at a meeting of the Council held at least 5 days prior to such meeting and setting out the substantial effect of the proposed bylaw. (93 words)	**AMENDING OR REPEALING THIS BYLAW 235** To amend or repeal this Bylaw, Council must: (1) unanimously pass a bylaw at a regular or special meeting of Council at which all Councillors are present, or (2) pass a bylaw at a regular meeting of Council following written notice of Council following written notice of motion openly announced at a meeting of Council held at least five days prior to presentation of the bylaw for first reading. (62 words)

The meticulous recrafting of bylaw material into plain language required endless meetings and continual rethinking about audience needs. Finally the imperatives of deadlines and working in a large organization forced a final draft. I know the drafters would admit to areas for improvement, and I have chosen three typical problems on which to make suggestions.

The cart before the horse

One way to ensure that the ordering focuses immediately on the subject is to formulate a question which the clause will answer. Consider this clause from the 9999 Bylaw:

> If a question relating to the procedures of council or committees is not answered by this Bylaw, the answer to this question is to be determined by referring to the most recent revision of *Robert's Rules of Order Newly Revised*.

Sometimes the bylaw language sounds a bit like "in the house that Jack built" language. Instead, ask the question, "What is the authority for any question not covered in the bylaw on procedures?" The answer is:

> The most recent *Robert's Rules of Order Newly Revised* is the authority for any council or committee procedural question not answered by this Bylaw.

The second version is easier to read, down from 40 words to 24, focuses the subject on answering the question, and eliminates passive voice and redundancies.

Establishing appropriate tone

If you begin a clause with a prohibition, chances are the reader will pick up on the negative tone. Here is one clause where a City may prefer to emphasize the positive:

> Council may not give a bylaw more than two readings at a meeting unless all Councillors present at the meeting vote in favour of allowing a third reading at that meeting.

One rewrite looks like this:

> Usually, only two bylaw readings are allowed at a meeting. However, Council may give a third reading if all Councillors present vote to allow it.

The positive phrasing is easier to read. The rewrite substitutes two short sentences, a 10- and a 15-word sentence, for one 31-word sentence.

Those old chestnuts

Bylaw 9999 avoids most ancient stereotypical clauses (including making the masculine stand also for the feminine) which appear in bylaws almost by rote. One that is particularly well entrenched did manage to survive in the *Procedures and Committees Bylaw*:

> RULES FOR   3. The marginal notes and headings in this bylaw
> INTERPRETATION   are for reference purpose only.

Michele Asprey responded to the use of this old chestnut in her 1991 *Plain Language for Lawyers*: "We are free to put in headings, and we can provide that they are to be disregarded in interpreting the document—although it is hard to understand why anyone who has drafted their document carefully would want to do that."[6] She's said it all.

Bylaw readings

The medieval clarion call of this bylaw vestige persists. Sometimes it proclaims:

> READ A FIRST TIME THIS 20TH DAY OF MARCH 1994 A.D.
> READ A SECOND TIME THIS 20TH DAY OF MARCH 1994 A.D.
> THIRD READING AND PASSED THIS 27TH DAY OF MARCH, 1994 A.D.
>   AS AMENDED

The A.D. is unnecessary. Choose the simpler format and modern syntax below:

> **First reading**   March 20, 1994
> **Second reading**   March 20, 1994
> **Third reading and passed**   March 27, 1994 as amended

Since this is not strictly part of the bylaw itself, that is, not a numbered clause, it could be boxed at the bottom of the last page along with the signature lines.

---

[6] Michele M. Asprey, *Plain Language for Lawyers* (Annandale, Australia: The Federation Press, 1991), p. 165.

Visual aids

Legal writers may dismiss the importance of visual aids as add-ons or mere frippery when compared with text. That is unfortunate as both media have their own distinctive purposes, strengths, and contexts.

I like the Law Reform Commission of Victoria's comments on visual aids:

> [A] cause for confusion is the habit of relying on words when some other form of communication could do the job better. An example is the use of a lengthy section to describe a geographical area, process, procedures or formula. In such a case, the words could be replaced by a map, chart or the formula itself.[7]

In a world where visual literacy is taught as a subject, and where computers are as common as telephones, it is practical to transpose long dense masses of words into visual layouts. In legal texts, we need more white space, headings and subheadings, tabular formats, charts, graphs, diagrams, explanatory notes, and examples.

Official reluctance to use visual aids in legislation is exemplified in the current Alberta Legislative Counsel Office Drafting Style Manual.[8] Though many plain language principles are incorporated, a few injunctions remain.[9]

Examples and explanatory notes

Some legal writers give as their reason for not including examples and explanatory notes that they are "not part of the law", or that they do not look formal enough. According to the Australian *Access to the Law*[10] report, that view begs the question. Whether they are part of the law or not is decided by Parliament, not by an ancient theory about the form that laws must take.

It is ironic that examples were a distinguishing feature of the *Indian Evidence Act 1872*, and of other Indian legislation in the nineteenth century. *The United Kingdom's Consumer Credit Act 1974* is also cited as legislation which makes good use of examples.[11]

Though Bylaw 9999 did not require explanatory notes, an early plain language draft of Alberta's new *Municipal Act* provided helpful explanatory footnotes and flow charts. Both were removed in the next draft.

Drafters of the City of Edmonton's *Nuisance Bylaw*, passed December, 1993, included two plain language forms as schedules in their bylaw. Both attachments aid the City and its citizens to solve nuisance issues promptly.

---

[7] As above, note 1, p. 7.
[8] *Alberta Legislative Counsel Office Drafting Style Manual* (Edmonton: June, 1991).
[9] These include: "15.(1) Headings should be used sparingly and should be of a general nature. (3) Note that the heading is part of the Act and, unlike marginal notes, tables of contents, and historical citations, is not there just for ease of reference. 17. Explanatory notes are used only in amending Bills and are deleted when the Bill is printed as an Act", p. 3.
[10] As above, note 1, p. 12.
[11] As above, p. 12.

Headings and subheadings

The City of Edmonton's Bylaw 10140 makes excellent use of question headings and subheadings to provide a clear map of the territory for readers. In the previous City Auditor General bylaw, the six-page bylaw had no headings. In this new bylaw, the document was divided in this manner:

THE AUDITOR GENERAL BYLAW

Part I	Purpose and Definitions[12]
Part II	What are the Auditor General's terms of employment?
Part III	What is the Auditor General's relationship to the administration and organizations?
Part IV	What are the Auditor General's responsibilities?
Part V	How are investigations commenced?
Part VI	Who does the auditor general report to?
Part VII	What types of reports does the Auditor General issue?
Part VIII	How does the administration respond to an Auditor General's report?
Part IX	How will the auditor general's report be presented?
Part X	What information is the Auditor General entitled to?

Note the question format for these main headings which speaks directly to questions readers would themselves raise. (In the City's later plain language *Nuisance Bylaw*, Mavis felt more comfortable about mixing up the question and more regular headings. Forcing the question pattern may cause awkwardness.) Each part of the *Auditor General Bylaw* is segmented into clear margin headings as well. For example, the layout of Part II looks like this:

Part II What are the Auditor General's terms of employment?

APPOINTMENT   _____

                            _____

                            _____

EMPLOYMENT TERMS   _____
AND PERFORMANCE   _____
APPRAISAL   _____

DISMISSAL   _____

                            _____

                            _____

The capitalized margin headings could be changed to the easier-to-read one capital and lower case format.

---

[12] I have replaced the City's capitalized bylaw headings with opening capitals and lower case in the rest.

Changing substance

In the work of plain language bylaw revisions, a drafter could be authorized by council to make the necessary changes to clarify what is considered to be the meaning of the bylaw. In Bylaw 9999, some of the terms were so cloudy that drafters analyzed options and decided on the most reasonable ones. Similarly, even improving the expression of the bylaw can produce new content. That content may have been implicit in and may be compatible with the original.

Though authorizers of plain language revisions do not usually expect substantial change in a document, experience in redrafting shows that significant change is quite common. The *form follows function* dictum is at work here. Sensitive communication and negotiation of proposed changes with affected City personnel or special publics are essential.

Bylaw reform

A common difficulty in bylaw writing is the parroting of words from an enactment or legislation because the writer doesn't know what they mean. Such writing perpetuates confusion in legislation.

Bylaws establish legal rules within our communities, and plain language is beginning to make these rules more accessible. So much remains to be done, and Canadian municipalities could undertake joint projects to save money and time. Some municipalities have more advanced technology and experience than others. Sharing and collaboration are the talismans of the plain language movement.

Generally speaking, bylaws have not kept pace with the drafting improvements in Acts. It is time they caught up.

Chapter 8
Legislation
Chapter Consultant: David Elliott
Legislative Drafting Consultant
Former Associate Chief Legislative Counsel of Alberta

What this chapter does
The chapter:
1   outlines reasons why plain language is essential in legislation
2   profiles Australian, New Zealand and British initiatives for plain language legislation
3   examines the "required by statute" controversy
4   discusses where and how definitions should be included in legislation
5   provides a checklist of plain language features for legislation

Before and *after* segments of legislation are on pages 205 to 238.

Reasons for plain language legislation

A monstrous morass. A mass of obscurity. A jungle. Structurally incoherent. These are descriptions judges and others have given of traditional legislation. It is time for a massive rewriting of old laws and a consistent commitment to plain language drafting of new legislation. Plain language initiatives to reform legislative drafting on several continents reveal compelling reasons for change.

In a 1985 talk to the Statute Law Society in Britain, Richard Thomas spoke of his conviction

> . . . that there remains an overwhelming need to achieve much greater clarity and simplicity [in statutes] and overwhelming scope to do just that. The need is manifest: complexity and obscurity cause massive waste—unnecessary expense for commerce, for professionals, for government and for the public; complex detail brings its own uncertainty before the courts . . . complexity brings contempt for the law, for parliament and for democracy itself.[1]

Plain language:
(1) Is in everyone's interest
It is in everyone's interest that the law be understandable—for governments, the legal profession, civil servants, business people, citizens, and the courts. Clear legislation saves everyone time, effort, and money.

(2) Increases respect for law
Baffling legislation diminishes respect for the law. The mythology that citizens know the law (ignorance of the law is no defence) is further exacerbated by incomprehensible Acts (citizens know even less than they could know).

---

[1] Richard Thomas, "Plain English and the Law" in *Statute Law Review*, 1985, pp. 139-51.

(3) Bolsters our democratic rights

It is bewildering, and unconscionable, that freedom in our society is based on often inscrutable statutory text. In a curious way, poor statutory drafting violates our *Canadian Charter of Rights and Freedoms*.[2] It discriminates against those who fall outside the linguistic culture of legislation.

(4) Is written for primary users

Far too many Acts are not written for the primary users of legislation, the millions of citizens with average literacy levels and average intelligence. The Law Reform Commission of Victoria tested the readability levels of selected legislation and found it required 10-14 years of university education. The report noted cryptically that hardly anyone qualified.[3]

(5) Continues reform

Though some Acts are more intelligible than they used to be, the format and organization of much legislation remains largely unchanged and there are still substantial language problems. The computerization of legislation has reawakened interest in law as communication.

(6) Provides accuracy and certainty

The assumption that traditional legislative drafting is precise is plainly wrong. Time after time, rewrites uncover ambiguities, omissions or mistakes. Legislation can be written more plainly without sacrificing legal concepts or essential details for precision.[4]

(7) Eliminates social costs

The social costs of incomprehensible law are high. When legislation is enacted without being understood, citizens unknowingly commit offences or are unaware of their legal opportunities. Further, community participation in decision-making is reduced.

(8) Develops international impetus

The pace of reform of legal writing has increased. Government departments around the world are doggedly eliminating the dense legalese of yesteryear. The Inland Revenue in Britain has directed its staff to remove legalese from tax forms and notices.[5] In 1997, the Internal Revenue Service in the United States reported it intends to rewrite all its publications and correspondence in plain language.[6] The reform, in its infant stages, should not stop. In varying degrees, plain language for legislation is being pursued in Sweden, South Africa, Australia, New Zealand, Canada, and the European Community.

(9) Provides a context for more

Clearer Acts will create a context for clear documentation generated from the Acts— regulations, reports, booklets, other publications, and Internet summaries.

(10) Is needed because of the volume and complexity of law

Constant elaboration of existing law results from the evolving complexity of modern life. The volume of tax legislation in the United Kingdom has exploded by 300% since 1970, in Australia over the last decade by 200%, and in New Zealand by 80%.[7]

---

[2] The right to liberty? The right not to be subjected to cruel and unusual punishment? What about the right to the assistance of an interpreter for a party who does not understand the language?

[3] Victoria Law Reform Commission (Australia), *Access to the Law: The Structure and Format of Legislation, Report No. 33*, May 1990, p. 1.

[4] As above, p. 3.

[5] Martin Cutts, *Lucid Law*, Plain Language Commission (Stockport, UK: Spectrum Press, 1994), p. 15.

[6] *Detroit Free Press*, "Clinton Defends IRS; Rubin Plans Changes", October 1, 1997.

[7] Tax Law Rewrite Project, Part II, *First Exposure Draft, Trading Income of Individuals*, 1997 (available on the Internet at: http://www.open.gov.uk/inrev/rewrite.htm).

(11) Reveals how confusing and inaccessible old law can be—even to judges
A New Zealand judge has written graphically about his own experience in recasting legislative provisions into plain language. He says:

> . . . we were asked to have a look at two provisions in the old Act . . . Our task was to present the full effect of the current provisions, but in an accessible, plain form. The first of the two provisions was long and complex. With the help of experts, we ascertained what it was really saying. We produced a clearer, crisper text. *The new provision was a third of the length of the old and no longer included some of its obscurities and contradictions.* It was much easier to understand and operate. So far as we and our expert advisors could determine, it included all the substance of the earlier provisions.
>
> When we turned to the second, apparently more straightforward, and certainly shorter, provision, we found to our dismay, and to the dismay of those advising us, that *no one could determine what the provision was about. It did not seem to make any sense at all.* That highlights a fundamental point about plain drafting. Something can be plainly drafted only if there is a good understanding about what is to be said.[8] [author's emphasis]

The judge then illustrated how the use of *notwithstanding any other provision in this section*, twice in the same Act and same section, resulted in two immovable objects or irresistible forces. "One, presumably," he said wryly, "must prevail over the other, but on their face they do not appear to allow that possibility."[9]

Yet the winds of change are blowing.

International initiatives in plain language legislation

Below are described key plain language legislative initiatives outside North America. In chronological order, these include commissions, new legislation, and conferences.

(1) Law Reform Commission of Victoria: *Access to the Law: The Structure and Format of Legislation*, Report No. 33, 1990

This ground-breaking report set out a strategy for the Australian government to implement its plain English policy on the language and structure of legislation. Research was based on extensive consultation and responses to questionnaires. The authors proposed remedies for each defect they uncovered:

Defects in legislation	Remedies
1. Long-windedness — sentences of 100-200 words	Use sentences averaging 20-30 words.
2. Complex sentence structures with embedded clauses	Untangle the clauses and write shorter sentences.
3. Sentences with conditions stated before the rule	State the rule first with exceptions or qualifications after.

---

[8] The Honourable Justice Sir Kenneth Keith KBE, speech from the *Conference Proceedings*, Tax Drafting Conference, November, 1996, p. 5.

[9] As above, p. 5.

Defects in legislation	Remedies
4. Unnatural hybrid language or artificial concepts	Use simple, comprehensible language.
5. Inappropriate over-reliance on text	Use charts, maps, and formulas when appropriate.
6. Delaying the main message and using an illogical structure	Place main message early and gather all related information together.
7. Material grouped too densely and schedule font smaller than that in legislation	Use white space, indents, comparable-sized font for schedules, and desktopping techniques for contrast.
8. 19th-century numbering system (alphanumeric)	Use a modified decimal system to clarify sequence, importance, and interrelationships between divisions and subdivisions. For simple legislation, use whole continuous numbers.
9. Repetitive explanatory memoranda printed separately from legislation and which are of little help	Produce explanatory memoranda using examples and graphic aids, and show why rights and duties are established or how they will operate. These should be printed with the legislation.
10. Legislation with virtually no finding aids	Provide indicators for definitions, marginal cross references, footnotes, and for complex legislation, appendices to indicate affected legislation.

Perhaps the single most egregious problem in legislative drafting highlighted in the report was following the rule that each clause should be made up of a single sentence. In 1850, that rule was actually abolished by Lord Broughton's Act[10] yet generations of drafters have overlooked that fact.

The report details how 18th- and 19th-century legislative reformers such as Jeremy Bentham, George Coode, Henry Thring, and Mackenzie Chalmers significantly improved the quality of legislative drafting.[11] Some of Chalmers' Acts are still regarded as "models of lucidity".

The report singles out the *Indian Evidence Act 1872* as remarkable because it included explanations and examples. Attempts to introduce similar legislation in Britain at the

---

[10] As above, note 3, p. 52.
[11] As above, note 3, pp. 48-53.

same time failed. In the 1970s and 1980s, the authors report that legislative "complexity and long-windedness reached their height".[12] The overly-long convoluted sentence was once again centre stage and greatly complicated the law. On a positive note, however, the British Renton Committee (1975), New South Wales legislation, and Lord Denning have all lent support to the idea of including examples in legislation.

This seminal report from Australia has been consistently referred to by plain language thinkers in the legislative field since that time.

(2) Martin Cutts, *Lucid Law: final report on an independent research project to rewrite and redesign a UK Act of Parliament*, 1994

Co-founder of the British Plain English Campaign in 1979 and director of the Plain Language Commission, Martin Cutts was challenged by government law writers to rewrite a law in plain language. This book is the story of how he rewrote the *Timeshare Act 1992*. Of special interest is the work Cutts did, as a typographer, in redesigning the Act.

The report's purposes are:

(i)   to stimulate interest and debate among statute users, writers and typographers

(ii) to provide a vision of statutes with transformed language and design

(iii) to put a statute into plainer language without losing significant meaning[13]

Cutts chose the *Timeshare Act 1992* because it was brief, recent, and represented UK parliamentary drafting. He delineated the primary audience for his new act as citizens, timeshare companies, and customers, and, as secondary audiences, judges, lawyers, and administrators.

Cutts found a number of weaknesses in the original Act. A selection follows:

Problem #1
Test participants found significant defects in the wording, layout, and design.
When Cutts tested the two Acts on readers, the original scored 32% and the revised, 82% for clarity of wording. For general layout and design, the original received 36% and the revision, 82%.

Problem #2
The structure of the Act did not help organize the reading.
The main points of the Act were scattered over five sections in a manner that did not allow readers to process material efficiently by bundling information. Few readers consulted section 1, where the definitions were placed, to garner main points.

Problem #3
The Act required a non-independent "chunk" of a section (with a 102-word sentence) to be included in the right-to-cancel notices issued to timeshare purchasers.
Readers' understanding of the "chunk" is contingent on references to other parts of the

---

[12] As above, note 3, p. 55.
[13] As above, note 5, p. 7.

Act which are not part of the notice. The passage also uses words such as *offeror* and *offeree* which are not defined in the notice or in the section to be used, and phrases which are difficult to understand.

Problem #4
The original Act has no Citizen's Summary.
Now this should surprise no one because Citizen's Summaries are not commonly part of English legislation. Yet in the world of business writing, summaries—often termed executive summaries because they are written for lay rather than technical or discipline-specific readers—have been around for decades in reports, proposals, and even in longer memos and letters. When there is more than one audience, or even if only one, they are a reader-friendly device.

Cutts' test participants overwhelmingly endorsed the idea of a Citizen's Summary: 97% said such a summary should be part of every Act of Parliament.[14]

In his commentary on the *Clearer Timeshare Act*, Cutts emphatically asserts that the summary would not be part of the law. Similar to other disclaimers that headings, margin notes, examples, explanations, and graphics (maps, charts, graphs, etc.) will not be part of the law, Cutts' assumption could be reconsidered. As long as these techniques were clearly executed, and the results compatible with the text of the legislation, why should they not be an integrated and integral part of the law? Drafters who are uncertain about the integrity of their summaries or graphics should be redrafting them as they redraft words. The cleaving to text and traditional format dies hard.

Problem #5
Introductory elements to the Act are not in plain language text or format
Cutts' measures to rattle ancient ritualized wording and format may seem as daunting as earlier changes to Latin rituals in churches. But the results are a breath of fresh air. The original enactment clause is not only ambiguous but archaically worded. Look at the two versions below with changes to the original bolded:

ORIGINAL
Be it enacted by the Queen's most excellent majesty by and with the advice and consent of **the Lords Spiritual and Temporal,** and **Commons in this present Parliament assembled,** and by the authority **of the same, as follows: —**[15]

REWRITE
This Act is now law by the authority of the House of Commons and the House of Lords, and by the assent of Her Majesty the Queen acting with their advice and consent.

---

[14] Remember when schools taught précis writing? Summary writing of various sorts is an art in itself and various types of summaries could be experimented with. (There is a difference between an abstract and an informative summary, for example.) Good summaries may also include graphics and descriptive headings. Summaries of key points in contracts or agreements, as well as Citizen's Summaries for legislation, are an acknowledgement that readers will benefit from optional and enhanced methods of reading. Summaries give readers preliminary maps before all the details. They act as memory refreshers when re-reading, and help readers who are working within time constraints.

[15] Most of these features identified by Cutts have been remedied in Canadian jurisdictions.

The reasons for the changes are:

Be it enacted is unwarranted. It is neither a command nor a prayer as the Bill has become law. As well, there is no referent for *it*.

the Queen's most excellent majesty is more simply worded as *by Her Majesty the Queen*.

by and with is an awkward doublet which can be deleted.

the Lords Spiritual and Temporal is unnecessary (and perhaps questionable).

Commons is not as quickly understood as *the House of Commons*.

in this present Parliament assembled Cutts considers redundant.

of the same is grammatically ambiguous.

as follows: — hearkens back to the complete sentence fallacy. It is semantically unnecessary to attach the enactment clause to the rest of the Act.

The ordinary reader will also confuse the date of royal assent in square brackets at the end of the long title in the original with the date the Act comes into force. Cutts deletes the long title from the Act.[16] Its wording is particularly vague in any case. Examine the differences in the opening elements below. You will see that Cutts has even told us what the Act is Chapter 35 of!

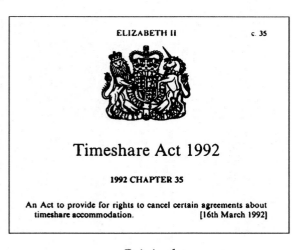

Original   Cutts' rewrite

---

[16] Cutts wants to keep long titles for Bills only because they serve the purpose of setting out the Bill's scope and so limiting amendments. At the Act stage, however, he substitutes a section 1 scope and purpose section headed **What this Act does; when and where it applies**. (See p. 3, centre pages of *Lucid Law*).

Problem #6
The text of the original Act reflects old-style typographical features
Cutts finds fonts that are too small in the schedule and sidenotes, the "ubiquitous Times" typeface, as he refers to it, (readable but tight-looking in comparison with his more open Plantin font choice), justified right text which causes uneven spacing, section beginnings which are "a messy juxtaposition of indent, section number, full point, em dash and bracketed subsection numbers"[17], running heads without section numbers, and footnote references that clutter the sidenote column. Cutts' typographical analysis and improvements are full of good sense and practical details that would help any computer user.[18] The following are size-reduced copies for you to compare original and revised page layouts:

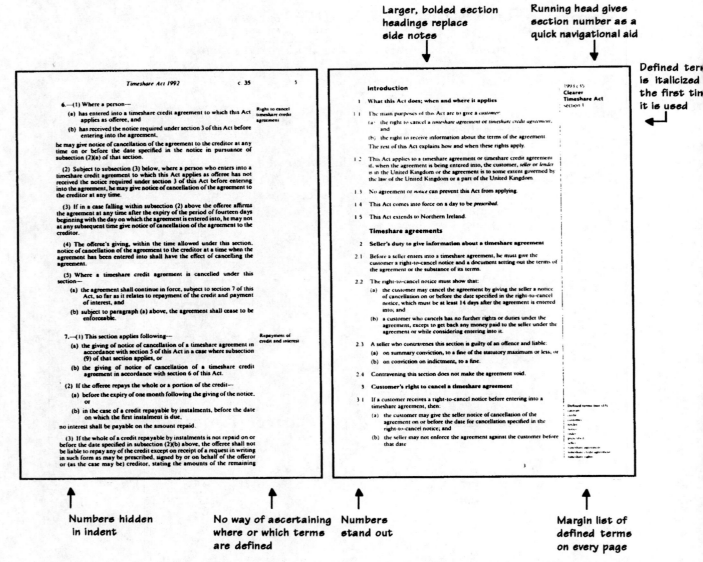

Figure 1: Layouts of Original Timeshare Act (left) and revised Act (right)[19]

---

[17] As above, note 5, p. 40.
[18] As above, note 5, pp. 39-43.
[19] Segments reproduced in this section with permission of Martin Cutts.

Consult the checklist on plain language features on pp. 94-95 for more of the specifications Cutts and this handbook recommend.

(3) *Tax Drafting Conference Proceedings*, hosted by the New Zealand Inland Revenue Department, Auckland, New Zealand, 1996

Participants from New Zealand, Australia, Canada, England, South Africa, and Hong Kong met to explore their interest in plain language drafting and how it related to tax legislation. All seemed committed to changing the view that tax law was necessarily complex and beyond the understanding of most taxpayers.

Audiences for simplified tax legislation

A United Kingdom (UK) speaker and Senior Parliamentary Counsel, Geoffrey Sellers, revealed the complexity of current tax law simplification rewrite projects in Australia, New Zealand, and the UK when he tackled the question of audiences. He reported that the New Zealand view was that, since taxpayers themselves seldom read tax legislation, the primary readers are tax specialists, lawyers, accountants, members of parliament, tax revenue staff, and the courts. The Australians, on the other hand, felt their purpose was to "give the law back to the people".[20]

In UK, parliamentarians are considered the first (presumably chronologically first, not primary) audience. Sellers revealed that parliamentarians are very attached to traditional parliamentary layout (not surprising in Britain). This attachment to a traditional "look", an emotional or sentimental attachment, helps explain some of the resistance to change. Yet Sellers said they hoped to persuade parliament to allow innovation and the following of best modern practice.

In establishing the audience for the UK tax simplification rewrite project, Sellers wondered if it were the actual current audience or some hypothetical future audience resulting from the rewrite. UK Inland Revenue Research had indicated that only about 3% of professionally qualified tax agents are solicitors. Their research from the Consumers' Association indicated that "the rewrite should enable many more taxpayers to have a real say in how their tax affairs are managed".[21]

A further interesting question in the audience research was whether the audience should be the same for all parts or sections of the legislation. Should rules that affect all taxpayers be in simpler terms than those that apply to only the more sophisticated payers? Sellers answered: "Our aim will be to redraft all of the law in as clear and simple terms as we can achieve. We are not going to stop at the point where the tax is intelligible [only] to professionals. If we can go further, we will".[22]

The Honorable Justice Sir Kenneth Keith from New Zealand extended the analysis of audience as it relates to Parliament. He felt the democratic legitimacy of legislation was greatly enhanced when law is comprehensible and accessible to approval or criticism. Noting that for the past 30 years legislation has been scrutinized beyond Parliament, that is, by Committees, individuals, and interested groups who make submissions on legislation, he emphasized careful pre-legislative processes.[23]

---

[20] *Tax Drafting Conference Proceedings, 1996*, New Zealand Inland Revenue Department, Auckland, New Zealand, p. 92
[21] As above, p. 96.
[22] As above, p. 97.
[23] As above, pp. 7-8.

Visual techniques for plain language legislation
In his conference paper, David Elliott (consultant on this chapter), described tools to help readers understand text. He proposed legislative drafting including tables of contents, diagrams, flow charts, explanatory text, question headings, formulae, drafting in the second person, combining questions with a second-person perspective, and algorithms.[24]

As a postscript to his paper published a year later (see footnote below) Elliott writes:

> I wrote this paper before becoming aware of the excellent work of the Commonwealth of Australia in their Tax Law Improvement Project. Virtually all the techniques I outline in this paper are well demonstrated in the *Australian Income Tax Assessment Act 1997* (1997 No. 38).

Needless to say the next initiative is the *Australian Act*.

(4) *Income Tax Assessment Act 1997, No. 38, 1997* (Australia)
This Act is currently the leading example of plain language legislation. Its first page subtitle is not an *act respecting* or *with respect to* but *an Act about income tax and related matters*. Its second page, Contents, not Table of Contents, features a strikingly clear and reader-accessible organization. The work shines with clarity and the imaginative use of words and design.

I can do little more than reproduce examples of the fine work represented in this 400-page Act. You will find these on pp. 221 to 238. Feature boxes highlight the plain language techniques.

(5) Inland Revenue, *First Exposure Draft of the Tax Law Rewrite Project* (United Kingdom), 1997
Described in its press release as an attempt to rewrite direct tax legislation so that it is clearer and easier to use, the *First Exposure Draft* features rules central to the income tax treatment of trading income. Certain features make the Rewrite Project unique—the basic rules for taxing the trading income of individuals were not conceived or expressed in ways relevant to modern business. Their operation can only be understood through extensive case law. As well, practices have resulted from the common understanding of users. The *First Exposure Draft* attempts to reflect this material clearly and more logically. It distills numerous judicial interpretations and translates into statute Inland Revenue practices and two extra-statutory concessions. One extra-statutory concession is abolished.

Method
The Tax Law Rewrite Project emphasizes two aspects to its method: one is full consultation as the key to success and the other is publishing work-in-progress early to ensure all users have a chance to influence the style of the rewritten statute. The *First Exposure Draft* kickstarts the five-year direct tax legislation rewrite.

---

[24] David Elliott, "Tools for Simplifying Complex Legislation", *New Zealand Journal of Taxation Law and Policy* (Brooker's Legal Information, 1997), pp. 153-168.

Proposed rewrite changes to simplify legislation, and described as "minor", fall into four categories:

- changes in the statute, but not the underlying law
- changes to law and policy
- changes to law but not to policy, such as enacting extra-statutory concessions
- removal of unnecessary material

Shortcomings of the present UK tax legislation

The authors report that the 6000 pages of current tax legislation are so poorly organized that it is difficult to get an overview of the law or find where certain issues are dealt with. The quality of tax legislation is compromised by severe time constraints imposed by the Budget and Finance Bill cycle (a fact all legislative drafters discuss). The existing tax code is "almost unintelligible to anyone but an expert".[25]

An early consultative document (July, 1996) concluded:

- Commentators felt that the experimenting with second-person drafting became confusing when provisions affected more than one party. They decided the other examples drafted in the third person achieved a suitable direct impact.

- Similarly, there was little enthusiasm for gender-neutral drafting when, in the main user's views, it made the text less clear and precise. Nevertheless, the rewrite team chose to use a gender-neutral approach unless the clarity and precision would be compromised.

- Unlike the Australians, the United Kingdom drafters do not want to leave gaps in numbering provisions and will adapt a multi-character numbering system.

- When further simplification can be obtained by minor changes to rules (and subject to Parliament's approval), they will only be done if "flagged up clearly for public consultation".[26]

The following is one example of a rewritten clause with the type of extensive explanation and consultation British legal counsel are involved in:

---

[25] *Tax Law Rewrite: First Exposure Draft, Trading Income of Individuals*, Key Points (London: Inland Revenue, 1997). (available on the Internet at: http://www.open.gov.uk/inrev/rewrite.htm), p. 3.

[26] As above, p. 4.

3.1.9 Surplus business accommodation

1. A person carrying on a trade may treat rent obtained from a letting of surplus business accommodation as a receipt of the trade, and treat expenses of the letting as expenses of the trade, if the following conditions are met.

2. The conditions are:

   a. the rent must be in respect of part of a building of which the rest, or part of it, is used to carry on the trade;

   b. the rent must be relatively small;

   c. the accommodation must be temporarily surplus to requirements.

3. Accommodation is regarded as temporarily surplus to requirements only if:

   a. it has been used within the last three years to carry on the trade, or has been acquired within the last three years, and

   b. the trader intends to use it to carry on the trade at a later date, and

   c. the letting is for a term of not more than three years.

4. If any of the rent and expenses from a particular letting are treated as receipts or expenses of the trade under this section, all subsequent rent and expenses from that letter must be so treated, unless the conditions cease to be met.

5. If the conditions are met at the beginning of an accounting period, they shall be treated as continuing to be met until the end of that period even if the condition as to the accommodation being temporarily surplus to requirements ceases to be met before the end of the period. An *accounting period* means a period for which the person carrying on the trade draws up accounts.

6. This section does not apply to accommodation which consists of property held as trading stock.

   Defined terms: *trade* - section 3.1.4; *expenses* - section 3.2.3; *receipt* - section 3.2.3.
   Origin: new.

Commentary on Clause 3.1.9

1. This clause has a non-statutory source. It comes from a long-standing practice, well-known to tax practitioners but never formally published. It was described in an article in *Tax Bulletin* issue 10 (page 115, February 1994) headed "Revenue decisions: Schedule D: Cases I and II: Surplus Business Accommodation". *Tax Bulletin* is an Inland Revenue publication giving the views of the department's technical specialists on matters thought to be of interest to practitioners. The article is identified in some reference books as Revenue Decision 9.

2. The practice allows, subject to conditions, income from letting surplus space in business premises to be included in Case I/II computations rather than being assessed under Schedule A. Such inclusion is acknowledged to be contrary to the strict application of the law, but for many years Inspectors have been authorized to accept this treatment to save both them and taxpayers from having to dissect accounts to exclude relatively small amounts of rent and expenses.

Commentary on Clause 3.1.9 (cont'd)

3. As is usually the case with non-statutory material, the statement is expressed in much less rigorous terms than legislation. Subsection (3) attempts to give greater precision to the expression "temporarily surplus". It must not be assumed that it is an exact reflection of current Revenue practice. That would be impossible since the concession is administered with appropriate flexibility. It is hard for legislation to be so flexible, especially when taxpayers are required to assess themselves.

4. We are considering whether to define "relatively small" in the clause itself in terms of a cash limit. This is an example of a wider problem which will recur in the rewrite. A figure gives precision but updating it for inflation is a cumbersome process. A descriptive phrase is more flexible but taxpayers may then look to the Inland Revenue for public guidance on its interpretation. **We welcome views on this general problem.**

5. There are some changes from the published concession. Firstly, subsection (1) provides that, as well as treating rent as a receipt of the trade, a person may treat letting expenses as expenses of the trade. This is implicit in the operation of the concession but needs to be spelled out in legislation.

6. Subsection (4) likewise brings out into the open what is normally assumed to be the case. Once a person opts to have trading treatment for the letting of surplus accommodation, then the treatment must be applied for the rest of that particular letting. Without this condition, someone could switch from one treatment to another from year to year, which would add to the complexity of the tax computations. This would be inappropriate for a concessional practice which owes its existence to the need to simplify the drawing up of computations.

7. Similarly, the rewrite benefit would be reduced if taxpayers had to change treatment halfway through an accounting period. Subsection (5) permits a taxpayer to continue treating the rent and expenses as trading receipts and expenses once the accommodation has been let for three years, up until the end of the accounting period.

The above example illustrates the commitment to analyse and rewrite complex law thoughtfully. The partnering potential British Inland Revenue is offering to its public via the Internet is indeed admirable.

The next section deals with a particularly troublesome controversy for plain language proponents.

Is "required by statute" a red herring?

As George Hathaway argues, "Nothing has a more chilling effect on the promotion of plain [language] than the two simple razor-like little words—'it's statutory'".[27] Hathaway, however, claims that defending the use of certain words as statutory is deceptive: statutes often do not require the use of the *exact words* but words that are in substance the same. Other statutory requirements say "shall contain language that...".

---

[27] George Hathaway, "The Search for Legalese 'Required by Statutes'", *Michigan Bar Journal*, December 1990, p. 1286.

In practice, what often results is the slavish mimicry of even the most badly drafted statutory prose. Is there a need to copy poorly-written law to make something legal?

The phrase, "required by law", is used in Alberta's *Financial Consumers Act* (1990), the first Commonwealth Act to require the use of plain language in certain documents. Section 13(1) requires four categories of documents to be "in readily understandable language and form", but 13(2) declares "subsection (1) does not apply to words or forms of documents that are required by law".

The seemingly contradictory statements illustrate the "required by law" dilemma. Subsection 13(2) can be justified as providing a defence for those whose forms have followed the requirements of the law to the letter. It would indeed be unfair to hold anyone liable for a non-plain language document if another law *required* the person to use non-plain forms or words. However, such practices may inadvertently encourage maintenance of obscure statutory wording. Drafters, therefore, need to consider the latitude they have in drafting so they do not blindly follow a set of words.

In his analysis of specifications for a plain language statute, Reed Dickerson argues that the mandating of specific language and forms makes it more difficult to maintain high standards of drafting. He suggests a uniform or model simplification Act requiring language that is clear to "a modest level of readership". That Act could exempt the mandated provision or "require that mandated provisions likely to cause significant trouble . . . be supplemented by appropriate definitions, examples or explanations". Finally Dickerson urges drafters to scrutinize a form mandated by statute carefully and amend it appropriately.[28]

Drafters of new legislation might be better advised not to prescribe exact wording of the law but to emphasize that the intent or the effect of the legislation be required in words or forms. Alternatively, Martin Cutts argues that, in the same way that British government departments require plain language in their public forms, so too, should the same commitment be made to prescribed wordings in statutory notices.[29] For older legislation, it is a continuing dilemma which may lock drafters into unplain language and design.

Definitions in legislation—where and how?

In modern legislation, reform drafters have experimented with the location and style of definitions. Traditionally, some Acts clog up their texts with pages of definitions at the beginning. Some refer readers to a later section of an Act for the definition, yet use the term many times before the section. And some provide definitions which make no sense to readers without context.

Here are some common sense rules for definitions in legislation:

1.   Decide on the best location for definitions. At times, they may be better placed at the end with locators on each page.[30] (The margin locators are an excellent

---

[28] Reed Dickerson, "Readability Formulas and Specifications for a 'Plain English' Statute-Part 2", *Michigan Bar Journal*, July 1985, p. 715.

[29] As above, note 5, p. 19.

[30] See Martin Cutts' margin lists of definitions in his *Clearer Timeshare Act (1993)*, pp. 2-3, in *Lucid Law*. He justifies his placement of definitions at the end because the Act is short and the number of definitions small. Both

feature no matter where definitions are placed.) If the definitions carry with them their own context,[31] they may be placed at the beginning or the end.

2.   If the definition is difficult to understand without context, and only applies to one section, define the term within the section where it will be more easily understood.

3.   Decide on visual indicators to alert the reader to the non-dictionary defined terms in legislation: italicized terms are easier to read than the traditional capitalization. Yet beware of the pockmarked appearance of too many italicized words on the page. In his *Clearer Timeshare Act*,[32] Martin Cutts italicizes only the first appearance of a defined term; yet every page carries with it the margin list of all defined terms. (See example of this layout of margin definitions on p. 86.)

4.   An alternative to the margin list of defined terms would be to include a boxed instruction to the reader on the top right of each page:

> ***Defined terms*** in this Act are italicized in text, and defined on pages ___ to ____.

Another method is to asterisk the defined word. The Income Tax Assessment Act 1997 (Australia) unobtrusively sets the unbolded asterisk before the defined term or phrase. In addition, the Act contains a boxed footer on every page that looks like this:

> * To find definitions of asterisked terms, see the Dictionary starting at section 995-1.

The boxed instruction, expanded margin note, asterisked list, and margin list act as aids to partial reading and re-reading, and to reading by those unfamiliar with legislative linguistic protocol. Use the following checklist as a guide in writing new legislation and as an audit tool in reviewing old law:

New Zealand's *Income Tax Act 1994*, and Australia's *Income Tax Assessment Act 1997* have positioned long sets of definitions at the back of their respective Acts. In their dictionary, the New Zealand drafters also consolidated definitions—there are no longer seven definitions for "arrangement", for example.

[31] For example, the definition in the *Financial Consumers Act (Alberta)* of *commission* which means "compensation, reward or benefit, but does not include salary", is easy to understand.

[32] As above, note 5, centre pages.

Checklist of Plain Language Features for Legislation	
Architecture of sentences	• Limit sentences to an average of 30 words or less. Parallel segments can be counted as single sentences. • Place core idea first and exceptions after, unless the syntax is a simple **If . . . then** construction. • Break long sentences with comparable chunks into parallel segments. • Use question headings when appropriate.
Boxes	• Use boxes for methods statements, explanatory notes, or others.
Citizen's Summary	• Consider using these summaries to help ordinary readers.
Concept checklist	• Consider a concept checklist to augment the definitions when the act is long or complex (see the *Australian Tax Act*).
Diagrams and charts	• Use diagrams, charts, tables, or other visual aids to replace words when they make reading easier.
Indexes	• Indexes are indispensable for long complex acts.
Navigational aids	• Use tables of contents, tables of sections (in long acts), preliminary guides (the *Australian Tax Act* uses **How to use this Act** and **How to find your way around**), transitional notes, cross references and visual indicators for definitions.
Numbers	• Make numbers stand out in their own white space. • Consider a decimal numbering system or numbers separated by dashes as in the *Australian Tax Act* on pp. 221 to 238.
Typography (Martin Cutts suggests most of these for his *Clearer Timeshare Act*)	• **Size -** Choose a minimum x-height (height of lower case 'x') of 1.5 mm. He used 1.8 for his text. • **Typeface -** Consider a font other than Times (designed for the narrow columns of newspapers). I have used Palatino in this book for main text similar to Cutts' choice of Plantin. They "breathe" a little easier and are more pleasing to the eye.

Checklist of Plain Language Features for Legislation (cont'd)	
Typograph (Martin Cutts suggests most of these for his *Clearer Timeshare Act*) (cont'd)	• **Justification** - Research suggests ragged right is easier to read. • **Headings** - Ensure headings stand out visibly from the text with size and boldness. • **Leading** - Times typeface which has a larger y-height, requires generous leading for long, dense subsections. Cutts' leading is 1.5 points but is generous between sections. • **Line width** - Cutts' rule of thumb is 50-70 characters and spaces to the line for good legibility. • **Margins** - Keep the inside margins to 30 mm so text can be easily seen at the spine when bound. • **Style** - Reading research recommends a serif font for text. Sans-serif fonts may be used contrastively for headings.
Vocabulary	• Provide plain language for common legislative legalese such as *shall* (*must*, *may* or *will* or another tense of the verb), *in respect of, respecting* (*about* or *for*), *notwithstanding* (*despite* or *even if*) , *where* (*if*), *thereunder, thereof, hereby, provided that* (*but* or *if*) and *pursuant to* (*under*)
What is operative?	• One commentator at the New Zealand Tax Conference emphasized that the arrangement of the Act was a *system*—you don't look at the parts in isolation.[33] The *Australian Act* makes as parts of the Act all of the following: • chapter, part, division, and subdivision headings • guides • section and subsection headings • notes and examples that follow provisions It declares as not parts of the Act: • footnotes and endnotes • tables of subdivisions • tables of sections There is a whole section on the role of guides in interpreting the Act.

---

[33] Tom Reid, as above, note 19, p. 148.

Finally, the unintelligibility of many laws results in high economic costs: extra costs for legal regulations and compliance, a distorted demand for legal services, obstacles to corporate decision-making, and costly administration.

The costs to a democracy are incalculable. Making law understandable to the people it rules is the founding principle of plain language legislation. The Attorney General of Victoria (Australia) wrote in 1985:

> What needs to happen now is to have a process whereby Parliamentary Counsel draft Bills . . . from the outset in plain English. This requires a radical departure from tradition. . . . [i]t requires *imagination, a spirit of adventure and a boldness* not normally associated with the practice of law or with the drafting of legislation . . . [34] [author's emphasis]

It is heartening to see plain language reforms abroad.[35] Yet there are miles to go before we sleep.

---

[34] Victoria Law Reform Commission (Australia), *Plain English and the Law, Report No. 9, 1987*, p. 1.

[35] Happily, here in Canada, a November, 1998 presentation to the Canadian Association of the Administration of Justice described an ambitious plain language redrafting of the federal *Employment Insurance Act*. Drafters are experimenting with many of the features described in this chapter. "Designing Clear Documents: The Art of Compromise, Employment Insurance Act Plain Language Project", presented by Irene Gendron and Philippe Hallée, both Legislative Counsel, Department of Justice of Canada, Ottawa.

Chapter 9
Collective Agreements
Chapter Consultant: Peggy Kobly, LL.B.

What this chapter does
The chapter:
1 explores the nature, purposes, and readers of collective agreements
2 examines selected research on the readability of collective agreements
3 looks at potential effects on readers of common collective contract language
4 uses as a case history a clause from a Canadian provincial government master collective agreement. The clause has required three levels of judicial interpretation.
5 provides *before* and *after* plain language examples from that agreement

> As an arbitrator who has looked at hundreds of collective agreements, I am convinced that time, money, grievances and arbitrations could be saved if more time were spent creating understandable language.
>
> David Elliott

The nature, purposes and readers of collective agreements

Their nature

Collective agreements have been described as the cornerstone of collective bargaining in North America. Though vital to national and regional policies, many collective agreements are astonishingly badly written. Competitiveness in national and international markets is impeded when parties to agreements are forced to seek interpretations of their words. The latter are expensive, waste time, create conflict, and undermine good labour relations.

Collective agreements are important to millions of workers. Not only do they serve as rule books for labour-management relations, they reflect broader purposes, according to researchers:

> By reflecting the economic, legal, social, ethical, and even political concerns of both parties, [these agreements] delineate the environment in which labour and management operate. In effect, the agreements communicate important attributes of a company's culture and value system.[1]

The authors then argue that the "tangled language" of the collective agreements they examined produced distrust in workers, and undercut, rather than supported a coherent value system.

---

[1] James Suchan and Clyde Scott, "Unclear Contract Language and Its Effect on Corporate Culture", *Business Horizons*, Jan/Feb 1986, p. 23.

Their purposes

Collective agreements should serve to
1. communicate information and state legal requirements
2. communicate clearly to their readers and still be legally effective
3. reflect a common ground acceptable to both parties after negotiators have bargained for their respective positions

For difficult clauses which may subsequently be interpreted by an arbitrator, *acceptable* may mean some *dissatisfaction*, but both are willing to "live with it".[2]

It is the second purpose which is widely overlooked as the research (below) shows.

Their readers

The readership of collective agreements is vast. In 1986, James Suchon and Clyde Scott estimated that there were then roughly 20 million union workers in North America alone, the majority of whom have difficulty understanding their work rules laid down in collective agreements.[3] The Alberta Union of Provincial Employees, a 1998 example, one of the parties to the collective agreement discussed later in this chapter, encompasses some 20,000 employees. The other party, government civil servants who supervise or manage union employees, will have as diverse skills and background as union employees—few of them with a knowledge of legal language.

Potential readers of collective agreements include employees, their family members, union representatives, managers, supervisors, shop stewards, various executive-type officers or officials, negotiators, lawyers, arbitrators, and judges. Collective agreements are frequently interpreted by people who *were not part of* the negotiations: union representatives, personnel managers, arbitrators and the courts.

What should be most significant to drafters of collective agreements are the numbers of readers who never sign the agreement and the enormous range of their reading skills. Collective agreements are not written for business people skilled in manoeuvering through the torturous waters of legalese.

Research on collective agreements

For nearly 50 years, researchers have pointed to the hazards of unclear or difficult-to-read collective bargaining agreements.[4] No matter how professional the union (public teachers, the film industry, nurses, universities), there seems little progress in developing excellent standards for plain language collective agreements.

---

[2] In "Writing Collective Agreements in Plain Language" 1992, p. 2 (unpublished paper in my collection), David Elliott states that such clauses, which both parties acknowledge may in future require interpretation by an arbitrator, are few. Most clauses, he maintains, are not constrained by this type of tension.
[3] As above, note 1, p. 22.
[4] For examples, see Leanne Lauer and D.G. Patterson, "Readability of Union Contracts", *Personnel*, Vol. 28, No. 1, 1951, pp. 36-40; Joesph Tiffin and Francis X. Walsh, "Readability of Union Management Agreements", *Personnel Psychology*, Vol. 4, No. 4, 1951, pp. 327-338; as above, note 1, pp. 20-25; and as above, note 2.

Why are collective agreements so poorly written?

1. The negotiating process itself

One hypothesis is that the process of negotiation itself, by representatives who are not writing specialists, results in poor products. Clearly, the main focus of collective bargaining representatives is producing documents they perceive to be legally effective and which maintain positions those they represent will accept. These drafters do not take the extra step to ensure that all other readers, especially primary readers, will understand their documents.

This is not to castigate negotiators whose expertise is negotiating, not writing. They may have had little or no training in plain language techniques. They may have spent years reading poorly drafted clauses. (Including a plain language specialist as an adjunct to the negotiating team would seem a practical solution.)

2. Standard clauses

Another plausible reason for poor drafting of collective agreements is labour negotiators' reliance on precedent agreements and encyclopedias of collective bargaining contract clauses. Negotiators choose and tailor clauses that fit their issues. Using overly-long, complicated, and prefabricated segments produces incomprehensible text.

3. Different linguistic culture

Unlike their readers, negotiators are used to reading the labyrinthine legalese that dominates collective agreements. Thus their minds are conditioned to spew out the same language. Yet non-negotiator readers are used to the language of the public media—short sentences, concrete wording, helpful headings and active voice verbs. The *hereunders*, the *aforesaids*, the *said articles*, and the *and/ors* create a foreign world for them.

Research on the readability levels of collective agreements

Suchan and Scott's 1986 research analyses the readability[5] of a seniority clause, a discipline clause, and a grievance clause in each of 196 bargaining agreements. Their sampling ranged from Teamsters and the United Auto Workers to the Motion Picture Guild. They examined clauses from contracts with only 17 employees to those covering 160,000 workers in both public and private sectors.

Using three time-tested readability formulas, Flesch's Reading Ease Formula, Gunning's Fog Index[6], and Farr-Jenkins-Patterson's Reading Ease Index, the two researchers proclaimed the results of their research "surprising and sad".

According to the first and third tests, 95 to 99 percent of collective agreements were either difficult or very difficult for the rank and file to understand. Gunning's Fog Index indicated readers of their 196 agreements would need 18 years of education to unscramble a typical union-management agreement.

---

[5] See Chapter 5 of this *Handbook* for a more detailed explanation of readability.
[6] Chapter 5 includes Gunning's Fog Index. You can easily assess the readability of any legal text using this method. Note, however, as explained in the chapter, readability is only *one of several* factors indicating how easy or difficult a text is to read and comprehend.

In 1990, David Elliott tested 30 randomly selected Alberta collective agreements. Following Suchan and Scott, he tested the readability level of the seniority, discipline, and grievance clauses, restricting his study to the first 100 words of each. Elliott used the Flesch formula because it is well organized, easy to apply, and had been adopted by a number of states to assess whether insurance policies met their legal requirements for plain language.

Elliott's conclusions were similar to the American researchers. The clauses were either difficult or very difficult to read. Later in this chapter, we look at a current government collective agreement which shows little progress since that time.[7]

Consequences of poorly written collective agreements

1. Lessens sense of job ownership

Union members to an agreement who are bound by it, but never sign anything, may be suspicious of agreements. Their past experience may have shown them that control of their job rights was more restrictive than they expected. Feeling uncertain about the meaning of their collective agreements may create anger over their dependence on others to explain the terms of their employment. The sense of ownership of their jobs which managements want to engender diminishes. Controlling the language and comprehension of a collective agreement results in a parent/child relationship, not worker autonomy.

2. Causes or complicates grievances or arbitrations

Plain language collective agreements will not stop all grievances. Yet it stands to reason that eliminating avoidably ambiguous words and phrases means less interpretation. Plain language agreements lay out more clearly the rights and responsibilities of the parties. Some grievances will be avoided altogether; others will allow parties and the arbitrator to concentrate on the problem instead of untangling the incomprehensible text of the agreement. Rewriting an agreement in plain language will pay for itself if it stops just one arbitration. (There will, as noted above, always be the "compromise wording" of hard-fought clauses. It is not these I refer to here.)

3. Results in fewer informed workers and managers

There are detrimental effects when organizations use difficult-to-read collective agreements. People are less likely to read and understand a poorly written document, and less likely to comply with its rules and respect them. This in turn negatively affects the work environment.

Case history of a 1998 public sector collective agreement clause

To make the discussion in this chapter less abstract, we have used an Alberta collective agreement to illustrate both the consequences of poor drafting and the result of redrafting selective segments in plain language.

Article 15 of the Collective Agreement between the Government of the Province of Alberta and the Alberta Union of Provincial Employees deals with the process for "Position Abolishment". The Article has 14 sub-paragraphs dealing with employees'

---

[7] I am, however, always always on the lookout for examples of new plain language collective agreements.

rights when positions are "abolished". These rights include the right to compete for comparable positions within the Public Service, the right to "bump" wage employees, and the right to severance pay. These rights, however, are available subject to certain conditions. Article 15.05 reads:

> An Employee whose position is declared abolished and for whom the Employer has not arranged continuing employment in the Alberta Public Service or with any successor employer, or with any other Crown agency (including Boards, Corporations, Agencies and Commissions) shall be eligible for placement through limited competition as follows:

Alberta abolished all the Corrections Officer positions at the Grade Cache Correctional Centre, after negotiating the transfer of the facility to the Federal Government. As part of the terms of the transfer, the Federal government offered, and the Corrections Officers accepted, continuing employment at the institution.

The Corrections Officers sought severance pay under Article 15, but the Government of Alberta argued that the officers were not eligible because it had arranged continuing employment within the meaning of Article 15.

The officers took the matter to arbitration, alleging that the Government had breached Article 15, and arguing that their continuing employment with the Federal Government was not "continuing employment with the Alberta Public Service or with any successor employer, or with any other Crown agency (including Boards, Corporations, Agencies and Commissions)". The Union argued that the phrase "any successor employer" must be interpreted within the context of the other types of employers mentioned in the list of provincial public sector employers.

The Arbitrator agreed with the Union's argument, and noted that the rationale underlying this interpretation was:

> . . . to relieve the Employer of certain obligations under that Article when it arranges ongoing employment with a successor employer within the (provincial) public sector because in that situation the employee is more likely to retain such things as recognition of seniority, continuation of pensions, etc. Why else would the Employer be relieved of these obligations with respect to the specifically enumerated categories of employers under this Article?

Alberta unsuccessfully sought judicial review of this decision in the Court of Queen's Bench and appealed the Queen's Bench decision to the Court of Appeal. The Court of Appeal has not yet given its decision.

Had the parties drafted the article in plain language, their differences would have become apparent much earlier. For example, the employer might have used language like this:

> 15.05   An employee whose position is abolished is eligible to compete in limited competitions for other available positions, unless the Employer has arranged continuing other employment with any other employer. The procedures to be followed in limited competition are: . . .

The Union's approach might have been:

> 15.05   An employee whose position is abolished is eligible to compete in limited competition for other available positions, unless the Employer has arranged continuing other employment with the Government of Alberta or an Alberta Crown Corporation. The procedures to be followed in limited competition are: . . .

Both rewrites are unambiguous, yet it is highly unlikely that the parties would have agreed to each other's rewrite without further hard bargaining. This is not to suggest that either party deliberately left the language ambiguous. It is not unusual in collective bargaining that parties have distinctly different interpretations of what was bargained for and agreed to.

This example demonstrates that plain language often highlights substantive differences, and is not merely aimed at clarifying difficult-to-read passages. The parties in collective bargaining face two choices:

a. Negotiate language that is as clear and unambiguous as possible, or

b. Agree on less precise language, which may be open to interpretation.

The first option, admittedly easier said than done, may result in a more protracted negotiation process, but one in which the parties are less likely to disagree about future contract interpretation. Plain language reduces the risk of lengthy and expensive arbitration proceedings in which a third party could impose an interpretation of the agreement that one, or even both, parties did not anticipate.

The following table shows how format and clauses in the collective agreement leave readers nonplussed. We have changed both style and substance to illustrate plain language collective agreement writing.

5. Selected *before* and *after* examples from the Alberta Government and Union of Provincial Employees Collective Agreement

Original	Reasons for change	Plain language version
This Agreement made the 4th day of October, 1994 BETWEEN	Wordy, no title, capitalization, unconventional placement of *between* (for lay readers)	Collective Agreement October 4, 1994 between
THE CROWN IN RIGHT OF ALBERTA (hereinafter referred to as the Employer) - and - THE ALBERTA UNION OF PROVINCIAL EMPLOYEES (hereinafter referred to as the Union)	Capitalization, wordy, needs a clarification of "Crown" for non-legal readers	The Crown in Right of Alberta (The Employer, the Alberta Government) and the Alberta Union of Provincial Employees (the Union)
WHEREAS, the Union has the sole right to negotiate and conclude a Collective Agreement on behalf of the Employees of the Crown pursuant to the Public Service Employee Relations Act; and (31 words) WHEREAS, the parties are mutually desirous of entering into a Collective Agreement consisting of a master and subsidiary agreement, with the intent and purpose to promote a harmonious relationship between the Employees and the Employer, and to set forth in this Collective Agreement rates of pay, hours of work and conditions of employment. (53 words)	Ancient, wordy WHEREAS clauses, incorrect punctuation (commas and period). This section is a sentence fragment. There is ambiguity between the master and subsidiary agreements. How many agreements? Which takes precedent? What is the relationship between them? (We have not settled these matters in our rewrite.)	**Background** Under the Public Service Employee Relations Act, the Union is the exclusive bargaining agent for the Alberta Government. (18 words) This Collective Agreement, a master and ____ subsidiary agreements, sets out pay rates, work hours and employment conditions. (18 words)

Original	Reasons for change	Plain language version
NOW THEREFORE, the Parties mutually agree as follows	Tautalogous. Delete.	
Article 15 **POSITION ABOLISHMENT** 15.01 Employer will make a reasonable effort to effect reduction in the workforce through attrition prior to and during the position abolishment process.	Overly officious and wordy language. High readability clause. Question: Is there any practical effect? Other than trying to persuade employees to take early retirement? Could this be deleted?	**Article 15** **Abolishing Positions** 15.01 The Employer will make a reasonable effort to reduce the workforce through attrition (retirement, sickness, death) before eliminating any filled positions.
15.02 The Employing Department shall give a permanent Employee at least ninety (90) calendar days prior written notice that his position is to be abolished. The Employing Department will provide a copy of the written notice to the Union. The Employing Department will notify the Union thirty (30) calendar days in advance of any formal position abolishment notice being provided to Employees.	The ambiguous *shall*. Sexist language: *his*. Passive voice verbs. Numbers duplication. Wordiness. The "30 days" is confusing—use "120 days". Consider no subheadings?	15.02 Employers must give a written notice to: (a) the Union about eliminating any position 30 calendar days before giving final notice to an employee (120 days before the position ends): (b) a permanent Employee at least 90 calendar days before eliminating his or her position. They must send a copy of the Employee's notice to the Union.

Original	Reasons for change	Plain language version
15.03 The Employee may resign in writing and receive pay at his regular rate in lieu of part of the notice specified in Clause 15.02 to a maximum of two (2) months' pay. If eligible, the Employee may retire pursuant to the Public Service Pension Act with such retirement to be effective on or after the date notice pursuant to 15.02 expires, however, if the Employee resigns and retires before the end of the notice period, he shall not receive pay in lieu of the notice.	Run-on sentence. Sexist language. Wordiness. Ambiguous *shall*. What does "part of the notice specified in Clause 15.02" refer to? Does it refer to a failure to notify the Union on time, or to a failure to notify the employer on time? Both? (The rewrite assumes the reference refers to both.) Duplication of numbers and words.	15.03 If the employer fails to meet the notification requirements specified in Clause 15.02: (a) Instead of working the entire notice period, an employee may resign in writing before the end of the 90 days, and receive a maximum of two months' severance pay at his or her regular rate; (b) An employee who is eligible to retire under the Public Service Pension Act, may retire at the end of the notice period. If the employee chooses to retire before the end of the notice period, he or she will not be paid severance pay.

This chapter has discussed the significant consequences of hurriedly written and often ambiguous clauses in collective agreements. As well, agreements may contain spelling inconsistencies, grammatical mistakes, inaccurate cut and pastes of former agreements and indecipherable legalese. For example, in the AUPE agreement there are three spelling variants on one page for the noun *layoff* (see the *Canadian Oxford Dictionary*, 1998).[8] They are *lay-off* (this is the version given in definition), *lay off* (which is the spelling of the verb to *lay off*), and *layoff*.

On the next page of the agreement, a 55-word sentence includes a dangling participle, an ambiguous *shall*, and confusion between singular and plural references:

> In determining which of similar Employees are to be recalled to positions within a classification, at a location and work unit as determined by the Employing Department, recall shall be on the basis of the seniority of such similar Employees, provided the Employee recalled is qualified and able to perform the work that is available.[9]

Collective agreements will become more valuable to employers and unions alike if they use drafters skilled in plain language styles and techniques.

---

[8] *Master Agreement between the Government of the Province of Alberta and the Alberta Union of Provincial Employees*, October 4, 1994, p. 13.
[9] As above, Article 12.06, p. 14.

Chapter 10
Family Law
Chapter Consultant: Jane Bergman, LL.B

What this chapter does
This chapter:
1 provides a context for plain language changes to traditional family law language
2 compares *Before* and *After* segments from a Minutes of Settlement
3 presents a practical, detailed plain language information letter to clients describing the steps and issues to consider in the process of obtaining an uncontested divorce

---

A context for audience-sensitive divorce agreements

The decisions made by separating or divorcing spouses carry with them an intense emotional context. Parties are required to sign documents when they are still in shock, grieving, angry, or emotionally fragile in other ways. Presenting documents which are written primarily for lawyers or judges adds to the difficulties of separating spouses. The need for plain language is transparent.

There are many actual and potential readers of an agreement between separating spouses or common law partners. They include the separating parties, their lawyers, older children, trusted relatives and friends, new partners, accountants, government agencies, possible mediators, psychologists or psychiatrists, and judges.

I have chosen two documents to illustrate how plain language may be used in this area. The first is common, and the second is not, but perhaps should be. The common one, Minutes of Settlement, is burdened by a forbidding-sounding title for non-lawyers. The Alberta Law Reform Institute's plain language draft of a Minutes of Settlement[1] was pleasingly retitled *Child Custody, Support and Property Division Agreement*. The After document in this chapter, an adaptation of the Institute's work, retains that title, many of their words and emphasis, and suggests some revisions. For the *Handbook*'s purposes here, the focus is only on the first half of the document.

Some changes may seem trite to a lawyer who has automatically used the traditional forms for years. Yet to the parties, reading the words *wife* and *husband*, in a document which describes the terms of their separation, can be painful. Or consider a client who has never read a legal document, or is a new immigrant. Even the phrase "suit for divorce" may be bewildering. The primary audiences here are the separating spouses who may refer to the document many times over the years to clarify details, or to refresh their memories.

---

[1] Presented at the *Just Language Conference*, Vancouver, BC, October 1992.

The rewritten portion of a *Minutes of Settlement* carefully delineates the terms *joint custody* and *access*, terms which are open to interpretation by each judge and lawyer. The document provides unambiguous guides for the separating parties, with the objective of reducing unnecessary future dissent. This document represents one couple's decisions, and one model of plain language. The section on spousal support, for example, follows the Alberta Law Reform Institute's assumption in their plain language draft that the parties intend the arrangement on spousal support to be final. Thus, they worded the agreement to be as final as possible. Every settlement agreement, however, must be tailored to the particular parties' needs.

The second document, a client reporting letter, contains information which lawyers in family law usually just discuss with their clients, but don't write down. The purpose of the letter is to provide clients with a record of the steps they can anticipate in order to obtain a divorce. The consultant to this chapter tested this letter on clients and received comments on its usefulness. Clients often forget the information they have been given verbally, or remain confused about the process in spite of conscientious discussions with their lawyers. Accompanying the letter is a flow chart to allow a visual overview of the road to divorce, its possible backroad options, detours, and byways.

Title Page BEFORE   **Title Page AFTER**

CHILD CUSTODY, SUPPORT AND PROPERTY DIVISION AGREEMENT BETWEEN JOHN SMITH AND MARY SMITH	Agreement about Separation, Child Custody, Support, and Property Division between Mary Smith and John Smith March 20, 1994

TITLE PAGE — CHANGES
- increased the font point size [type in box not proportionate to page sizes above]
- eliminated the capitals to increase readability
- added the last signature date for ease of reference
- created space before the parties' names for emphasis
- added the word *Separation* to the title to reflect that aspect as well

Table of Contents

TABLE OF CONTENTS—CHANGES
- No table of contents in the original
- * Instead of the original heading, *Miscellaneous*, we substituted these headings: *Payment of legal fees*, *How to change or cancel this agreement*, and *Governing Law*.

The Facts BEFORE

THE FACTS

1. This agreement is between MARY SMITH (called "the wife" in this agreement) AND JOHN SMITH (called "the husband" in this agreement).

2. The following is true

    a) the husband and wife were married on 15 June 1982;

    b) the husband and wife separated on 15 March 1992;

    c) there are two children of the marriage: SUSAN SMITH, born on 1 February, 1984 and ROBERT SMITH, born on 15 April 1986;

    d) the husband and wife are joint owners of [street address] on lands legally described as [legal description] (called "the home" in this agreement);

    e) The wife has started a suit for divorce in the Court of Queen's Bench of Alberta, Judicial District of Edmonton in action number XXXXX applying for:

        i)   a divorce judgment;

        ii) an order for joint custody of the children;

        iii) an order requiring the husband to pay child support to the wife of $500 a month for each child;

        iv) an order requiring the husband to pay spousal support to the wife of $250 a month for three years.

Background AFTER

Background

1. This agreement is between Mary Smith and John Smith.

2. John and Mary were married on June 15, 1982. They separated on March 15, 1992. There are two children of the marriage: Susan Smith, born February 1, 1984 and Robert Smith, born April 15, 1986.

3. John and Mary are joint owners of [street address] on lands legally described as [legal description] (called "the house" in this agreement).

4. Mary has begun divorce proceedings in the Court of Queen's Bench of Alberta, Judicial District of Edmonton (Action Number XXXXX) applying for:

    a) a divorce,

    b) joint custody of the children,

    c) child support from John of $500 a month for each child, and

    d) spousal support from John of $250 a month for three years starting June 1, 1998.

THE FACTS—CHANGES
- changed the heading to *Background*, a more natural term for the information here
- eliminated the references to *wife* and *husband,* and substituted the parties' names using first names only after the initial full names
- deleted *The following is true* as it added nothing
- regrouped the information into four points: names of the parties to the agreement; details of the marriage, separation, and children's births; house ownership; and Mary Smith's divorce proceedings applications
- substituted *divorce proceedings* for *suit for divorce*
- substituted *house* for *home* because of the emotional connotations of the word *home*
- eliminated the unfamiliar syntax of *in action number* and used a parenthesis instead
- cut out the unnecessary legal terms *judgment* and *order*
- redrafted the last two points more concisely
- reduced the three levels of numbering to two
- changed the semicolons to commas in the new 4 a) to d)

Separation BEFORE

3. The husband and wife will live apart from one another, as though they are not married.

Separation AFTER

5. **Separation**
   John and Mary will live apart from one another.

Child Custody, Access, and Support BEFORE

4. The husband and the wife have joint custody of the children.

5. The husband and wife will put the best interests of the children before their own interests. They will help both children have a good relationship with both of them. They will talk to one another about important questions of the children's upbringing, for example, about their

    -   religious upbringing,
    -   education,
    -   social environment,
    -   health care (unless there is an emergency).

6. The children will live primarily with the wife.

7. The husband will have reasonable and generous access to the children.

Child Custody, Access, and Support AFTER

6. **Child Custody**
6.1 Mary and John will have joint custody of the children, that is, have equal say in major decisions affecting the children.

6.2 John and Mary will put the best interests of the children before their own interests. They will help both children have a good relationship with both their parents. They will talk to one another about important questions of the children's upbringing, for example, about their

    -   religious upbringing,
    -   education,
    -   social environment, and
    -   health care (unless there is an emergency).

7. **Living Arrangements for the Children**
    The children will live primarily with Mary. On alternate weekends, one mid-week night per week, and one month each summer, the children will live with John, unless Mary and John mutually agreed to a change in this schedule.

8. **Parental Access to the Children**
    Both parents will have reasonable and generous telephone access to the children when living with the other parent.

SEPARATION—CHANGES
- substituted John and Mary for *husband* and *wife*. This was done throughout the rest of the document, too, changing the order of the names regularly to ensure that one party was not prominent
- deleted *as though they are not married*. Its inclusion does not ensure anything nor make any condition clearer

CHILD CUSTODY, ACCESS, AND SUPPORT—CHANGES
- reorganized Part 2 with subheadings and clearer specifics, for example, defining what *joint custody* means for this separating couple, and clarifying what John Smith's rights are in terms of *generous access*
- added the subheadings "Living Arrangements for the Children" and "Parental Access to the Children" for easier reference.
- changed the verb in Clause 4, *have* to *will have*, to make it consistent with the Clause 3 verb, *will live apart*
- eliminated the referent ambiguity in Clause 5 (*with both of them*) by substituting *with both their parents*
- grouped Clauses 4 and 5 since both points referred to child custody

The final segments are presented only as *After* examples with comments on changes.

9. **Child Support**
9.1 John will pay child support to Mary
   a) of $800 a month until otherwise agreed or ordered, and
   b) 60% of all extraordinary expenses which include:

   (i) daycare costs
   (ii) extracurricular activities
   (iii) medical and dental costs

9.2 John will stop paying child support to Mary for a child who:

   a) is not attending school full time or
   b) is under the age of 18 who stops being dependant on Mary or
   c) gets married

9.3 Every May 15th, John and Mary will exchange Income Tax Returns and review the amount of child support John pays based on the Federal Child Support Guidelines. The new payment, if any, will start on June 1st of each year.

9.4 John will include each child on any extended medical or dental benefits in the insurance plan that is available to him through his employment for as long as he is obliged to pay child support for that child.

CHILD SUPPORT—CHANGES
- Due to change in the laws regarding child support, the agreement provides for a global child support payment that can be reviewed annually based on the parents' incomes.

10. **Resolving disputes about the children**
    If Mary and John cannot agree on a matter affecting one or both of the children, they will first try to resolve the disagreement through mediation or assessment by an agreed upon professional (such as a child psychologist or psychiatrist). If this fails, the matter will be settled by applying to the Court of Queen's Bench of Alberta.

11. **Spousal support**

RESOLVING DISAGREEMENTS—CHANGES
- substituted the word *professional* for *assessor*
- changed the title to more accurately relect the subject matter—otherwise it was too generic

The second family law document (below)* illustrates how a client information letter in plain language can provide a useful overview of the process ahead. Such handouts can eliminate the anxiety associated with trying to remember unfamiliar language and steps. Your clients will find that these resource "maps" contribute to their peace of mind. Plain language interpretations create good will and can be referred to with friends and family.

---

*Jane Bergman writes: "The responses that I have had to the client information letter are somewhat limited. My clients are usually content to have it, yet they rarely comment directly on it. Unfortunately, (or perhaps fortunately for them), they have not been through the process before so they have no other experience to compare it with. They seem to think it is ordinary and appropriate for them to have it. I suggest it should be. I can say that it is easier for me, as their lawyer, to be able to direct them to an outlined procedure when they contact me with questions. I also find I have fewer calls from clients wondering about the timing or the next stage than I used to.

Barristers & Solicitors
#242, 123 - 4th Street S.W.
Calgary, AB T0X 0X0
Phone: (403) 555-1212
Fax: (403) 555-6666

> **Client-help Sheet**
> **Keep for Reference**

July 8, 1998

Mary Jane Client
Address
Address

Dear Mary Jane Client:

Client Information Letter

This letter will help you with the process we have begun today. As it is difficult to remember all the information we covered, this letter explains the steps you can anticipate in obtaining your divorce. Depending on the decisions you and (*spouse's name*) make, the steps may include options. The accompanying flow chart maps those processes.

Your preparation for our next meeting
1. Obtain the following documents to bring to our next meeting:

    (i)   Marriage Certificate*
    (ii)   Statements on RRSPs, investments, or pensions
    (iii)   Bank balances, accounts
    (iv)   Income tax forms (last three years for both spouses)
    (v)   Mortgage Statement
    (vi)   Certificate of Title (to house)
    (vii)   Any credit card or loan statements for current debts

    *   If you do not have your certificate, phone my office, and I will order one for you from a registry office.

If your husband refuses to allow you access to any of the above information, please telephone me. I will then arrange for a *Notice to Disclose* (a document requiring your husband to give us the information) to be delivered to your husband.

2. Discuss with your husband whether he is prepared to move out, and when. If he is unwilling to do so, I will file a *Notice of Motion* along with an *Affidavit* to obtain an *Order for Exclusive Possession of the Matrimonial Home*.

3. Review the following **Issues to consider when you decide to separate** below, pages 2 and 3. If possible, discuss these issues with your spouse. Make notes on your answers and concerns.

Client Information Letter - page 2

Issues to consider when you decide to separate

1. **Marital status**

   (a) Do you want to live separately but remain married, or do you want a divorce?

   (b) Are there "grounds" (reasons accepted by law) for a divorce? To apply for a divorce, you must be able to prove **one** of the following:

       (i) that you and your spouse have not lived together for at least one year,

       (ii) that your spouse has had an affair recently, or that you have recently found out about the affair,

       (iii) that your spouse has recently emotionally, or physically abused you **[some lawyers may not want to include this item.]**

2. **Support payments for either spouse**

   (a) Can you financially support yourself without help? Can your spouse financially support himself/herself without help?

   (b) How much money do you (or does he) need as support? For how long?

   (c) If no payments are to be made at this time, will both spouses agree not to apply for support later?

   (d) Do you both understand the tax implications of support payments? (For example, if your spouse pays you spousal support payments, those payments are deducted from his taxable income. The payments to you are added to your taxable income. Payments you receive as child support are not taxable.)

3. **Children**

   (a) Who will be responsible for making important decisions about the children's lives?

   (b) Where will the children live, and when will they live there?

   (c) When will the children be able to stay or visit with your spouse?

   (d) What are your respective incomes? Which spouse will be paying the child support?

   (e) What expenses are paid for each child? Do any of the children have:

       i)   daycare costs
       ii)   extracurricular costs
       iii) school costs
       iv) medical or dental costs

   (f) How long will the support for children be payable?

Client Information Letter - page 3

4. **Property**

    (a) Will you or your spouse stay in the house? Who owns the house?

    (b) How will the remaining property be divided?

    (c) Are there pension plans, savings or investments to be divided?

    (d) Does any of the property belong solely to one of the spouses? (Categories for sole ownership of property can include: (i) property owned by a spouse before marriage (ii) property received as an inheritance or gift (iii) money received by settlement from an accident.)

5. **Costs**

    (a) Who will pay for the legal costs?*

    *Please see notes on legal costs at the end of this letter.

Many clients cannot answer all these questions. One of my roles as your lawyer is to make recommendations about average payments based on your incomes. As well, I will recommend a mediator if you are having difficulty resolving separation or divorce issues. The mediator will meet with you and your spouse to help you decide on terms which will be written into an Agreement.

If you are unable to negotiate terms with your spouse, it may be necessary to prepare a *Court Application*. A judge then decides what the terms should be.

If you and your spouse agree on all issues related to separation, child support, custody, and property division, your divorce will be treated as an uncontested divorce. The next set of information describes the process for obtaining an uncontested divorce.

Client Information Letter - page 4

The process for an uncontested divorce

Person responsible	Action
Client	1. delivers (or mails) required documents to lawyer.
Lawyer	2. prepares a *Statement of Claim for Divorce*.
Client	3. reviews the *Statement of Claim for Divorce*.
Lawyer	4. files the *Statement of Claim* at the Court House. In practice, court filing is done by a *court runner* who takes the document to the Clerk of Court who officially stamps the document and provides stamped copies for the lawyer.
	5. arranges for a filed copy of the *Statement of Claim* to be served on (personally given to) your spouse. Our office asks your spouse to come to the office for his copy of the *Statement of Claim*.
	6. records in a sworn statement for the Judge (called an *Affidavit of Service*) the day your spouse was given the *Statement of Claim*.
Client's spouse	7. within 15 days*, reviews the *Statement of Claim* and decides if he wishes to hire a lawyer to fight the divorce. Then he or his lawyer must file *a Statement of Defence*. *If* he is not opposing any part of the Divorce, your spouse need not do anything further. Or, he may file a *Demand of Notice*, which is an acknowledgement that he will not contest the divorce, but wants to approve documents before the divorce is finalized.

*If the *Statement of Claim* is served outside Alberta, but in Canada, the time allowed is 40 days. If it is served outside Canada, other procedures apply.

Client Information Letter - page 5

Person Responsible	Action
Lawyer	8. if the divorce is uncontested, on the 16th day after your spouse has been given the *Statement of Claim*, prepares a statement, called an *Affidavit*, for you to sign. This document asks the judge to give you a divorce, and provides all the information the Judge needs in order to grant the divorce. The *Affidavit* represents your voice speaking, without the need for you to go to Court.
Client	9. signs the *Affidavit*.
Lawyer	10. prepares and sends three documents to accompany the *Affidavit* for the Judge: *Request for Divorce Judgment*, the *Divorce Judgment*, and the *Affidavit of Service*. If your spouse has filed a Demand of Notice, both Divorce documents require your spouse's signature. If he or she has not filed the Demand of Notice, a fourth document must be included, a *Praecipe to Note in Default*.
Judge	11. reviews and signs the documents if they are satisfactory. This can take from 2 to 8 weeks.
	12. occasionally, may request more information requiring another *Affidavit* and client's signature.
	13. signs and dates the *Divorce Judgment*. The *Divorce Judgment* is finalized on the 31st day after the Judge dated and signed it.
Judge's clerk	14. mails copies of the *Divorce Judgment* to your home address, to your spouse's home address, and to me at our law office.
Lawyer	15. calls you as soon as her copy is received.
	16. obtains a *Divorce Certificate* for you on the 32nd day after the *Divorce Judgment* is signed, thus completing the process.

Note: Our office supplies another Client Information Letter on the processes for a contested divorce.

Client Information Letter - page 6

The attached fee schedule describes my hourly fees as your lawyer, and the usual costs when (i) a spouse agrees to all terms and (ii) there are no changes. The costs sheet also explains when the payment is due.

This *Information Letter* has been prepared in plain language to help you through a difficult time in your life. Remember that you can call me with questions. I'm here to help you.

Yours truly,

Jane Bergman

/JB

Enclosures

Finally, you could create a picture of the complex alternatives on the road to divorce. The flow chart which follows is not exhaustive but comprehensive enough to show common detours to the final destination. Because the insider legal language can be baffling to clients from a wide range of educational backgrounds, a glossary of legal terms is included to help the client understand.

Flowchart of possible roads to divorce

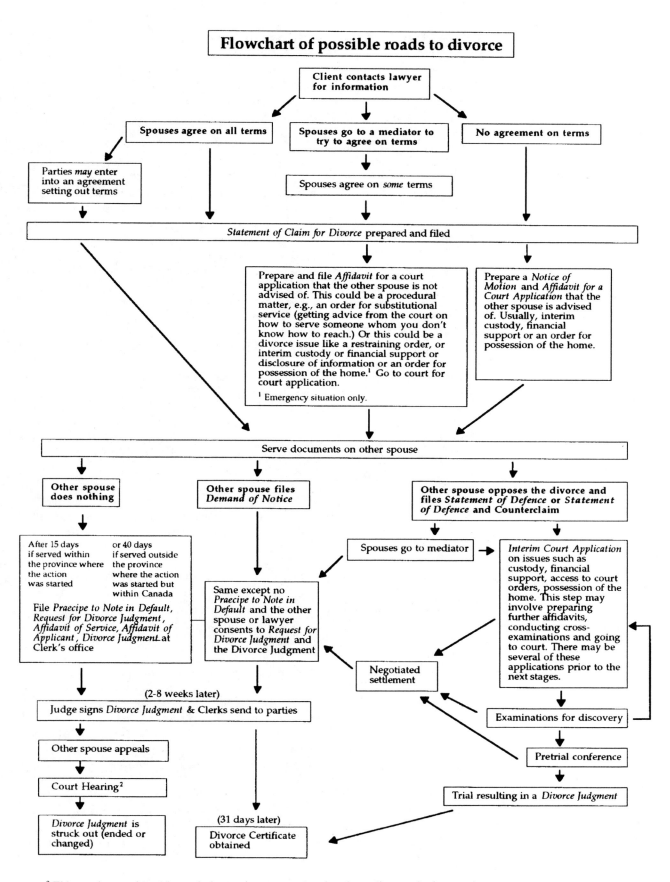

Client contacts lawyer for information

- **Spouses agree on all terms**
- **Spouses go to a mediator to try to agree on terms**
- **No agreement on terms**

Parties *may* enter into an agreement setting out terms

Spouses agree on *some* terms

Statement of Claim for Divorce prepared and filed

Prepare and file *Affidavit* for a court application that the other spouse is not advised of. This could be a procedural matter, e.g., an order for substitutional service (getting advice from the court on how to serve someone whom you don't know how to reach.) Or this could be a divorce issue like a restraining order, or interim custody or financial support or disclosure of information or an order for possession of the home.[1] Go to court for court application.

[1] Emergency situation only.

Prepare a *Notice of Motion* and *Affidavit for a Court Application* that the other spouse is advised of. Usually, interim custody, financial support or an order for possession of the home.

Serve documents on other spouse

- **Other spouse does nothing**
- **Other spouse files *Demand of Notice***
- **Other spouse opposes the divorce and files *Statement of Defence* or *Statement of Defence* and Counterclaim**

| After 15 days if served within the province where the action was started | or 40 days if served outside the province where the action was started but within Canada |

File *Praecipe to Note in Default, Request for Divorce Judgment, Affidavit of Service, Affidavit of Applicant, Divorce Judgment* at Clerk's office

Spouses go to mediator

Interim Court Application on issues such as custody, financial support, access to court orders, possession of the home. This step may involve preparing further affidavits, conducting cross-examinations and going to court. There may be several of these applications prior to the next stages.

Same except no *Praecipe to Note in Default* and the other spouse or lawyer consents to *Request for Divorce Judgment* and the Divorce Judgment

Negotiated settlement

Examinations for discovery

(2-8 weeks later)

Judge signs *Divorce Judgment* & Clerks send to parties

Other spouse appeals

Court Hearing[2]

Divorce Judgment is struck out (ended or changed)

Pretrial conference

Trial resulting in a *Divorce Judgment*

(31 days later)

Divorce Certificate obtained

[2] This can be considerable work done prior to court hearing depending on the issues.

Plain language glossary of terms

Affidavit

This document (usually prepared by a lawyer and signed by a client) sets out the facts for a judge's information. The client must swear that the facts set out in the Affidavit are true. As a result, the client having to go to Court.

Affidavit of Divorce

This affidavit is signed by the person who has personally given it to, or otherwise served, the other spouse.

counterclaim

This document prepared and filed at Court is very similar to the Statement of Claim for Divorce, but sets out the other spouse's claims for divorce.

court applications

These represent the process of bringing an issue to a Justice for a decision. There are many different issues that a Justice may be asked to decide upon so there are many kinds of applications. Usually the applications involve preparing Affidavits and then going before a Justice based on the facts in the Affidavits. Some applications may be short (less than 20 minutes of court time) and some may be longer than 20 minutes and require a *Special Hearing*.

cross-examinations

These are meetings in which the lawyers may ask questions of the spouse for whom they are not acting. The questions are restricted to the contents of the other spouse's Affidavit(s) or, if they have given any verbal testimony, to their verbal testimony. This is done at an office with a court reporter in attendance. The court reporter takes a record of everything that is being said for future reference.

Demand of Notice

This document is filed by the other spouse when he or she has no objection to the claims made in the *Statement of Claim for Divorce* but wants to review the *Divorce Judgment* before it is filed and made final.

Divorce Judgment

This document, signed by the Justice, states that after 31 days the spouses will be divorced. It may also include decisions about child custody and access, child and/or spousal support or a Restraining Order. If it includes these other things, it is called the *Divorce Judgment and Corollary Relief Order*.

examinations for discovery

These are meetings providing opportunities for lawyers in a contested divorce to ask questions of the spouse for whom they are not acting. The questions relate to all possible divorce issues and facts. This is done at an office with a court reporter in attendance. The court reporter takes a record of everything that is being said for future reference. This is used to get more facts and information and also to see how the spouses react under questioning.

Interim Court Application

This is a court application that is brought before the actual final divorce trial. Because it takes a long time (years) to get a divorce trial, the spouses may need to have decisions made by a Justice before the trial or before a settlement is reached. An Interim Court Application accomplishes this.

Plain language glossary of terms (cont'd)

Praecipe to Note in Default   This document advises the Court that there has been no formal response from the other spouse to the *Statement of Claim for Divorce* (the other spouse has not filed a *Demand of Notice, Statement of Defence,* or *Statement of Defence and Counterclaim*).

Restraining Order   This is an order that may be obtained from the Court that provides that a person may not contact another person and/or may not go to particular locations. It could refer to a spouse not contacting the other spouse or to a spouse not contacting the children.

serve a document on a spouse   The spouse who has not started the divorce proceedings is entitled to be made aware of the proceedings. This is done by "serving" (delivering) a copy of the documents that have been filed at Court about them. If possible, the spouse must be personally given the documents—this is often done by a process server. If the documents cannot be given personally, it is possible to apply to the Court for directions on how else the other spouse may be notified of the divorce proceedings.

Statement of Claim for Divorce   This document starts the legal process for a divorce and sets out all claims the spouse starting the divorce is making. It must be filed at the Court and then served on the other spouse.

statement of defence   The other spouse may file this document after being served with the Statement of Claim for Divorce. The statement of defence sets out reasons why the other spouse opposes the claims made by the initiating spouse.

The samples in this chapter exemplify the potential for plain language documents in the area of family law.

Chapter 11
Release Forms
Chapter Consultant: Cassandra Haraba, M.A., LL.B.

> ## What this chapter does
> The chapter:
> 1   tells the story of how the need for a plain language release form came about
> 2   critiques the traditional language of a release used to settle a case, and presents a redraft release in plain language

The conundrum: plagiarism—a plain language story

Some time ago, a consultant—we'll call him Douglas Palmer—had some of his training materials plagiarized by Company B for whom he had conducted workshops. Organizations often use their own employees to instruct specialized courses when economic times are bad.

When the bad times were over, the organization requested that Palmer return to instruct his course. As it turned out, Palmer discovered that the interim instructor had plagiarized his copyrighted educational materials, and, with small changes and additions, had, for several years, used the materials to conduct the training.

Douglas Palmer felt angry. Not only had he suffered the theft of his intellectual property, but he had lost income and saved Company B time and money at his expense. Palmer felt he needed "justice to be served", but he was not prepared to enter into a potentially lengthy court case.

Palmer spent considerable time documenting his case in a letter. He decided to request an apology and a modest monetary settlement.

He set up an interview with the new director of the department in which the plagiarism had occurred. The director was appalled and embarrassed on behalf of his company to hear about the theft of Palmer's intellectual property. His immediate acknowledgement of the seriousness of the problem was reassuring. The director referred the matter to an executive to negotiate. Copies of the documentation letter were sent to the executive. Two negotiating meetings later, the executive promised to send him a cheque and an agreement for him to sign releasing his legal rights against Company B. Of course, Company B hired a lawyer to draft the release agreement.

The release was a collage of legal garble, beginning with a 221-word sentence. No attempt had been made to clarify with Douglas Palmer what would be acceptable to him as a signee. Here is the *before* release:

RELEASE

KNOW ALL MEN BY THESE PRESENTS THAT **[1]** in consideration of **[2]** the sum of **[3]** _____ dollars ($_____) and other good and valuable consideration, the receipt and sufficiency of which is hereby **[4]** acknowledged, DOUGLAS PALMER and PALMER INC. do hereby **[4]** for themselves, their heirs, executors, administrators, agents, servants, employees, sucessors, insurers and assigns **[5]** (hereinafter called the "Releasors") **[6]** remise, release and forever discharge **[7]** _____ (hereinafter called the "Releasee") **[6]** its directors, officers, agents, servants, employees, successors, insurers and assigns and each of them from any and all manner of action and actions, cause and causes of action, suits, debts, due sums of money, claims and demands **[8]** whatsoever at law or in equity **[9]** which the Releasee ever had, or now has, can, shall or may hereafter **[4]** have, be it within contemplation or not, **[10]** or by reason of, or arising out of, any cause, matter or thing whatsoever done or omitted to be done, occurring or existing up to and inclusive of the date of these presents, **[11]** including without restricting the generality of the foregoing, **[12]** any claim, demand, or cause of action, **[8]** arising out of or in any way relating to the use by any agent, servant or employee of _____ of any program structure or materials owned or written or developed by the Releasors or any agent, servant or employee of either of them.

THE RELEASORS **[6]** hereby **[4]** agree to indemnify and save harmless the Releasee of and from any and all future claims that may be commenced against the Releasee **[13]** with respect to any and all matters relating to the use by any agent, servant or employee of _____ of any program structure or materials owned or written or developed by the Releasors or any agent, servant or employee of either of them.

THE RELEASORS FURTHER acknowledge that the terms of this release and the settlement of the matters in issue between the Releasors and the Releasee as referred to herein, **[3]** are confidential, and the Releasors agree to keep confidential all matters relating to any matter or thing relating to or arising out of this Release, and any other dealings between the Releasors and the Releasee.**[14]**

IN WITNESS WHEREOF I have set my hand and seal **[15]** at the City of Montreal, in the province of Québéc, this 20th day of March, A.D. 1998.**[16]**

SIGNED, SEALED AND DELIVERED **[17]**)
in the presence of)

)
) COMPANY B

_____)
WITNESS) DOUGLAS PALMER

Figure 1: Original release sent to Douglas Palmer

Palmer refused to sign the release. Contentious issues lurked in that amazing morass of words:

1. Because the release extinguished Palmer's right to action for future claims, he felt Company B might be able to plagiarize again, with impunity.

2. The release extinguished Palmer 's right to action not only for the plagiarism but also for any sort of claim Palmer might have—now and forever—for any wrongdoing by Company B up to the date of the release. Although Palmer did not think he possessed any other causes of action, the wide sweep of the release nonetheless made him anxious.

3. Paragraph 2 of the release seemed to make Palmer responsible for protecting Company B from other peoples' claims for Company B's use of materials owned, written, or developed by Palmer or his agents, servants, or employees.

4. Palmer could not promise to maintain confidentiality about the plagiarism because he had already discussed it with family, friends, and colleagues.

5. Palmer could not promise to keep confidential "any other dealings" between him and Company B because he intended to continue to conduct courses for the company.

One solution

First, weed out the archaisms and inaccuracies. The table below lists candidates which correspond to the numbers on the original release. The numbers are placed immediately after the offending word or phrase in the original release.

Original	Rewrite	Reason
[1] KNOW ALL MEN BY THESE PRESENTS THAT	delete	archaic phrase *Legal Writing: Sense and Nonsense,* p. 191
[2] in consideration of	delete this phrase which is generally unknown to layreaders	If the consideration is not here, using the word will not help. The "other good and valuable consideration" is too vague. Since consideration is the essential term of the contract, it should be specific.
[3] the sum of	delete	redundant
[4] hereby, hereafter, herein	delete	The archaic "here" words are thrown in gratuitously.

Original	Rewrite	Reason
[5] for themselves, their heirs, executors, administrators, agents, servants, employees, successors, insurers and assigns	See Reason	When Palmer releases his own right to action, he releases it for his heirs, executors, employees, administrators, agents, servants, successors, insurers and assigns. However, if he is releasing his *insurer's* right to action, he might need his insurer's consent, because of the nature of insurance contracts. As well, if Palmer were to release *all* his claims against Company B, he might also release his right to an action his insurer would have wanted to pursue.
[6] (hereinafter called the "Releasors") (hereinafter called the "Releasee")	(The "Releasors") (The "Releasee") (use lower case, too)	long and archaic
[7] remise, release and forever discharge	use *release* only	excess baggage
[8] from any and all manner of action and actions, cause and causes of action, suits, debts, due sums of money, claims and demands	from all claims	verbose, repetitive
[9] whatsoever at law or in equity	delete	*Whatsoever at law* is redundant. Garner identifies seven meanings for "the chameleon-hued" word *equity* (*A Dictionary of Modern Legal Usage*, p. 220)
[10] be it within contemplation or not	delete	redundant
[11] or by reason of, or arising out of, any cause, matter or thing whatsoever done or omitted to be done, occurring or existing up to and inclusive of the date of these presents	delete	an abomination which needs severe editing or extermination

Original	Rewrite	Reason
[12] including without restricting the generality of the foregoing	*includes*	That is what *includes* means.
[13] agree to indemnify and save harmless the Releasee of and from any and all future claims that may be commenced against the Releasee with respect to any and all matters relating to the use by any agent, servant or employee	delete	This paragraph seems to make Palmer responsible for protecting Company B from *other peoples' claims* for Company B's use of materials owned, written, or developed by Palmer or his agents, servants, or employees.
[14] Releasors and the Releasee	substitute names	easier to read, humanizes the document
[15] IN WITNESS WHEREOF I have set my hand and seal	delete	ancient language
[16] at the City of Montreal in the province of Québéc, this 20th, A.D., 1998.	Montreal, Québéc, March 20, 1998	redundancies
[17] SIGNED, SEALED AND DELIVERED in the presence of	signed in the presence of	inappropriate ancient language and capitalization

Table 1: Critique of the traditional release

Ater plucking out the legalese, tailor the release to the facts and the clients' desires. Company B will pay Palmer some compensation for its employee's plagiarism of his materials but does not want to admit legal responsibility for the plagiarism. Palmer will release Company B for past plagiarism only, and he does not want Company B to plagiarize his materials in future. If Palmer is releasing Company B for past plagiarism only, then Company B does not want to plagiarize Palmer's materials in future either. (It doesn't make sense for Palmer to release Company B today for plagiarism it might commit tomorrow.) Company B would like Palmer to agree not to discuss the plagiarism with the media.

Release Agreement

1. Company B will pay Douglas Palmer $10,000.00.

2. In exchange for the $10,000.00, Douglas Palmer will release Company B from any claim to damages relating to Company B's employee's unauthorized use of Douglas Palmer 's copyrighted educational materials ("materials") in the past.

3. Company B does not admit legal responsibility for its employee's unauthorized use of Douglas Palmer 's materials.

4. Company B will educate and monitor its employees to ensure that they do not use Douglas Palmer 's materials in the future.

5. Douglas Palmer will not release to the media any information about Company B's employee's unauthorized use of his materials.

Date: _____

Signatures: _____   _____
            Witness   Douglas Palmer

                                          By: _____
                                              Company B

Figure 2: The rewritten release

In reality, Douglas Palmer was paid $10,000 by the company, and he never signed the original release. The company left itself open to being sued. Had it negotiated a more even-handed plain language release, Douglas Palmer would have signed.

Too often releases are offered in the most general of terms, straight from the badly written precedent. Releases could be improved if they were more audience-sensitive, part of a sound negotiating process, and based on the law of the area. The above release is tentatively offered. There are many other approaches.[1]

---

[1] The discussion of vicarious liability is beyond the scope of this chapter.

Chapter 12
Public Forms

Chapter Consultant: Susan Barylo, B.A., Plain Language Forms Co-ordinator for Alberta Agriculture, Food and Rural Development (1993-1998)

What this chapter does

This chapter:

1 defines *form*
2 lists audiences for forms
3 identifies common problems with forms
4 describes the behaviors of form fillers
5 discusses selected design principles
6 examines the importance of testing
7 looks at *before* and *after* examples of forms
8 reproduces a case history on a government plain language forms project and money saved

---

"You'll have to fill out a form."

For most of us, the word *form* has negative connotations—tied to the sense of being forced to fill in boxes, of fitting letters into awkward spaces that do not match our data, and of endless lines, pages, and restrictions. From the public's point of view, forms represent a high percentage of government and legal documents. The British government estimated 2000 million central government forms used each year—36 for every individual in the country.[1] Many of those forms are essential to compile information to meet the requirements of legislation.

What is a form?

A *form* is a document or computer screen which acts as a turnstile to an organization's services. A form collects and gives information which allows operating, management, or policy decisions. Form design is crucial to the success of plain language forms. And of course, text rewriting is as important here as in any other plain language document. The banking and insurance industries, and tax, health, and social service departments are representative of groups which have rewritten and designed forms over the past decade. In many countries, court forms have been simplified as well.[2] Many legal forms, however, remain as vestiges of "old form"—labyrinthine and frustratingly obtuse.

Who are the users of forms?

Users of forms include the sponsoring firm, department, group, or individual author, and the form filler. The form processor may add data after the form is filled, enter the

---

[1] Reported in Robert Barnett's "Forms for the General Public: Do They Really Work?", *Occasional Paper No. 5* (Revised 1989), Communication Research Institute of Australia, Canberra, p. 1.
[2] For examples, see 19 excellent forms reproduced in James P. Ryan et al, "Plain Language—Michigan Court Form: 'The Divorce Package'", *Michigan Bar Journal*, February 1987, pp. 172-177.

data into a computer system, or retrieve data later from the form. A final user is the person who handles public inquiries. The key user or audience, however, is the form filler. To ensure the data collected is valid, analyse the characteristics of your form fillers by asking questions. What can you predict about their knowledge of the form's subject matter? What levels are their language and numerical abilities likely to be at? What is the user's probable attitude towards your organization or subject? Are there users who might be unfamiliar with the form's method, layout, and logic?

Common problems with forms

Forms not written for their audiences

Forms are often too sophisticated for the public who use them. The Communication Research Institute of Australia found that most public forms don't work. They typically find error rates of 90%.

Poor or too many instructions cause inefficient reading

Form fillers do not read instructions. Or they misread them. Or they skip them because they think they know them from previous years, or because they seem obvious.

Readers conditioned by bad forms skip daunting passages

Form fillers have been conditioned by poor forms not to have the confidence in their ability to understand text segments. They leave out questions or segments with legalese or long, circuitous syntax.

Forms are written for managers, not form fillers

Managers of forms often exhibit an imperialist attitude to their forms. A common defence is, "Readers better smarten up and learn how to read the form". Forms creators and administrators often sidestep the key to successful forms which is looking at forms *from the user's point of view* and gauging the consequences if the form is misunderstood.

The following table lists the most predominant weaknesses in public forms[3]:

The "look" of the form	• cluttered appearance • too many pages • inappropriate answering space or letter dividers • inconsistency of graphic symbols • confusing mixture and placement of columns and boxes • inappropriate use of captions instead of plain language questions in full sentences
Questions	• inconsistent form of questions or sequence of *yes* and *no* • contradictory methods of answering questions

---

[3] The list draws on research described in "Forms for the General Public: Do They Really Work?", *Occasional Paper No. 5* (Revised 1989), Communication Research Institute of Australia, Canberra.

Questions (cont'd)	• long difficult questions (should be broken into several simpler ones) • ambiguous questions • poor sequencing of questions • questions only answered by "educated guesses" • questions about information the form filler would not likely have access to or remember • too many open-ended questions resulting in too much or inaccurate information
Logical linkages	• unclear routing information throughout the form • instructions separated from the pertinent questions • requests for private information without giving a reason • distracting headings or separations • not telling the form filler where to go next at the end of a column
Process	• creating the graphics before drafting and testing the questions • no testing of forms
Technical aspects	• esoteric punctuation (use only periods, question marks, and commas) • lines that are too long for small font size • font that is too small for seniors to read • using all capital letters for text or captions • not using the same typeface for the same functions (questions, explanations, and headings) • using words only the computer or lawyer knows, not the form filler

What do we know about form fillers' behavior?

A 1988 Dutch study into practical problems experienced by 98 users filling out government forms made use of think-aloud protocols to research why and when users experienced problems. Researchers concluded that form fillers' main strategies can be described as a "kick-and-rush" technique. Form fillers almost never reread their answers or calculations. They skipped explanatory notes and other segments they considered unnecessary. They didn't have the background knowledge to satisfactorily interpret and decide on answers. Finally, many lacked the necessary language skills and familiarity with graphic signals to answer questions satisfactorily.[4]

---

[4] Michaël Steehouder & Carel Jansen, "Optimizing the Quality of Forms", *Studies of Functional Text Quality*, eds. Henk Pander Maat and Michaël Steehouder, Utrecht Studies in Language and Communication (Amsterdam: Rodopi, 1992), p. 161.

Selected design principles

Though most guidelines have exceptions or are useful only in specific contexts, I am including several guidelines that forms specialists generally agree on.

1)   Use forms for action, not information

Since a form requires a series of actions, the form should provide clear, specific tools and directions for form fillers to complete the actions accurately. The form should only provide enough background information to steer the form filler towards appropriate answers.

2)   Separate adjunct information

When it is optional to read adjunct information such as general background, functional reasons, and information about outcomes, separate it from questions and other explanations.

3)   Use definitions for action, not information

Instead of presenting definitions as descriptions, give them as instructions.

Before   What is meant by compounded interest?

After   How to assess your compounded interest

4)   Frame questions for answers, not guesses

Do not ask abstract questions that could result in guessing.

Before   Are you eligible for a spousal rebate?

After   Does your spouse earn less than $ _____?

5)   Use columns with precision

Use a multiple column grid to organize several visual elements in a form. It works well when you need to combine background information (column #1), the questions (column #2), and the answer space (column #3). Yet, ensure the instructions are precise and not open to misinterpretation as below:

Before

Explanatory notes	Questions	Answers
If you are a married woman, only fill out your maiden name here.	1 Your surname:	_____
	2 Your initials:	_____
If you are married but not living together with your spouse, tick the "no" box.	3 Are you married?	☐ yes ☐ no

There are three sources of confusion here. The first explanatory note, "If you are a married woman, only fill out your maiden name **here**" could be misinterpreted. *Here* looks as if it refers to the column #1 space which separates it from the second explanatory note. Yet, the header says the column is only for explanatory notes, not answers. Secondly, if you are not married, do you fill out your surname (which happens to be your maiden name) or does the question not apply to you? Finally, because the graphic dividers are the vertical column lines, the eye does not naturally flow horizontally across the table. A clearer version appears below:

If you are a married woman, fill out your maiden name (your surname before marriage).	your maiden name	your initials (given names)
If you are an unmarried woman, fill out your surname.	your surname	your initials (given names)

A second confusion arises with the second explanatory note. If you are married but not living with your spouse, you are directed to tick the box. But the question asks, "Are you married?" and the answer is also *yes*. Form fillers might tick both boxes. To overcome this problem, the drafter should add *only* to the directive: "If you are married but not living with your spouse, tick **only** the *no* box."

6)   Avoid negatives

Avoid double negatives, a negative image, or creating questions with mostly no answers. Responders to forms prefer to write *yes*. An original form[5] to inform livestock owners about a payment procedure had an overwhelmingly negative image (see below left) with *Warning—Incorrect Manifest* and *Bad Manifests Cost Money* as the key elements the eye is directed to. The revised form (below right) is more positive. Number-indexed information makes the form easier to fill out.

---

[5] *Plain Language Forms Project*, Alberta Agriculture, Food and Rural Development, Edmonton, 1995.

Before   *After*

Figure 1: Livestock Owners form[6]

7)   Give your form a header

It is the most prominent item on the form. When a form begins near the top without the visual indicator, it looks overwhelmingly complicated. The header should identify the issuing authority and have a descriptive title that is meaningful to the user, not just to the issuing group. Alberta Agriculture, Food and Rural Development improved its headers as follows:

Before	**After**
Apiculture Registration Form	Beekeeper Registration
Soil Conservation Planting Plan for Field Windbreaks Only	Map for Field Windbreak
Production Animal Registration Certificate	Elk and Deer Registration Certificate

---

[6] Reproduced with permission of Alberta Agriculture, Food and Rural Development.

8) **Make your text readable and your design clear and practical:**[7]
- Use serif typefaces for continuous text.
- Keep typesize at least 10-point or 12-point if there are readers 40 years and older.
- Use upper and lower case, not all capitals, even in headings or captions.
- Do not underline text for emphasis. Instead use boldface, italics, subheadings, bullets, and sidebars.
- Use symbols such as → , • or ☞ as indicators.
- Use examples, especially for calculations.
- Consider separate instruction booklets for multi-page forms.
- Give the responder the least amount of work to do. For example, checking a box is quicker than writing out *yes*.
- Leave plenty of space for responding. Allow 2 to 4 lines per inch for minimum 1/4" handwritten responses.
- Allow for ample margins and spacing between sections. Use back-to-back forms rather than cramming pages.
- Decide on a practical size for your reader. Least desirable is the traditional 8.5" x 14" size.
- Project a friendly, helpful image.
- Investigate the requirements of your entry system. Usually the entry order on screen should parallel the way the data entry staff read the form.

The importance of testing

Because forms are used by so many people and have significant implications for the time and costs in an organization, it is imperative that evaluation be built in to the plain language process. Analysis of *the public* or *target publics* is the first step to shaping the best evaluation. One government agency says plain language forms should be directed "at the people in your *audience who will likely have the most difficulty understanding the document*"[8] (author's emphasis).

Here are some of the factors to consider before testing:

- literacy level
- English as first or second language
- age range
- cultural sensitivity

- experience with forms
- information needs
- knowledge-specific vocabulary
- appropriateness of visuals and general appearance

Focus groups

To test an early version of your revised form, assemble a focus group composed of representative users. These may include form users and staff who process or use data from the form. Tests may be in the form of interviews, observations, or think-aloud

[7] Some of these details were synopsized from "Creating user-friendly forms", *Plain Language Forms Guidelines*, Government of Alberta, March 1993.
[8] As above, p. 4.

protocols. In the latter, users talk through their reactions, including both answers and obstacles to answers.

A range of tests

The Australian Centre for Plain Legal Language recommends a series of tests in the process of revising a form:

a)   Begin by evaluating the current form to decide if a new form is needed.

b)   After setting criteria for the new form and preparing initial questions, prepare and test a question protocol.

c)   If there are amendments to the initial questions, test and revise until you are satisfied.

d)   Follow a series of steps on design and testing with a final, more elaborate usability test. The Centre recommends regular revisions after the document has been implemented.

Testing of the early stages does not require large groups of people. Major problems will be uncovered in small groups of up to ten people.

Befores and afters

Bank Form Segments

Traditional mortgage and bank loan forms have intimidated customers with the bulk of legalese and mountainous paragraphs. Two decades ago, the American Citibank led the way in simplifying its loan application form. Buried under the verbiage was a relatively simple contract between the borrower and the lender. Here is one example:

Before	After
In the event of default in the payment of this or any other Obligation or the performance or covenant contained herein or in any note or other contract or agreement . . . undersigned shall deem itself to be insecure . . . whereupon such Obligations shall become and be immediately due and payable, and the Bank shall have the right to exercise all the rights and remedies available to a secured party . . . . . . If any provision of this paragraph shall conflict with any remedial provision contained in any security agreement or collateral receipt covering any Collateral, the provisions of such security agreement or collateral receipt shall control. **(374 words)**	**Default** I will be in default: 1. If I don't pay an installment on time; or 2. If any other creditor tries by legal process to take any money of mine in your possession. **(31 words)**

Citibank installment loan application made understandable[9]

Below is another example from a mortgage rewrite:

Before	After
Severability of Provisions 32. IF for any reason any covenant contained in this agreement, or the application thereof to any party or circumstances, is to any extent held or rendered invalid, unenforceable or illegal, then such covenant shall: (a) be deemed to be independent of the remainder of this agreement and be severable and divisible therefrom, and its invalidity, unenforceability and illegality shall not affect, impair or invalidate the remainder of this agreement or any part thereof; (b) continue to be applicable and enforceable to the fullest extent permitted by law, against any party and circumstance other than those to which it has been held or rendered invalid, unenforceable or illegal by a Court of competent jurisdiction. **(121 words)**	**Independence of Provisions** 32. If any part of this agreement is ruled invalid, all other parts remain in effect. **(15 words)**

---

[9] "Firms Learn to Keep Language Simple", *The Globe and Mail*, December 5, 1996.

To see a makeover of a complete form, refer to the dramatic recasting in plain language of a *before*, a *Release and Indemnity* form, into the *after*, a *Parent or Guardian's Consent Form*, shown on pages 21 and 22 of this *Handbook*.

A case history of government plain language forms

The article that follows tells the story of the plain language forms project carried out over two years by Susan Barylo, the consultant to this chapter.

Alberta Agriculture Saves Money with Plain Language Forms Project
by Christine Mowat[10]

Thanks to Susan Barylo and her plain language committee, the Alberta government now has clear evidence that plain language forms have already saved money for Alberta Agriculture, Food and Rural Development (AAFRD). Few plain language project coordinators bother to measure *before* and *after* changes. Barylo's results are a welcome addition to plain language research.

In July 1993, AAFRD hired Barylo as the plain language forms coordinator. By April 1996, 92 of the 646 forms had been revised in plain language. Over a million (1,034,530) of the 92 forms are used each year. The longest revision is a 35-page scholarship application booklet; most, however, are one to two pages.

First steps involved choosing cross-department representation and narrowing to an initial 24 forms. The process varied from one-to-one rewriting to gathering a team of people who used the form.

Beware of resistance to plain language changes
Barylo says newcomers to a plain language process react in predictable ways: some resist the policy changes that clarifying language often lead to; some are fearful of changes to their job context, especially with the question,

"Is this form needed?" People find it difficult to rethink familiar forms and the process. And some teams do not agree to testing.

Another problem is that some don't like the team approach, and others procrastinate or stall. Initially, certain team members allow only small changes, then months later, when they see the value of the changes, are ready for more. Barylo claims that plain language by edict doesn't work, and that the process must be a gradual, seductive one. News of project successes throughout the department helps add credibility.

How do you start a plain language process?
The plain language writer may begin by sitting down with the user, administrator or "owner" of the form and assuming the "play-dumb" approach. She may ask, "What does this mean? What kinds of questions do you get on the form? Where and how is the form used? What do you do with the information?"

Barylo outlines the whole process before a project begins, and suggests obtaining data on the *before* form before changing it. For example, her collection of data on the original, Operating Application-Class B Agricultural Societies made possible

/more

---

[10] This article was previously published in *LawNow*, Legal Resource Centre, University of Alberta, Edmonton, August/September 1996 and *CLARITY*, No. 38, January 1997.

this comparison: staff processing time on a grant application was reduced from 20 minutes on the original to 3 minutes on the redesigned form. On the original of a Grant Report Form, the department had only had a 25% return rate. With the new plain language form, the return rate doubled. An Annual Report of Agricultural Societies form, originally 8 pages, is now reduced to 1 fold-over page. Mailing costs are one-third less. *Before* and *After* data on using a Tree Nursing Order Form is especially persuasive. See the chart below.

Design is crucial to plain language forms

A dramatic example of a visually enhanced form is the new Elk and Deer Registration Certificate. Formerly the Game Protection Animal Registration Certificate, the original was a crowded typed page with segments for data on the animal and its owner and another for applying to transfer ownership. The old form had gaps in the required information for users and confusing requests for information. For example, instead of asking for the genetic status, the new form asks for the species of animal.

On one side of the new form is the registration certificate designed as a certificate and enhanced with lightly monogrammed deer and elk heads.

There are clear instructions for using both sides of the form. The second side, a notice to change registration, and a newly designed tear-off notice to update inventory, makes the form efficient and multi-functional. The form breathes and is visually welcoming.

Cost savings tell the story

Barylo describes her research as "anecdotal" though she has used surveys, focus groups, and participant descriptions. She reports that not all the groups who participated in the forms improvement projects have as yet measured efficiency improvements between the old and new forms.

In AAFRD, the cost savings from the plain language forms project are real. With 400 administrative support staff (average salary of $24,000), and 200 managers (average $60,000), Barylo uses as a base an average AAFRD-person-year valued at $38,154. With 1,034,530 forms processed a year, and savings in staff time at least 10 minutes per form, she calculates the annual savings to the government is an astounding $3,472,014.

Barylo further qualifies that figure. "This is average," she says. "The real savings based on a detailed evaluation may be significantly higher." She refers to a detailed analysis of six redesigned forms from the Rural Development Division. Total staff time saved on six forms was 62.1 work days or a total of $9076.83. Coincidentally, the public's time saved on these forms was 235 days!

In my view, AAFRD's plain language initiative is beginning to produce some of the most significant measurements on plain language this province has seen. The department stands as a model to others in government and business. "Putting their money where their mouth is" has a new plain language meaning now.

Tree Nursery Order Form		
	1993 Original Form	1994 Plain Language Form
Number of applications	2900	3540
Error rates	40%	20%
Staff time to correct errors	10-minute telephone calls per form (almost 27 work days)	5-minute telephone calls to correct (8.5 work days)

Perhaps the most interesting of Alberta Agriculture's projects was the rewriting of their Feeder Agreement and Promissory Note (see pp. 243 to 246 in the *Befores and Afters* section). Over four years, the manager of the Feeder Association program, the Plain Language Co-ordinator, and a lawyer worked on the form.[11] Approximately 20,000 people use the form in 250 Alberta feeder associations.

The feeder agreement results from local community co-operatives banding together to borrow money from the banks at lower bank rates to buy baby cattle. Farmers who signed the original feeder agreements didn't understand that the feeder association owned the cattle. If the farmer doesn't follow a number of specifications, the association has the legal right to reclaim the cattle. Feeder association staff processing the form were thrilled with the form's new design and clarity.

The best forms software and books we know of on plain language forms are included in the Bibliography, pp. 361-66.

---

[11] Interestingly, the co-ordinator never met with the lawyer. Instead, the manager and co-ordinator worked on the drafts, then sent them to the lawyer. This pattern was repeated thoughout the process. My experience is that when all parties work together on drafts, the process can be streamlined.

Chapter 13
The Future of Plain Language

What this chapter does
This chapter:
1 tackles the question of whether plain language should be legislated or allowed to develop voluntarily
2 looks at suggestions for encouraging plain language in the university law faculties, bar admission courses, and law societies
3 examines reasons for plain language standards and more collaborative or national initiatives
4 acknowledges continuing obstacles and resistance to plain language
5 connects the need for plain language and the globalization of English

---

How should we promote plain language?

In the 1990 Canadian Bar Association (CBA) and Canadian Bankers' Association Joint Committee Report, *The Decline and Fall of Gobbledygook: Report on Plain Language Documentation*, the authors suggested that promoting plain language should be left to voluntary efforts, not legislation. In 1991, Peg James and I conducted a plain language audit on the report itself and wrote:

> It seems to us that a fuller commitment to promotion is required. The CBA needs "disciples" to more actively promote plain language education and practice. Those with experience of plain language "selling" know how difficult a sell it is, and how plain-language-illiterate many lawyers still are. Affirmative action policies are required. The reformist theme of the report is at odds with the tame proposals for promotion. Is there a logical fallacy in the Joint Committee's position that because they view plain language as a process they must favour a voluntary approach? We believe that legislation regulating certain kinds of documents might also be a valuable strategy. We wish the committee had examined this subject in greater detail.
>
> [*The report had further stated that legislation is not effective when it requires individuals to undertake some positive action that needs time, skill, effort and commitment.*]

The Alberta legislature has taken a different position. Alberta's *Financial Consumers Act* is the first Commonwealth legislation to require the use of plain language in financial documents. Section 13 of that *Act* is modelled on subjective[1] U.S. plain language laws, but with some innovative enforcement provisions. For instance, a Director appointed under the *Act* can order that

---

[1] Carl Felsenfeld and Alan Siegel have summarized the differences between subjective and objective standards in American plain English statutes. The first, New York's plain language law, simply required consumer contracts after 1978 to be written in non-technical language and in a clear and coherent manner using words with common meanings, and to be appropriately divided and captioned by sections. Other "subjective" descriptors in legislation included *lay language, easily understandable, readable*, and *language that a reasonable person could understand*. The authors then reviewed many similar subjective standards in the law. The Massachusetts plain language statute selected a recognized readability test, the Flesch test, as their objective standard of compliance. Connecticut's plain English law used both subjective and objective tests. See Carl Felsenfeld and Alan Siegel, *Writing Contracts in Plain English* (St. Paul, MN: West Publishing Co., 1981), pp. 215-224.

language or forms be improved. As well, arbitration can be ordered when individuals claim consequential loss from an unclear document. Consumer organizations can seek a declaration that the *Act* has been contravened and obtain an injunction and costs (designed to be embarrassing but not punitive).

Even if earlier plain language legislation has been ambiguous, poorly written, unclear, too sketchy, or in legalese — and all of these are true — it does not mean that good plain language legislation cannot be written. Plain language advocacy of all types should be encouraged.[2]

I still believe what we wrote then.

In her *Drafting Legal Documents: Principles and Practices*, Barbara Child notes the continuing expansion of plain language, attributing its growth to self-policing by industries, organizations and individuals.[3]

Another level of "legislating plain language" is through the drafting policies and practices of legislative counsel who draft legislation. This is not just legislating plain language for documents, but writing the legislation *itself* in plain language. Chapter 8 of this *Handbook* explores new models of plain language legislation.

A plain language glossary for legislation

Philip Knight, former head of the British Columbia (Canada) Plain Language Institute and plain language legislative drafter in Canada and South Africa, has recently reported on two significant changes for the new *Revised Statutes of British Columbia*. The following table demonstrates the first change required — plain language vocabulary for legislation:

Table 1 — Traditional Expressions Replaced in the *Revised Statutes of British Columbia*, 1997[4]

Traditional Expression	Replacement
adequate number of	enough
an equality of votes	a tie vote
ascertain	find out, determine
attain	reach
body corporate	corporation
bona fide	in good faith, genuine, properly but "bona fide" retained in commercial contexts, when used as a term of art, and in the *Human Rights Act*
by reason (only) of / by virtue (only) of	because
by means of	by
chairman	chair

---

[2] Christine Mowat and Margaret James, "A Plain Language Audit on 'The Decline and Fall of Gobbledygook: Report on Language Documentation'", *Papers for the Third Annual Meeting of the Canadian Corporate Counsel Association*, Toronto, 1991, pp. 49-50.

[3] Barbara Child, *Drafting Legal Documents: Principles and Practices*, 2nd ed. (St. Paul, MN: West Publishing Co., 1992), p. 405.

[4] Philip Knight, "New Words and Old Meanings", *The Advocate*, Vol. 56, Part I, January 1998, pp. 27-29.

Traditional Expression	Replacement
commence	begin (except for legal proceedings)
construction (in the context of determining meaning)	interpretation
deemed	considered (except for legal fiction effect)
expend	spend
fiscal year	financial year
fix	set, establish
forthwith	promptly, immediately, without delay, or at once
frequently	often
guardian ad litem	litigation guardian
in camera	in private
in case	if
in lieu	instead, or in place
in loco parentis	in the role of parent
in the event	if
in whole or in part	all or some, all or part of
institute, used as a verb	start, begin, establish (most contexts) commence (in the context of initiating legal proceedings in court)
is binding upon	binds
natural person	individual
notwithstanding	despite, as an exception to, even though
pending (as a preposition) (as an adjective)	until changed
prior to	before
pro rata	prorated, or proportionately
province	British Columbia (if geographic) Government (if Crown)
said	the, that, those
same (used as a pronoun)	it, he or she, him or her
subsequent to	after
such (used as a demonstrative adjective)	the, that, those, it
sufficient number of	enough
the manner in which	how
under the provisions of	under
until such time as	until
upon	on
utilize	use
vendor	seller
within (referring to a place)	in

Traditional Expression	Replacement
where (except where it is used to denote location)	if (used to introduce a condition that may or may not occur)
	when (used to introduce a condition that will certainly occur, but whose timing is uncertain)

Knight describes this glossary of 45 words as an important but modest beginning.

Kicking *shall* out of the court

Even more exciting than the glossary is what Knight refers to a new *code of words of authority* for that seemingly innocent, yet irascible, word *shall*. I won't list all the authors who have complained bitterly and at length about the troublesome *shall*. Bryan Garner did it best, as Knight points out, when he referred to *shall* as a "horrific muddle"[5], the most egregious example of legal imprecision documented. *Words and Phrases* contains 76 pages of cases interpreting *shall*.

Table 2 below captures the nuances of the former one-word-fits-all *shall* and mandates the careful discriminating uses of substitutes: *must, may, is* or *are entitled to*, appropriate verb tenses, or *will*.

Table 2 — for words of authority used in the *Revised Statutes of British Columbia, 1997*[6]

Purpose	Rule	Example
To impose a duty, obligation, or requirement	Use *must*	Law Society Rule 55(7): If a vote is required . . . it *must* be conducted by secret ballot.
To create a right or entitlement	Use *may*, or *is (are) entitled to*	Law Society Rule 103: Any person *may* deliver to the Secretary a written complaint against a member.
		Law Society Rule 92(11): A Bencher who is present at a Bencher meeting *is entitled to* one vote.
To create a discretion	Use *may*	Law Society Rule 72: The Executive Committee *may* . . . extend any date stated in this Part.
To prohibit an action or to create a duty to avoid doing something	Use *must not*	Law Society Rule 315(2): Any time taken for matters referred to in subrule . . . *must not* be included in the calculation of . . .

---

[5] Bryan Garner, *A Dictionary of Modern Legal Usage*, 2nd ed. (Oxford: Oxford University Press, 1995), p. 942.
[6] As above, note 4, p. 30. The rest of Philip Knight's article contains cautions on the use of the new code which drafters need to be aware of.

Purpose	Rule	Example
To disallow the exercise of a right, create a disentitlement, or limit a discretion	Use *may not* or *is not entitled to*	Law Society Rule 311(3): A person whose application for enrollment has been rejected . . . *may not* apply for enrollment until . . . Law Society Rule 92(13): A Bencher *is not entitled to* vote by proxy.
To declare a state of being	Use the appropriate tense of the verb *to be*.	Law Society Rule 5: The Secretary is designated as head of the Society . . .
For the future indicative	Use *will* This may be used in private documents, but should not apply often in statutes, since legislation is written in the present tense.	

Teaching plain language

In "The State of Legal Writing: Res Ipsa Loquitur", George Gopen carefully analyses the sources of poor legal writing and writes candidly:

> In light of the importance to lawyers of controlling the language and particular rhetorical difficulties that confront the legal profession, *the absence of care of competence in the teaching of writing at law schools is stunning.*[7] (my emphasis)

The Canadian Bar Association/Canadian Bankers' Association Report also made, and later passed, these recommendations for the teaching of plain language writing courses:

- Canadian law schools and Bar Admission courses should be urged to include a plain language drafting course in their curriculum in an effort to instruct law students on how to write better, plainer, and clearer.

- Law societies should design and offer Continuing Legal Education courses on writing in plain language.[8]

Though short courses are offered through some of these institutions, they need to be more comprehensive and finely integrated with other courses. If substantive law professors and instructors of other courses continue to teach in legalese, there will be contradictory standards for students' legal drafting. Instructors and law professors themselves often have only sketchy information about plain language. There are now thousands of texts, monographs, booklets, research studies and reports about plain language. Libraries need to recognize and amass collections to support the teaching of plain language.

---

[7] George D. Gopen, "The State of Legal Writing: Res Ipsa Loquitur", *Writing in the Business Professions*, ed. Myrna Kogen (Urbana, IL: National Council of Teachers of English and the Association for Business Communication, 1989), p. 165.
[8] The Canadian Bar Association and Canadian Bankers' Association Joint Committee Report, *The Decline and Fall of Gobbledygook: Report on Plain Language Documentation* (Ottawa, 1990), p. 47.

Traditionally, legal research and writing have been taught in one course with most energy given to the research methods and little emphasis on the writing. The lack of support we see in university English departments for tenure-track professors to teach writing is, unfortunately, also the case in law faculties. George Gopen noted that only one law school in the USA had been "bold enough to do what logic and sound pedagogy demand — to implement a three-year writing requirement for all law students."[9]

A 1992 American Bar Association survey on the role of law schools in preparing lawyers to practise law shows that practising lawyers rank writing skills number 2 out of 17 skills the firm expects a new associate to bring to the job. They believe that 91% of competence in writing should be developed by law schools and that only 9% should be developed on the job.[10]

Reasons for plain language standards

Because plain language means different things to different people, there is a case to be made for consolidating knowledge and providing some uniformity of standards.

1. **Education**

   Plain language standards research will help educate legal writers, and help overcome the discrepancy between paying lip service to plain language and the reality of producing excellent plain language documents. A recognition of standards will promote plain language in a way that practising the craft behind closed doors never will. We need to structure and systemize the practice and study of plain language to make it more easily accessible and understood. I often hear references to "plainer but not extreme" writing that suggest a lack of familiarity about plain language principles. Plain language is not *extreme*: it is clear.

2. **Regulation**

   Plain language groups need to develop clear criteria or credentials showing a basic common knowledge and practice. Those in the field need to consider the interdisciplinary nature of the study of plain language. Professional associations could consider the merits of certification.

3. **Quality assurance**

   Many individuals and groups are now claiming proficiency in plain language techniques. A prestigious law firm in Australia is selling its services under the banner of plain language. Soon that will happen in Canada, and other countries, too. Professional law associations may want to ensure that plain language legal writing services provide clients with a match between the documents and the purposes they are intended to serve. Developing checks on quality will help protect the public.

---

[9] As above, note 7, p. 165.

[10] *Legal Education and Professional Development—An Educational Report of the Task Force on Law Schools and the Profession: Narrowing the Gap*, American Bar Association, July 1992.

4. **Cooperation**

I speak for Canada here but similar challenges probably face other countries and regions. The Canadian plain language field is fragmented by geography, by the diversity of organizations with plain language mandates, and by the number of plain language groups who have had funding cuts over the last few years. A more concerted effort to plan strategically for the future of plain language requires pan-Canadian initiatives. For example, Plain Language Sections of Canadian Bar Association across Canada could contribute to a standards task force. We need more sharing of innovation, successes, and obstacles in the plain language field.

Several international plain language conferences over the last decade have created strong global bonds among plain language theorists, practitioners, and advocates. Publications such as *CLARITY* (England) and the *Scribes Journal of Legal Writing* (USA)[11] continue to sustain and inspire the plain language movement. Perhaps it is at this international level that standards development is most likely, and most profitably, to occur.

Resistance phenomena

This *Handbook* has examined many examples and tools for success in plain language projects. Yet, we cannot be too sanguine. There are still obstacles to overcome:

1) *Writers with insufficient knowledge to produce plain language documents*
    Legal writers who have not internalized the interdisciplinary aspects of plain language may continue to produce inferior legal documents — in fact, the writing may reflect an uncomfortable blend of two legal writing codes. Hastily trained plain language learners may adopt components of plain language piecemeal. In-depth training with supervised practice and group drafting sessions seems the most successful route. Faculty members, managers, executives, and senior partners who value excellent writing and are knowledgeable about plain language will make a difference.

    Half-day or even one-day "show and tell" sessions without any writing and feedback will not produce quality plain language writing. Writers improve their writing by writing, talking, thinking, reading, redrafting, and collaborating. They need time to make the plain language philosophy and process theirs. Overly hasty and partial approaches result in mechanical, superficial or even contradictory writing techniques.

2) *Educating only law students, articling students or new young lawyers in plain language drafting*
    Senior partners, senior counsel, directors or heads of departments and even professors need to demonstrate their commitment to plain language by learning about it themselves. Writing is a great leveller: age is neither the cause of, nor a necessary obstacle to, quality writing.

3) *The study of law and learning legalese*
    To learn the history of the law, legal principles and reasoning, law students must read thousands of pages of traditional legal language. Over three or more

---

[11] See *Handbook* Bibliography, pp. 361-66.

years, their minds are continuously steeped in outmoded phraseology and overly-embedded syntax. That is why a parallel study of plain language expression is imperative, for legal writers must "unlearn" legalese — or learn to be interpreters.

4) *Lawyers used to the elitism of legalese*
Legalese is a learned academic discourse, a language which helps initiate lawyers into their profession. Yet the gatekeeper function of legalese is one which must be abandoned in communicating legal matters to non-lawyers.

Neophyte professionals often draw the security of their discipline's exclusionary language around them: using the language provides an identity, a kind of membership card to the club. Some willingly take on the voice of their academic discourse. Some are seduced by the surface dimension only, learning to mimic it while still failing to engage fully in the genuine rhetorical task of writing clearly for their readers. The use of legalese is often combined with tortuous, convoluted prose.

There are lawyers who write and speak clearly and powerfully for their audiences. We need more plain language role models — both plain language leaders and plain language documents to create new levels of legal literacy.

5) *"The words retained have accepted meanings in law"*
This defensive reaction to holding on to legalese is becoming less common. Some objectors are so concerned with how courts have ruled that they are blind to the reality: words and phrases which require judicial interpretation might have been the wrong word and phrases in the first place. In fact, they could have been poorly chosen and poorly drafted. No one will take a document to court because it is too clear.

6) *Assuming that plain language writing will remove all complexity*
Two underlying plain language principles are little understood:

i) Complex subjects may be written at a low readability level (The "I think; therefore, I am" axiom) but the complexity of the subject matter remains.

ii) With complex legal matters, the use of plain language at least removes the compounding difficulty of convoluted language. Complexity does not demand complicated syntax nor legalese. Ironically, some plain language writing is complex; not everything can be simplified. But the language and format can be clear.

The resistance phenomenon is usually based on a common resistance to change, ignorance, or misinterpretations of the international plain language movement. Resistance is slowly being eroded by plain language education from universities, bar associations, and plain language projects and training in the public, corporate, legal and government sectors.

Plain language and the globalization of English

A pressing reason for plain language legal documents is the evidence of a surge to global economy. English, a language which did not exist 2000 years ago when Julius

Caesar landed in Britain, has become the language of the planet, a first fairly global language.

Used by 750 million people (some estimates put it closer to 1 billion), English is the mother tongue of barely half of those who speak it. It is the language of international business, politics, and science and the medium for 80% of the information in the world's computers. English is the language of technology from Silicon Valley to Shanghai. Half of European business is conducted in English and many multinational corporations write international memoranda in English. Russia, Germany, and Japan have been invaded by English. English is taught in China, Saudi Arabia, Kuwait, Singapore and others, and is a second language in India and Singapore.[12]

The sheer numbers of legal documents which will be, and are already, produced to support the globalizing of the world economy cry out for legions of plain language writing experts.

Plain language offers advantages both to the legal profession and to populations at large. Our freedom is extended by the plain language open-door policies to the law. We should be able to understand our mortgages, wills, collective agreements, consumer contracts, divorce agreements, legislation, regulations, international trade documents and even our lawyers' letters.

Plain language represents a cultural and political change in attitude to legal writing. Past marginalizing of the public by incomprehensible legalese is beginning to end. Rather than diminishing the law, plain language bolsters its authority. Under the flag of plain language where the law is accessible to wider audiences, our justice system may be more widely accepted and respected.

For too long, legalese has alienated the public from the legal community. The urgency for continued growth of plain language is an ethical and civic issue of major proportions. Courts in England and Australia have argued that unintelligible documents may be legally ineffective.[13] A recent U.S. appeal court decision found an Immigration and Nationalization Service Notice was not clear and therefore the agency's procedures did not meet constitutional requirements.[14]

It would be rash to predict the future evolution of plain language. Oh, let's be rash! I believe a time will come when the public, government, and corporate sectors will choose only lawyers (and judges) whose documents they can understand.

---

[12] Robert McCrum, William Cran and Robert MacNeil, *The Story of English* (New York: Viking Penguin Inc., 1986), pp. 1-2.
[13] Robert D. Eagleson, "Taking the Gobbledegook Out of Legal Writing", *Queensland Law Society Journal*, April 1990, pp. 114-115.
[14] Cheryl Stephens, "U.S. Pushing Forward with Plain Language", *LawNow* (Edmonton: Legal Studies Program, University of Alberta), October/November 1998, p. 44.

Appendices:
Before and After Samples

On each *before* document, you will find a **Problem Index box** and on each *after* document is a **Plain Language Features box**. We acknowledge that the plain language samples produced could likely be improved or at least done in a different way. However, the models are provided for discussion — there is always one more perfect draft.

Appendices: *Before and After Samples*

Appendix 1
Will

Before and After

(Reproduced with the permission of The Continuing Legal Education Society of British Columbia)

Original precedent will   **BEFORE**

THIS IS THE LAST WILL AND TESTAMENT of me, PETER JOSEPH JONES, of 5555 West Water Street, Vancouver in the Province of British Columbia, V0J 7T1.

1.   I HEREBY revoke all Wills and Testamentary Dispositions heretofore made by me and DECLARE this to be my Last Will and Testament.

2.   I APPOINT my wife, GENIE JEAN JONES, to be the EXECUTOR of my Will and TRUSTEE of my estate. If my wife should die before me, will not or cannot act or continue to act as Executor and Trustee or dies before the completion of the trusts set forth in this Will then I APPOINT my brother, BARTON LOUIS JONES, to be the Executor of this my Will and Trustee of my estate in place of my wife (the Executor and Trustee who shall be acting from time to time is hereinafter referred to as "my Trustee"), and I GIVE to my Trustee all my estate upon the following trusts:

(a)   to use my Trustee's discretion in the realization of my estate with power to my Trustee to sell, call in and convert into money any part of my estate not consisting of money at such time or times, in such manner and upon such terms as my Trustee may in my Trustee's discretion decide upon. And my Trustee will have the separate power to retain any of my assets in the same form as they are at my death at my Trustee's discretion and the assets so retained will be deemed to be authorized investments for the purposes of my Will;

(b)   except where otherwise provided in my Will, to pay out of and charge to the capital of my estate my just debts, funeral and testamentary expenses and all duties and taxes that may be payable in connection with my death;

PROBLEMS INDEX

- antiquated language (e.g., "lapsed residue", "issue")
- no contents page or headings
- long, circuitous sentences
- doublets and triplets
- the ambiguous "shall"
- awkward syntax
- overly long signage segment
- capitalization
- dense layout

Original precedent will

and I hereby authorize my Trustee to pay such duty or tax prior to the due date thereof or to commute the duty or tax on any interest in expectancy;

(c)   to pay or transfer the residue of my estate to my wife, if she is living at my death;

(d)   if my wife shall die before me, to divide the residue of my estate into as many equal shares as there shall be children of mine alive at my death, PROVIDED that if any child of mine shall then be dead and if any ISSUE of such deceased child shall be living such deceased child of mine shall be considered alive for the purposes of such division.

My Trustee shall set aside one of such equal shares for each child of mine who shall be living at my death and shall keep such share invested and pay the net income derived from such share to or for such child until he or she attains the age of TWENTY-FIVE (25) years when ONE-HALF (1/2) of such share shall be paid or transferred to him or her and thereafter the net income from the remainder of such share shall be paid to or for such child until he or she attains the age of THIRTY (30) years when the remainder of such share shall be paid or transferred to him or her. If such child should die before becoming entitled to receive the whole of his or her share in my estate, such share or the amount thereof remaining shall be held by my Trustee, in trust, for the children of such child who survive him or her in equal shares. If such child should leave no child him or her surviving, such share or the amount thereof remaining shall be held by my Trustee, in trust, for my issue alive at the death of such child in equal shares per stirpes.

My Trustee shall set aside one of such equal shares for the issue of each child of mine who shall have predeceased me but shall have issue alive at my death and shall divide such share among the issue of such deceased child then alive in equal shares per stirpes.

(e)   In the event there is a lapse or failure in the distribution of the residue of my estate or any part thereof (the "Lapsed Residue") to divide the Lapsed Residue in equal shares among such of my mother-in-law, ROBERTA Tina RUSSELL, my father, DONALD CAMERON JONES, my mother, SUSAN LANGE JONES, my sister, HOPE INA JONES, my brother, BARTON LOUIS JONES and my sister, WILMA CINDY JONES, as shall be living at the date of such lapse or failure.

3.   NOTWITHSTANDING any other provision in my Will I AUTHORIZE my Trustee to pay to or to apply for the benefit of any child of mine such part or parts of the capital of the share held in trust for such child as my Trustee in my Trustee's discretion considers advisable.

4.   EXCEPT AS OTHERWISE specifically provided, if any person should become entitled to any share in my estate during his or her minority, the share of such person shall be held and kept invested by my Trustee and the income and capital or so much thereof as my Trustee, in my Trustee's discretion, considers advisable shall be used for the benefit of such person until he or she attains the age of majority.

5.   I AUTHORIZE MY TRUSTEE to make any payment, transfer or delivery of any part of my estate passing to a beneficiary during his or her minority either

Original precedent will

directly to such beneficiary or to the surviving parent or guardian of such beneficiary, AND the receipt of such payment, transfer or delivery by such beneficiary, parent or guardian shall be a sufficient discharge to my Trustee notwithstanding the minority of the recipient or that the recipient may not be bonded or may be insufficiently bonded.

6.   SHOULD MY TRUSTEE be required to make any investments for my estate my Trustee shall not be limited to investments authorized by law for trustees but may make any investments which my Trustee in my Trustee's discretion may consider advisable. Nor shall my Trustee be liable for any loss that may happen to my estate in connection with any investments made by my Trustee in good faith.

7.   I AUTHORIZE my Trustee in the distribution of my estate in my Trustee's discretion to allocate and appropriate any item or items which form part of my estate to the account of any portion of or interest in the residue of my estate and to place a value thereon for the purposes of such allocation and appropriation and the decision of my Trustee as to such allocation and appropriation and distribution shall be final and binding upon all persons interested in my estate.

8.   SO LONG AS any real or leasehold property forms part of my estate and remains unsold, my Trustee may let or lease the same for such period, upon such terms and subject to the covenants and conditions as my Trustee shall think appropriate. Further my Trustee may accept surrenders of leases and tenancies, expend money in repairs and improvements, give options, subdivide, and generally manage the property.

9.   My Trustee, in carrying out the trusts set forth in my Will, may in my Trustee's discretion borrow or raise money by way of mortgage or charge upon any part of my estate or otherwise, with power to execute all documents necessary for so doing and my

Original precedent will

_____

Trustee shall be at liberty to pay the normal rate of interest whether or not this sum of money

has been borrowed from a Trustee or a beneficiary in this my Will.

10.   I HEREBY APPOINT my sister, HOPE INA JONES, to be the

guardian of my infant children upon the death of the survivor of me and my wife.

                          IN WITNESS WHEREOF I have hereunto set my hand this first day of

September, 1992.

SIGNED, PUBLISHED AND DECLARED by   )
the above-named Testator, PETER JOSEPH   )
JONES, as and for his Last Will and Testament,)
in the presence us, both present   )
at the same time who, at his request,   )
in his presence and in the presence of each other,)
have hereunto subscribed our   )
names as witnesses:)
)
Name: _____   )
)
Address: _____   )
) _____
      _____   )
)
Occupation: _____   )
)
Name: _____   )
)
Address: _____   )
)
      _____   )
)
Occupation: _____   )
)
)

Plain language will

AFTER

WILL OF PETER JOSEPH JONES

CONTENTS

> **PLAIN LANGUAGE FEATURES**
> - contents page and headings
> - "per stirpes" defined and referenced to relevant clauses [12(a)(b) & 14]
> - short sentences, decreased readability level
> - no legalese
> - sentence architecture and parallelism
> - clear, natural language
> - streamlined signature section

WARNING

Continuing Legal Education Society publications are offered as an aid to developing and maintaining professional competence with the understanding that the authors and publishers are not providing legal or other professional advice.

Users of this will must exercise their professional judgment about its accuracy and applicability and must also refer to relevant legislation, case law, and other primary sources of information.

The Continuing Legal Education Society and the advisors, authors, and editors who have worked on this will expressly disclaim any responsibility for errors or omissions.

Plain language will

Last Will

1. This is my last will. I am Peter Joseph Jones, of 5555 West Water Street, Vancouver, British Columbia.

2. I cancel all my former wills and codicils. (A codicil is a legal addition or change to a will.)

Appointment of Personal Representatives

Executor and Trustee

3. In this will, my "Trustee" is both the Executor of my will and the Trustee of my Estate.

4. I appoint my wife, Genie Jean Jones, ("Genie") to be my Trustee.
   If Genie:
   (a) dies before me,
   (b) is unwilling or unable to act as Trustee,
   (c) is unwilling or unable to continue to act as Trustee, or
   (d) dies before the trusts in this will are completed,
   then I appoint my brother, Barton Louis Jones, to be my Trustee.

Guardian of my children

5. If Genie dies before me, I appoint my sister, Hope Ina Jones, to be the guardian of my children.

Administration of my Estate

Trustee to administer my Estate

6. I give my Trustee all my property of every kind and wherever located (my "Estate") to administer as I direct in this will. In administering my Estate, my Trustee may retain or convert my Estate as set out in paragraph 15 of this will.

Special gifts

7. I direct my Trustee to make the following gifts.
   If my brother, Barton Louis Jones, survives me, I give to him:
   (a) my 1925 Hardy fishing reel, and

Appendix 1
Page 7 of 12

Plain language will

    (b) my Campion boat, named the *Black Fish*.

If Barton dies before me, I give this reel and boat to my friend,
Dave Brown, if he survives me.

Debts to be paid from my Estate

8. I direct my Trustee to pay out of my Estate:

    (a) my debts,

    (b) my funeral and other expenses related to this will and my death, and

    (c) all duties and taxes that must be paid in connection with my death.

My Trustee has the authority to prepay or delay payment of any duties or taxes.

Distribution of remainder of my Estate

9. I direct my Trustee to distribute the remainder of my Estate as follows:

    (a) To give the remainder of my Estate to Genie if she survives me for at least 30 days.

    (b) If Genie does not survive me for 30 days, to hold the remainder of my Estate in trust in equal shares, one share for each child of mine who is alive at my death, and one share for each child of mine who died before me but who left descendants alive at my death. If a child of mine died before me but left descendants alive at my death, the descendants will take that child's share of the remainder of my Estate in equal shares per stirpes. (For the meaning of per stirpes, see paragraph 14.)

Terms of the trust for my children who are 25 years or more

10. If a child of mine is alive at my death and is at least 25, I direct my Trustee to give that child his or her share of my Estate outright.

Terms of the trust for my children who are under 25 years

11. I direct my Trustee to set aside the share of each child of mine alive at my death who is under 25, and to invest each share on these terms:

    (a) Until the child is 19, my Trustee may pay as much of the income or capital of that child's share as my Trustee decides, to or for the benefit of the child. My Trustee may pay these amounts to the child's parent or guardian, or may otherwise use the amounts for the child's benefit. I direct my Trustee to add any unused income to the capital of the child's share.

(b) When the child is 19 and until he or she is 25, I direct my Trustee to pay to the child the income from his or her share. My Trustee may also pay to the child as much of the capital from his or her share as my Trustee decides.

(c) When the child is 25, I direct my Trustee to give the child the rest of the capital of his or her share.

12. If any child of mine dies after me but before he or she is 25, I direct my Trustee to hold the rest of that child's share on these terms:

(a) If a child dies before he or she is 25 but leaves surviving descendants, I direct my Trustee to hold the rest of that child's share in trust for those descendants in equal shares per stirpes. (For the meaning of per stirpes, see paragraph 14.)

(b) If a child dies before he or she is 25 and leaves no descendants, I direct my Trustee to hold the rest of that child's share in trust in equal shares per stirpes for my descendants who survive that child. (For the meaning of per stirpes, see paragraph 14.)

(c) If any child of mine is under 25 and becomes entitled to some or all of the share of a deceased child of mine, I direct my Trustee to add my living child's part of the deceased child's share to the share my Trustee already holds for that living child and on the same terms.

Terms of the trust for others who are under 19 years

13. If a person other than a child of mine is under 19 and becomes entitled to any share in my Estate, I direct my Trustee to hold that share and keep it invested on these terms:

(a) My Trustee may use as much of the income and capital as my Trustee decides for the benefit of that person until that person is 19.

(b) My Trustee may pay these amounts to that person's parent or guardian, or otherwise use the income and capital for that person's benefit.

Plain language will

_____

(c) I direct my Trustee to add any unused income to the capital of that person's share and then to pay the capital to that person when he or she is 19. If that person dies before reaching age 19, I direct my Trustee to pay that person's share to his or her estate.

Meaning of per stirpes

14. Where I have directed my Trustee to distribute some part of my estate in equal shares per stirpes, I mean that my Trustee should do the following:

(a) Note the person the potential beneficiaries must be descendant from. In paragraphs 9 (b) and 12 (a), they must be descendant from a child of mine. In paragraph 12 (b), they must be descendant from me.

(b) For the noted person, determine which is that person's nearest generation of descendants.

(c) Divide the share into as many equal shares as there are living members of that generation plus deceased members of that generation who leave descendants then living.

(d) Give each living member of that nearest generation one share.

(e) Divide the share of each deceased member of that nearest generation among his or her descendants in the same manner.

Powers of my Trustee

To convert or retain

15. When my Trustee administers my Estate, my Trustee may convert my Estate or any part of my Estate into money, and decide how, when, and on what terms to convert it.

My Trustee has the separate power to retain my Estate or any part of my Estate in the form it is in at my death for as long as my Trustee wishes, even for the duration of the trusts in this will. My Trustee's power to retain any part of my Estate in the form it is in at my death applies even if there is a debt owing on my property or even if the property retained does not produce income.

To invest my Estate

16. My Trustee may invest my Estate as my Trustee decides and is not limited to investments authorized by law for trustees.

To manage real estate

17. As long as any real estate forming part of my Estate is unsold, my Trustee may manage the property generally, and may:

     (a) rent or lease the property for any period of time and on any terms that my Trustee decides,
     (b) spend money for repairs and improvements,
     (c) give options to purchase or lease, and
     (d) subdivide.

To employ advisors

18. My Trustee may employ qualified advisers to give advice or services for my Estate, and my Trustee may pay the fees and expenses of these advisers from either the income or the capital of my Estate. These advisers may include real estate agents, lawyers, accountants, counselors, and consultants.

To borrow money

19. In carrying out the trusts in this will, my Trustee may borrow money by placing a mortgage or other charge on my Estate. My Trustee may sign all necessary documents to do this. My Trustee may pay the normal rate of interest to the person who has loaned the money, even if that person is a Trustee or beneficiary of my will.

To allot my Estate

20. In this will I have directed my Trustee to divide my Estate into shares. When my Trustee distributes my Estate, my Trustee may allot any item that forms part of my Estate to any share or portion of a share. To do this, my Trustee may place a value on that item, and whatever value my Trustee decides upon will be final and will bind everyone interested in my Estate.

Plain language will

_____

Trustee's fees in addition to gift

21. My Trustee may charge a fee for acting as Trustee in addition to any gift or benefit I give to my Trustee in my will or in any codicil.

Signed by Peter Joseph Jones as his last will on _____ , 19 ___ .

At the request of Peter Joseph Jones, we were both present when he signed this will. Then, in his presence and in the presence of each other, we signed as witnesses.

Signature _____

Printed name _____

Address _____

_____

Occupation _____

_____

Peter Joseph Jones

Signature _____

Printed name _____

Address _____

_____

Occupation _____

Appendix 2
Municipal Lease Clauses

Before and *After*

(from Wordsmith Associates files)

Lease Rewrite

BEFORE

3.04   Provided that the Organization shall not then be in default of any of the terms, covenants and conditions of this Lease to be kept, observed and performed by the Organization upon the expiry of the Term, the Organization may, no later than six (6) months prior to the expiration of the Term, apply in writing to the City to renew this Lease for a further period of five (5) years upon the term, covenants and conditions herein contained excepting any further right to renew the Term of this Lease and subject to the then current policies of the city governing the terms and conditions of social recreation organization leases and the City hereby agrees that approval of such a written request for renewal will not be unreasonably withheld.

AFTER

3.04   To be eligible to renew this lease for five years, the Organization must:

a)   apply in writing to the City no later than six months prior to expiry of the term.

b)   agree to the city policies governing the terms and conditions of social recreation organization leases in the year 2000.

c)   not be in default of any part of this lease.

d)   accept that the right to renew this lease will occur only once.

The City agrees not to unreasonably withhold approval of such a written request for renewal.

Appendix 2

Appendix 3
The Right to Information Bylaw

After (segments)

```
┌─────────────────────────────────────┐          ┌────────┐
│      Right to Information Bylaw      │          │ AFTER  │
│      PLAIN LANGUAGE FEATURES         │          └────────┘
└─────────────────────────────────────┘
```

Opening

Unusual overview on title page—which is not considered legally part of the bylaw—but which creates an important signpost and context. And image-evoking language in a bylaw!

Table of contents

Drafters still need to lowercase the headings. But there *is* a table of contents.

Clear lay language

i) No legalese and no use of the word *shall*. Instead, drafters use *must, may,* or *will.*

ii) Short sentences or parallel segments.

Definitions

i) Definitions placed at back where they can be separated from the bylaw and used while reading.

ii) Italicized defined terms instead of capitals.

iii) Explanation of location and how to use definitions at beginning.

Use of "I" and "You"

You is a defined term. *I* is only used in the Part headings (not in the table of contents). This is very experimental for a bylaw. We are unaware of any other legislation which incorporates this plain language guide.

Action ending

i) Appeal forms at end as part of the bylaw certainly make action easy. Even the appeal forms use *I* and *you.*

ii) Flow chart of the appeal process.

Layout

Clear margin headings and good use of white space. (However, see page 15 as an example of capitals that are difficult to read.)

Gender-neutral language

The even-handedness in the language is admirable:

49(2) example
. . . but must inform **her or his** department head as soon as . . . .

Parts headings

Question headings for the Parts are reader-friendly and form excellent logical links in the "chain".

> **Selected pages from a
> municipal plain language bylaw**

THE CITY OF EDMONTON

BYLAW NO. 10999

The Right to Information Bylaw

Information is the lifeblood of a democratic society. The right to know what information governments have, why they collect it and what they do with it, is a fundamental right in the information age.

Governments have passed Access to Information legislation which recognizes that information in their custody belongs to the people who elected them. Unelected governments, dictatorships that have controlled power by controlling information, are falling as technology provides new ways of getting information.

The City of Edmonton was among the first municipalities to pass an access to information bylaw. The City recognizes that it is not only necessary to pass effective legislation, but that it is just as important to keep it up to date.

TABLE OF CONTENTS

THE CITY OF EDMONTON

BYLAW NO. 10999

The Right to Information Bylaw

Edmonton City Council enacts:

PART I PURPOSE, PRINCIPLES AND DEFINITIONS

PURPOSE

1. The purpose of this bylaw is:

   (1) to facilitate access to *information* in the possession of the *City*, and

   (2) to prevent release of *information* that would amount to an invasion of any person's privacy.

PRINCIPLES

2. The *City* acknowledges that:

Ownership of Information

   (1) the *information* that it has gathered and created is owned by the *citizens*,

   (2) *information* has value,

   (3) *information* must be kept safe from harm like any other valuable asset and must be guarded against misuse,

   (4) *information* can also be a marketable asset being managed by the *City* on behalf of its *citizens*,

Duty to Create

   (5) it has a duty to create records to document its functions, policies, decisions, procedures and transactions, and

Duty to Provide

   (6) it is responsible through its *employees*, to provide *information* to persons asking for it as quickly and conveniently as possible, unless there are clear and reasonable grounds to withhold the *information*.

Duty to Inform

3. The *City* acknowledges its obligation to inform *citizens* about its programs, activities, policies and the ways that *information* is collected, where it is kept and how it is used.

Eliminating Barriers to Access

4. The *City* will work with *citizens* to eliminate or reduce barriers to accessing *information* including cost, delay and unnecessary classes of *exempted information.*

Protecting Personal Privacy

5. The *City* acknowledges its duty to protect its *citizens* from any unauthorized or unwarranted use of *personal information* that the *City* possesses.

DEFINITIONS	6.	Words that appear in *italics* in the body of this bylaw are defined in Schedule I. The definitions are in a Schedule so that *you* can pull it apart from the rest of the bylaw and use it as a reference guide as *you* read.

PART II WHAT INFORMATION CAN I GET FROM THE CITY?

INFORMATION AVAILABLE	7.		*You* may access all *information* that is in the possession of the *City*, unless it is *exempted information*.
UNCERTAINTY	8.	(1)	If *employees* are uncertain about whether any particular *information* should be released or disclosed, they must consult with their *supervisors*.
		(2)	If *supervisors* are uncertain about whether any particular *information* should be released or disclosed, they must consult with their *department head*, who must make a decision on whether to release the *information*.
INFORMATION ACCESS BOARD	9.		The *Information Access Board* is established to hear appeals under this bylaw. If *you* are not satisfied with a decision on whether to release *information*, or if *you* wish to dispute fees charged or the format *information* is produced in, *you* may appeal to the *Information Access Board*.

PART III WHERE AND HOW CAN I GET THE INFORMATION I NEED?

RIGHT TO INFORMATION	10.	(1)		*You* have a right to view any *information* except *exempted information*, provided *you* comply with subsections (3) and (4). *You* may request copies of the *information* and *you* are entitled to receive it in any format that is reasonably available from the department or *organization* that has the *information*.
		(2)		Despite subsection (1), *you* have a right to view or obtain copies of *exempted information* if it is *personal information* about *you* as an individual. *Personal information* about *you* as an individual may only be withheld if:
			(a)	releasing it could reasonably be expected to threaten anyone's safety, mental or physical health, interfere with public safety,

Appendix 3
Page 5 of 12

(b)   releasing it could reasonably be expected to cause immediate and grave harm to your health and safety, or

(c)   the *information* is about collective bargaining, arbitration or ongoing investigations for the purpose of disciplinary action or personnel selection.

(3)   Reasonable fees as set out in Schedule III will be charged before *you* are entitled to receive the requested *information*. (*You* may ask for an exemption under section 58.)

(4)   *You* may be asked to make your request in writing to help the *employees* to find the *information* and prepare any necessary fee estimates.

BROCHURE AND INFORMATION DIRECTORY

11.   (1)   After June 1, 1995, the *City* must maintain and make available to the public the *Right to Information Brochure*. *You* may pick up a copy at any Edmonton Public Library, at the Citizen Action Centre or at the Office of the City Clerk. The Brochure must include:

(a)   a description of the mandate and functions of each department, office and *organization* of the *City*, and

(b)   the title, name, address and telephone number of each *department head* and *information coordinator*.

(2)   After January 1, 1997, the *City* must maintain and regularly update a directory of *information*. *You* may view a copy of the directory at the Office of the City Clerk. The directory must include:

(a)   all of the *information* contained in the *Right to Information Brochure*,

(b)   a description of the *information* held by each department, office and *organization*,

(c)   a subject index, and

(d)   a list of each collection of personal *information* including:

(i)   the title and location of the collection,

SCHEDULE I

DEFINITIONS

The following words when used in The Right to Information Bylaw mean:

Citizen	Any individual who resides in the City of Edmonton.
Council Committee	A council committee as defined in the Municipal Government Act, SA. 1994, c.M-26.1.
City	The municipal corporation of the City of Edmonton and any *Organizations* and any corporate entity created or controlled by the *City*.
City Manager	The Chief Administrative Officer appointed by Council under the Municipal Government Act, SA. 1994, c.M-26.1.
Department Head	The General Manager of any *City* department, the senior official in any *City* office, the Chair or other head of any *Organization* and Council as the head of Councillors.
Employee	Any individual employed by the *City*, and includes City Councillors, contract employees, independent contractors and any other individuals appointed to perform duties for the *City*, *supervisors*, *department heads* and the *City Manager*.
Exempted Information	*Information* described in Part V of this bylaw.
Information	Any *information*, regardless of its form or characteristics, within the custody and control of the *City*. *Information* includes correspondence, memoranda, books, maps, plans, photographs, drawings, diagrams, pictorial or graphic works, films, microforms, sound recordings, videotapes, electronic files, electronic mail transmissions, databases and spreadsheets. It does not include software, macros or any other mechanism that produces *information*.
Information Access Board	The *Information Access Board* is a tribunal established under section 40 to decide matters related to access to information.
Information Coordinators	Employees of the *City* who are appointed by *department heads* to assist you with any aspect of a request for *information* or an appeal to the *Information Access Board*.
Organization	*Organizations*, including boards, authorities and committees, which are created and controlled by the *City*.

Personal Information	Recorded *information* about an identifiable individual, including:

       (i)   name, address or telephone or fax number,

       (ii)   race, national or ethnic origin, colour or religious or political beliefs or associations,

       (iii)   age, sex, marital or family status, source of income or sexual orientation,

       (iv)   identifying number, symbol, or other particular assigned to the individual,

       (v)   fingerprints, bloodtype or inheritable characteristics,

       (vi)   health or health care history, including *information* about a physical or mental disability,

       (vii)   educational, financial, employment or criminal history, including criminal records where a pardon has been given,

       (viii) opinions about the individual, or

       (ix)   the individual's personal views or opinions, unless they are about someone else.

Public Interest	The general well-being of the community including safety, health and welfare.
Right to Information Brochure	A brochure described in section 11 that gives general information on *City* departments, offices and organizations.
Third Party	A person or a group of persons other than the person requesting *information* (*you*) or the *City*.
Supervisor	The person to whom an *employee* normally reports, or their designate. For the purposes of this bylaw, City councillors are considered to report only to City Council.
Working Days	Monday to Friday, excluding statutory and civic holidays.
You	Any person who wants or is requesting *information* from the *City*.

e:\mavis\foisched.I

SCHEDULE II

APPEAL FORMS

If *you* want to appeal a refusal to release *information*, if *you* are a *third party* requesting that *information* not be released or for any of the other reasons listed under section 41, *you* must fill out this Appeal Notice. If *you* want to appeal, *you* must mail or deliver this Appeal Notice to the *Information Access Board* within 20 days after receiving written notice of a refusal to release *information* or any other ground for appeal or within 60 days after *you* make your request for *information* if *you* have not received either the *information* or a written refusal to release the *information*.

A. APPEAL NOTICE TO INFORMATION ACCESS BOARD

TO: The Information Access Board DATE: _____
c/o Office of the City Clerk
3rd Floor, City Hall
#1 Sir Winston Churchill Square
Edmonton, Alberta
T5J 2R7

I requested *information* about: (please attach a separate page if necessary)

_____

_____

I am appealing the *City's* decision because: (if *you* have received written reasons, attach copy)

____ it has not released *information* ____ the *information* I received is not
____ it proposes to release *information* complete
that affects my interests ____ my request for fee adjustment was
____ the *information* is not in the format denied
I requested

I disagree with the *City's* decision (*you* may give reasons): (please attach a separate page if necessary)

_____

_____

_____ _____
Signature Name Printed

_____ Phone Numbers
Street Address Home: _____

  Work: _____

_____ Fax: _____
Postal Code

NOTE: **A hearing will be held by the *Information Access Board*. You will be informed of the date of the hearing.**

SCHEDULE II

APPEAL FORMS

If *you* want to appeal a decision of the *Information Access Board* or under section 48, *you* must fill out this Appeal Notice. If *you* want to appeal, *you* must mail or deliver this Appeal Notice to the Office of the City Clerk within ten *working days* after the *Information Access Board* hearing.

B. APPEAL NOTICE TO CITY COUNCIL

TO: City Council
c/o Office of the City Clerk
3rd Floor, City Hall
#1 Sir Winston Churchill Square
Edmonton, Alberta
T5J 2R7

DATE: _____

I requested *information* about: (please attach a separate page if necessary)

_____

_____

I am appealing the *Information Access Board's* decision because: (if *you* have received written reasons, attach copy)

___ it has not released *information*
___ it proposes to release *information* that affects my interests
___ the *information* is not in the format I requested

___ the *information* I received is not complete
___ my request for fee adjustment was denied

I disagree with the *Information Access Board's* decision (*you* **may** give reasons): (please attach a separate page if necessary)

_____

_____

Signature _____

Name Printed _____

Street Address _____

Phone Numbers
Home: _____
Work: _____

Postal Code _____

Fax: _____

NOTE: **A hearing will be held by the City Council. You will be informed of the date of the hearing.**

SCHEDULE III

Fees

(charges for each applicable item will be added together and applicable taxes will be added to the total owing)

ITEM	CHARGE
1. search time for locating and retrieving a record	$15.00 per hour after the first two hours
2. photocopies:	$0.25 per page; $0.50 per double-sided pages (copies will be double-sided whenever possible)
colour photocopies	$1.60 per page; $3.20 per double-sided pages
3. copies in other formats (if format is reasonably available)	floppy diskettes $10.00 each compact diskettes $20.00-$40.00 each microfiche $10.00 per fiche microfilm $40.00 per roll photographs $ 5.00 per photo plus: 5 x 7 $ 4.00 8 x 10 $ 5.00 11 x 14 $10.00 16 x 20 $15.00 slides $ 2.00 per slide audio cassettes $15.00 per cassette video cassettes $40.00 per cassette
4. programming services to produce the record	$55.00 per hour to extract data from an electronic data base
5. special orders and published information	Information in media other than that listed on this schedule will be available at a reasonable cost established by the department.
6. costs incurred by the City	If the City incurs any costs charged by third parties to access or produce the information, these will be charged to the person requesting the information.
7. created information	actual cost of creation, including staff time and materials used

SCHEDULE IV

Request and Appeal Process Summary

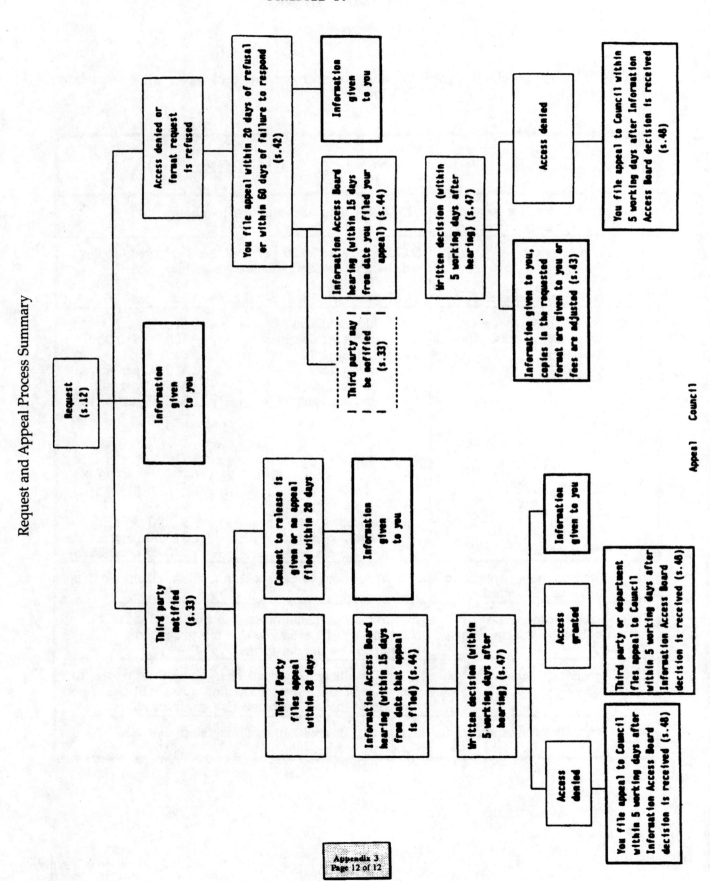

Appeal   Council

Appendix 4
Confidentiality Agreement

Before and After

(Permission to reprint given by Mallesons Stephen Jacques in Australia. The Confidentiality Agreement was prepared for them by Robert Eagleson and was originaly published in *CLARITY*, January 1997, pp. 47-50. Copyright continues to belong to Mallesons Stephen Jacques.)

Confidentiality Agreement   Contract Number: [INSERT CONTRACT NUMBER]
[INSERT NAME]   1

before

AGREEMENT made this   day of   199

BETWEEN: Heavy Weather Pty Ltd. (A.C.N   ) (hereinafter called "Heavy") of the first part

AND: [RECIPIENT'S NAME] of [INSERT RECIPIENT'S ADDRESS] (hereinafter called "Recipient") of the second part
WHEREAS:

A.   Heavy holds in its own right and/or as licensee, agent or trustee for other persons certain Confidential Information which has substantial value to it and such other persons and which it is unwilling to disclose to Recipient and/or other persons.

B.   Recipient is required to access and deal with such Confidential Information as part of his work with Heavy.

C   Heavy has agreed to permit or facilitate access by Recipient to such Confidential Information solely and strictly upon and subject to the terms and conditions of this Agreement.

NOW THIS AGREEMENT WITNESSES and the parties covenant and agree as follows:-

1.   **INTERPRETATION**:

1.1   In the Agreement, unless the context requires otherwise, the following words and expressions shall have the meanings set opposite them:-

"Confidential Information"   means and includes the whole or any part of all and any information or data of any nature or description possessed, controlled, retained or held by Heavy in any medium or form whatsoever, and directly or indirectly relevant to or derived from the Confidential Information described in the First Schedule hereto, but specifically excludes Confidential Information which is either:-

(i)   known to the Recipient at the Effective Date of the Agreement; or

29 July 1993
[REF]

PROBLEMS INDEX

- old style layout and language (e.g., *whereas, now this agreement witnesses, shall, same, in respect of*)
- capitalization
- incorrect grammar (neither . . . or)
- decimal numbering too heavy for short agreement
- doublets, triplets, repetition
- underlining
- passive voice / third person point of view

(ii)		public knowledge by virtue of any means, except as a result of breach of this Agreement; or
(iii)		obtained or received by the Recipient after the date hereof from any other person except Heavy, which other person shall not be in breach of any agreement with Heavy intended to secure or preserve to Heavy confidentiality in respect of the Confidential Information.
"Effective Date of the Agreement"		means 1st May, 1992, or the date on which Recipient first commenced performance of his duties for Heavy, whichever is the earlier date, notwithstanding the later execution of this Agreement.

2.   <u>CONFIDENTIALITY AND USE</u>

2.1   Heavy shall make available the Confidential Information, or so much thereof as it shall in its absolute discretion determine to Recipient for such period or periods it may from time to time determine, and for the purpose specified in Clause 2.2 or such other purpose as Heavy may from time to time determine or permit.

2.2   Recipient acknowledges that the Confidential Information shall be made available to it solely for the purposes of Recipient undertaking and executing the duties as specified in the agreement (Contract No.[CONTRACT NUMBER]) between Heavy and [COMPANY NAME], effective from [DATE EFFECTIVE].

2.3   Recipient shall keep and maintain absolute confidentiality and secrecy in respect of the Confidential Information and shall not disclose and/or communicate, directly or indirectly, the same to any person whatsoever other than as required for the performance of the duties as specified in Claues 2.1 and 2.2.

2.4   Recipient shall neither exploit or use the Confidential Information in any way whatsoever, nor cause or permit or any other person who shall obtain the Confidential Information from Recipient to exploit or use the same in anyway whatsoever, otherwise than for the purpose specified in Clause 2.2.

29 July 1993
[REF]

after

Confidentiality agreement

Owner of confidential information	Light Reading Pty Ltd ACN 000 000 000 Level 58, 302 Gonzales Street, Alice Downs 2087 phone (　　)　　　　　　　　fax (　　)
Contractor	[*name*] [*address*] [*phone*]　　　　　　　　[*fax*]
Contract number	
Confidential information covered	Any information in any form or medium we make available to you in connection with: [*specify relevant project*]
Date of agreement	/　　　/

We accept this confidentiality agreement.

The common seal of
Light Reading Pty Ltd
was affixed by the
authority of the Board

in the presence of

....
Director

....
Director/Secretary

Signed by the contractor

in the presence of:

....
Signature

....
Signature of witness

....
Name - print

....
Name - print

Page 1

PLAIN LANGUAGE FEATURES

- clear forms design (probably with colour)
- key summary information on page 1
- "we" and "you" perspective with definitions highlighted on page 2
- clear, natural language
- short sentences
- active voice verbs
- the consideration and signature are plainly placed on page 1

To improve:
Add *page 1 of 2* and *page 2 of 2*

Light Reading █ Confidentiality agreement █

General Terms

When must we disclose the information to you?

1.1 We must make that part of the confidential information available to you that we consider in our sole discretion to be necessary for you to carry out the project.

1.2 The confidential information always remains our property. This agreement does not give you any right, title or interest in it.

How must you treat it?

2.1 You must use the confidential information solely for the purpose of carrying out the project. You must not use or exploit it for your own benefit or for any other purpose, or allow any other person to do so without our written consent.

2.2 You must not disclose it, and must ensure that your employees, contractors and agents do not disclose it to any other person except as required to carry out the project and then only on a confidential basis.

2.3 You must take reasonable steps to protect the confidential information and keep it secure from unauthorised persons.

2.4 You must inform us immediately if:

(a) you become aware or suspect that there has

been a breach of these obligations; or

(b) you are required to disclose the information by law.

2.5 At the end of the project or if we ask for it earlier, you must return the confidential information, and all copies, notes and memorandums relating to it, to us as we direct.

2.6 You do not have to treat as confidential information

(a) which is or becomes part of the public domain, except information that is or becomes so because it has been disclosed without authority; or

(b) which is lawfully known to you before the date of this agreement; or

(c) which is or becomes available to you from another person who is in possession of it lawfully and can disclose it to you on a non-confidential basis; or

(d) which you are required by law to disclose but you must seek to limit that disclosure in any way we reasonably request.

Indemnity

3. You indemnify us against all loss, damage, expense

and costs arising because you do not observe the conditions of this agreement for any reason.

Duration

4. Your obligations under this agreement continue after the project ends.

General

5.1 This agreement contains the entire agreement between you and us and takes the place of all other statements about the confidential information.

5.2 This agreement may be varied only if you and we agree in writing.

5.3 If we do not exercise a right at any time in connection with a default under this agreement, this does not mean that we have waived the right or cannot exercise it later.

5.4 This agreement is covered by the laws of New South Wales. You and we submit to the non-exclusive jurisdiction of its courts and courts of appeal from them.

we means Light Reading Pty Ltd.

you means the contractor named on page 1.

Page 2

after

Appendix 5
Farmout Agreement Segment

Before and After

(from Wordsmith Associates files)

Farmout Agreement Section

BEFORE

AFTER

SECTION 14

14. INDEMNITY

The Farmee shall

(a) be liable to the Farmor for all loss, costs, damages, and expenses whatsoever which the Farmor may suffer, sustain, pay, or incur; and in addition

(b) indemnify and save the Farmor harmless from and against all claims, liabilities, actions, proceedings, demands, losses, costs, damages and expenses whatsoever which may be brought against or suffered by the Farmor or which it may sustain, pay or incur

by reason of any matter or thing arising out of, resulting from, attributable to or connected with the operations carried out by or on behalf of the Farmee on or with respect to the Farmout lands, other than operations carried out by or for it as Operator for the joint account pursuant to the Operating Procedure for which the provisions of the Operating Procedure shall apply. The losses, costs, damages, expenses, claims, liabilities, actions, proceedings and demands subject to the above liability and indemnity include, without limitation, those arising from damage to property or death or injury of persons or animals and those arising out of contract or otherwise. The costs subject to such liability and indemnity shall extend to legal costs on a solicitor and client basis.

14. Farmee's Responsibility

The Farmee:

(a) is responsible for all losses, costs and damages incurred by the Farmor;

(b) must compensate the Farmor for all (third party) claims, proceedings, losses, costs and damages brought against or incurred by the Farmor

resulting from operations connected with the Farmout Lands conducted by or for the Farmee as Operator under the Operating Procedure for the joint account.

The Farmee's obligations include responsibility for losses, costs, claims or proceedings arising from:

i) environmental damage
ii) property damage
iii) injury or death to people and animals, and
iv) legal costs on a solicitor/client basis

under contract or otherwise.

Appendix 6
Farmout Proposal Letter

Before and *After*

(from Wordsmith Associates files)

PROBLEMS INDEX

- tired or obsolete phrases: *Attention, Gentlemen, Re, further to, upon, should advise*
- poor layout
- no headings and thus confusing organization
- legalese: *representations, warrantees, shall, with respect to*
- confusing presentation of numbers and formulas in 4(a) and (b)
- passive voice
- that this offer is still subject to approval is buried at the end

May 6, 1998
DELIVERED BY COURIER

CALGARY, AB
T2P 0N0

Attention:

Gentlemen:

Re: Alberta Farmout Proposal

Further to our conversation on January 17, 1998 and your letter of October 30, 1997, Gushing Oil (Farmor) is prepared to grant a farmout to Crude Oil (Farmee) based on the following general terms and conditions:

1. The farmout lands shall comprise the Farmor's interest in all P&NG rights to the top of the Paleozoic underlying the following lands:

    Farmor 100%

2. The Farmor makes no representations or warranties as to its title to the Farmout Lands except that it has not disposed of or otherwise encumbered its interest in the Farmout Lands at the date hereof.

3. On or before _____, 1998, Farmee shall commence a well (the 'Test Well') at a location of its choice on the Farmout Lands. Farmee shall drill the Test Well, at its sole cost, risk and expense, to a depth sufficient to penetrate 15 meters into the Paleozoic or to a total subsurface depth of 1350 meters, whichever first occurs ('Contract Depth').

4. Upon drilling the Test Well to Contract Depth and either completing it to the outlet valve on the wellhead or abandoning same, and having supplied the Farmor with complete information obtained from the drilling of the Test Well, on a current basis, including the results of any representative production potential tests, Farmee shall have earned the following interests in the Farmout Lands:

    (a) in the Test Well Spacing Unit - 100% of the Farmor's working interest, reserving unto the Farmor a SSGORR of 5-15% based on 1/150th of monthly oil production, expressed in barrels, and a GORR of 15% (min.$.20/Mcf) on natural gas and related byproducts. Such overriding royalties shall be convertible at the Farmor's option, within (30) days of receipt of written notice of payout or abandonment of the Test Well, to 40% of the Farmor's prior working interest. Such conversion shall be effective as of the date on which payout or abandonment occurred; and

    (b) in the balance of the Farmout Lands - 60% of the Farmor's prior working interest.

5. Farmee shall be designated initial Operator of the Farmout Lands and shall reimburse the Farmor for all rentals attributable to the Farmout Lands on a per diem basis from the date hereof until the Farmee earns an interest in the Farmout Lands or such right to earn terminates. Thereafter, rentals shall be borne in accordance with the working interest of the parties.

6. Gushing Oil reserves the right to the option to take their product in kind.

7. Any cash or non-cash drilling or other credits or incentives granted on account of any drilling operation on the Farmout Lands by the Farmee with respect to any Test Well shall be retained by the Farmee and, except where prohibited by the Regulations, credited to the payout account for such well.

    The foregoing is expressly subject to the final approval of management.

    Should this proposal be acceptable, please so advise in writing and _____ will proceed with requesting final management approval. _____ incorporates the 1981 CAPL Operating Procedure and the 1983 PASWC Accounting Procedure in our Farmout Agreements. Attached is _____ preferred rates and elections.

    Should you wish to discuss the above, please contact me at 555-1313.

                                        Yours truly,

                                        Landman

AFTER

May 6, 1998
Delivered by Courier

Calgary, Alberta
T2P 0N0

Alberta Farmout Proposal

This farmout proposal is a follow-up to our January 17, 1998 discussions and your
October 30, 1997 letter. Although this agreement is subject to final approval by our management,
Gushing Oil (*farmor*) is pleased to offer the following general terms and conditions to
Crude Oil (*farmee*):

1. **Farmout lands**
   The lands to be farmed out are _____ (legal description). Gushing Oil owns
   100% interest in all P&NG rights in the farmout lands.

2. **Title to farmout lands**
   Gushing Oil affirms nothing about its title except that it had not disposed of or otherwise
   encumbered its interest in the farmout lands.

3. **Drilling start date and contract depth**
   Crude Oil will start drilling its test well by _____, 1998

   i)   at its own cost and risk, and

   ii) to a depth of either 15 meters into the Paleozoic, or to a
        total depth of 1350 meters, whichever comes first. That
        depth is the contract depth.

4. **Crude Oil's test well responsibilities**
   When Crude Oil has drilled the test well to its contract depth, it must:

   i)   test, complete, equip, or abandon the well according to
        good oilfield practices, and

   ii) regularly supply Gushing Oil with complete test well
        information (for example, log analysis and results of
        production potential tests).

5. **Interest to be earned by Crude Oil**
   Crude Oil will earn the following interest in the farmout lands:

Location	% of working interest
Test Well Spacing Unit	100% (minus the royalties described in Clause 6 below)
Balance of farmout lands	60%

> **PLAIN LANGUAGE FEATURES**
> * clear, full, purpose statement with qualification at top
> * short, succinct sentences with subpoints
> * readable format for numbers and comparisons in #5 and #6.
> * logical bolded headings create a clear organization
> * active voice verbs
> * no legalese
> * modern format with subject headings

...2

Farmout Proposal - Page 2
May 6, 1998

6. **Gushing Oil's royalties and conversion option**
Gushing Oil will earn the following royalties on the farmout lands:

Location	**Royalties**
Test Well Spacing Unit	*on crude oil* a SSGORR of 5 - 15% based on 1/150th of only oil production (in barrels) *on natural gas and related byproducts* a GORR of 15% (minimum $0.20/Mcf)

Within 30 days of Gushing Oil's receiving written notice of Crude Oil's payout or abandonment of the test well, Gushing Oil may request conversion of these royalties to 40% of its prior working interest. The conversion will be effective on the date of the payout or abandonment.

7. **Operator of farmout lands**
Crude Oil is the initial operator of the farmout lands.

8. **Rental payments**
Crude Oil will reimburse Gushing Oil at a daily rate for rent on the farmout lands from the start date until

    i)   Gushing Oil earns an interest in the farmout lands, or

    ii) such right to earn interest terminates.

Afterwards, Gushing Oil and Crude Oil will share rental payments in accordance with their working interests.

9. **Cash or product in kind**
Gushing Oil reserves the right to take either their cash or product in kind.

10. **Test well credits to the payout account**
Crude Oil will credit to the test well payout account

    i)   any cash or non-cash drilling funds, or

    ii) any other credits or incentives

which come from the drilling of any test well on the farmout lands.

If you wish to discuss any of this, please call me at 555-1313.

Yours truly,

Landman

Appendix 7
Schedule 10 of the *Finance Act* (No. 2), Britain, 1992

Before and *After*

(Permission to reprint the Rent-a-Room Relief Schedule granted by its author, Martin Cutts, Research Director of the Plain Language Commission, England, and by sponsors of the work, Barclays PLC, London, convenor for the Special Committee of Tax Law Consultative Bodies)

From a U.K. act, *Finance Act 1992*

BEFORE

SCHEDULE 10

Section 59.

FURNISHED ACCOMMODATION

Introduction

1. Paragraphs 2 to 8 below apply for the purposes of this Schedule.

2.—(1) An individual is a qualifying individual for a year of assessment if apart from this Schedule he would be chargeable for the year to income tax under Case I or Case VI of Schedule D (or both those Cases) in respect of all relevant sums accruing to him in respect of a qualifying residence or qualifying residences; and it is immaterial whether the sums are treated for income tax purposes as derived from one source or from two or more separate sources.

(2) Relevant sums are sums accruing in respect of the use of furnished accommodation in the residence or any of the residences or in respect of relevant goods or services supplied in connection with that use.

(3) In a case where—

    (a) the individual is chargeable for the year to income tax in respect of sums falling within sub-paragraph (4) below, and

    (b) any of those sums are treated for income tax purposes as derived from a source mentioned in sub-paragraph (1) above,

the individual is not a qualifying individual for the year (if he would be apart from this sub-paragraph).

(4) Sums fall within this sub-paragraph if they are not relevant sums accruing to the individual in respect of the residence or residences.

3. As regards a year of assessment a period is a basis period for a source mentioned in paragraph 2(1) above if it is a period on whose profits or gains income tax for the year falls to be finally computed in respect of the source.

4. A residence is a qualifying residence if it is the individual's only or main residence at any time in any period which as regards the year of assessment concerned is a basis period for a source mentioned in paragraph 2(1) above.

5.—(1) This paragraph applies to determine an individual's limit for a year of assessment.

(2) Subject to the following provisions of this paragraph, the limit is the basic amount for the year.

(3) For the purposes of sub-paragraph (4) below a relevant period is—

    (a) any period which as regards the year is a basis period for a source mentioned in paragraph 2(1) above;

    (b) any period of one year which begins at the same time as any period which is less than one year and falls within paragraph (a) above;

    (c) any period of one year which ends at the same time as any period which is less than one year and falls within paragraph (a) above.

SCH. 10

(4) In a case where—

(a) at any time in a relevant period sums accrue to a person or persons other than the individual in respect of the use of residential accommodation in the residence or any of the residences, or in respect of relevant goods or services supplied in connection with that use, and

(b) at that time the residence concerned is the individual's only or main residence,

the limit is the amount equal to half the basic amount for the year.

6. The basic amount for a year of assessment is—

(a) such sum as may be specified for the year by order made by the Treasury;

(b) £3,250 if no sum is so specified.

7. "Residence" means a building, or part of a building, occupied or intended to be occupied as a separate residence, or a caravan or house-boat; but a building, or part of a building, which is designed for permanent use as a single residence shall be treated as a single residence notwithstanding that it is temporarily divided into two or more parts which are occupied or intended to be occupied as separate residences.

8. Relevant goods and services are meals, cleaning, laundry and goods and services of a similar nature.

Exemption etc.

9.—(1) This paragraph applies if—

(a) an individual is a qualifying individual for a year of assessment,

(b) the amount of the sums mentioned in paragraph 2(1) above does not exceed the individual's limit for the year, and

(c) no election that this paragraph shall not apply to the individual for the year has effect under paragraph 10 below.

(2) Where this paragraph applies the following shall be treated as nil for the purposes of the Tax Acts—

(a) the profits or gains of any period which as regards the year is a basis period for a source mentioned in paragraph 2(1) above;

(b) the losses of any such period.

1990 c. 1.

(3) Where this paragraph applies no allowance or balancing charge shall be made for the year to or on the individual under section 24 of the Capital Allowances Act 1990 in respect of any machinery or plant provided for the purposes of any trade from which any of the sums mentioned in paragraph 2(1) above are derived.

(4) In a case where—

(a) apart from this sub-paragraph the preceding provisions of this paragraph would apply, and

(b) the amount of the sums mentioned in paragraph 2(1) above together with the amount of any relevant balancing charges would exceed the individual's limit for the year,

the preceding provisions of this paragraph shall not apply.

(5) For the purposes of sub-paragraph (4) above a relevant balancing charge is a balancing charge which (apart from this paragraph) would be made for the year on the individual under section 24 of the Capital Allowances Act 1990 in respect of any machinery or plant provided for the purposes of any trade from which any of the sums mentioned in paragraph 2(1) above are derived.

(6) In ascertaining the amount of sums for the purposes of this paragraph no deduction shall be made in respect of expenses or any other matter.

Finance (No. 2) Act 1992   c. 48

10.—(1) An individual may elect that paragraph 9 above shall not apply to him for a year of assessment, and (unless withdrawn) the election shall have effect accordingly.

(2) An election under this paragraph shall have effect only for the year of assessment for which it is made.

(3) An individual who has made an election under this paragraph for a year of assessment may give a notice to withdraw the election, and if he does so the election shall not have effect for that year.

(4) An election, or notice of withdrawal, under this paragraph—

(a) must be made or given before the end of the period of one year beginning with the end of the year of assessment concerned or such longer period as the Board may in any particular case allow, and

(b) must be made or given in writing to the inspector.

(5) In a case where—

(a) an election is made, or a notice to withdraw an election is given, under this paragraph, and

(b) in order to give effect to the election or its withdrawal it is necessary to make an adjustment by way of an assessment,

the assessment shall not be out of time if it is made before the end of the period of one year beginning with the day when the election was made or (as the case may be) the notice to withdraw was given.

Adjusted profits etc.

11.—(1) This paragraph applies if—

(a) an individual is a qualifying individual for a year of assessment,

(b) the amount of the sums mentioned in paragraph 2(1) above exceeds the individual's limit for the year, and

(c) an election that this paragraph shall apply to the individual for the year has effect under paragraph 12 below.

(2) In a case where—

(a) this paragraph applies, and

(b) the sums mentioned in paragraph 2(1) above are treated for income tax purposes as derived from a single source,

the profits or gains of any period which as regards the year is a basis period for the source shall be treated for the purposes of the Tax Acts as equal to the amount found by deducting amount B from amount A.

(3) For the purposes of sub-paragraph (2) above—

(a) amount A is the amount of the sums mentioned in paragraph 2(1) above;

(b) amount B is the amount of the individual's limit for the year.

(4) In a case where—

(a) this paragraph applies, and

(b) the sums mentioned in paragraph 2(1) above are treated for income tax purposes as derived from two or more separate sources,

the profits or gains of any period which as regards the year is a basis period for a separate source shall be treated for the purposes of the Tax Acts as equal to the amount found by deducting amount D from amount C.

F

SCH. 10

(5) For the purposes of sub-paragraph (4) above—

   (a) amount C is the amount of such of the sums mentioned in paragraph 2(1) above as are treated for income tax purposes as derived from the separate source, and

   (b) amount D is the amount found by multiplying the amount of the individual's limit for the year by the appropriate fraction;

and the appropriate fraction is the fraction whose numerator is equal to the number of pounds in amount C and whose denominator is equal to the number of pounds in the sums mentioned in paragraph 2(1) above.

1990 c. 1.

(6) Where this paragraph applies no allowance shall be made for the year to the individual under section 24 of the Capital Allowances Act 1990 in respect of any machinery or plant provided for the purposes of any trade from which any of the sums mentioned in paragraph 2(1) above are derived.

(7) In ascertaining the amount of sums for the purposes of this paragraph no deduction shall be made in respect of expenses or any other matter.

12.—(1) An individual may elect that paragraph 11 above shall apply to him for a year of assessment.

(2) An election under this paragraph—

   (a) shall (unless withdrawn) have effect for the year of assessment for which it is made and for subsequent years of assessment,

   (b) must be made before the end of the period of one year beginning with the end of the year of assessment for which it is made or such longer period as the Board may in any particular case allow, and

   (c) must be made in writing to the inspector.

(3) An individual who has made an election under this paragraph may give a notice to withdraw the election, and if he does so the election shall not have effect for the year of assessment for which the notice is given or any subsequent year.

(4) A notice of withdrawal under this paragraph—

   (a) must be given before the end of the period of one year beginning with the end of the year of assessment for which it is given or such longer period as the Board may in any particular case allow,

   (b) must be given in writing to the inspector, and

   (c) shall not prejudice the making of a fresh election for any subsequent year of assessment.

(5) Sub-paragraph (6) below applies where—

   (a) an individual is a qualifying individual for a year of assessment,

   (b) the amount of the sums mentioned in paragraph 2(1) above does not exceed the individual's limit for the year, and

   (c) an election under this paragraph has effect (apart from sub-paragraph (6) below) for the year.

(6) In such a case—

   (a) the individual shall be deemed to have given notice to withdraw the election for the year of assessment concerned,

   (b) the notice shall be deemed to have been given on the last day of the period of one year beginning with the end of the year of assessment concerned, and

   (c) sub-paragraphs (3) and (4)(c) above and (7) below shall apply accordingly.

Finance (No. 2) Act 1992   c. **48**

(7) In a case where—

  (a) an election is made, or a notice to withdraw an election is given, under this paragraph, and

  (b) in order to give effect to the election or its withdrawal it is necessary to make an adjustment by way of an assessment,

the assessment shall not be out of time if it is made before the end of the period of one year beginning with the day when the election was made or (as the case may be) the notice to withdraw was given.

Application of Schedule

13. This Schedule shall apply in relation to the year 1992-93 and subsequent years of assessment (whatever the basis period or periods for the source or sources mentioned in paragraph 2(1) above may be as regards the year of assessment concerned).

Schedule 10[1]

RENT-A-ROOM RELIEF

Introduction

1 The purpose of this schedule is to give individuals a tax relief for *rent* from a furnished *letting* or lettings in their only or main *residence*.

2 The tax relief is called rent-a-room relief.

3 The schedule applies in relation to the *tax year* 1995-96 onwards. Later paragraphs explain how it applies.

4 Definitions are shown in paragraph 24. The first time a defined word is used, it appears in italics.

Qualifying for rent-a-room relief

5 *You* are entitled to rent-a-room relief in respect of a tax year if:

(a) you charge rent for furnished letting in respect of the tax year;

(b) the rent would otherwise be assessable under Schedule A or Schedule D Case I or both of them;

(c) the furnished letting is in property which is your only or main residence at some time in the tax year or the *basis period* for that year;

(d) all your rent from furnished letting in your only or main residences in the tax year, from no matter how many sources, is included in the rent-a-room calculation; and

(e) the furnished letting is for residential use.

6 You are not entitled to rent-a-room relief for rent from furnished letting in a residence that is not your only or main residence.

7 You are not entitled to rent-a-room relief for income arising from unfurnished letting.

8 You are not entitled to rent-a-room relief for income arising from both furnished and unfurnished lettings in your only or main residence.

Limit for rent-a-room relief

9 If the rent is £3,250 or less in a tax year (or for a trader the basis period for that year), it is exempt from tax. If the rent comes from a trade or trades you carry on, you must add any *balancing charge* to the rent to see whether your limit of £3,250 has been exceeded. If it has, you are not entitled to the exemption but paragraph 18 may be relevant to you.

10 The limit for rent-a-room relief may be changed by Treasury order.

AFTER

1996 c100
Finance Act 1995
Schedule 10
paragraph 1

PLAIN LANGUAGE FEATURES
- helpful, visible headings
- "you" perspective
- definitions indicator in introduction
- definitions in paragraph 24 make it all understandable
- short, specific sentences
- natural, understandable language
- more readable typeface
- simplified numbering system
- formula in 19 (b) is clearly delineated
- reader-friendly calculation procedures
- the word "elect" and other unplain words are gone
- oops! #21 still says *in respect of*—substitute *for*

Defined terms
(see paragraph 24)
balancing charge
basis period
letting
rent
residence
tax year
you

Footnote
's59, 1992c48

Special Committee of Tax Law Consultative Bodies.
Redraft of Schedule 10, Finance (No. 2) Act 1992. Draft 9, 12/95

Appendix 7
Page 6 of 9

1

1996 c100
Finance Act 1995
Schedule 10
paragraph 11

11 Your limit is halved if rent is also payable to another individual or individuals for furnished letting in your only or main residence at some time in:

(a) the same tax year;

(b) the basis period for that year; or

(c) any other period of 12 months which includes such a letting for a shorter period.

Treatment of losses

12 Unless you opt out of rent-a-room relief (see paragraph 13), you are not entitled to relief for any losses arising from the letting.

Opting out of rent-a-room relief

13 If you are entitled to rent-a-room relief, you are also entitled to opt out of taking it, for instance if you have made losses from the letting. To opt out, you must notify your tax inspector in writing within a year of the end of the relevant tax year.

14 You are entitled to withdraw your opt-out for a particular tax year. To withdraw it, you must notify your tax inspector in writing within a year of the end of the relevant tax year.

15 Late notification of opt-out or withdrawal may be accepted at the discretion of the Board of Inland Revenue.

16 If you opt out for one tax year, the opt-out lasts only for that year. To opt out for any other tax year, again follow paragraph 13.

17 When you opt out or withdraw your opt-out for a tax year, the Board of Inland Revenue may need to assess you or adjust your existing assessment for that year. The Board may do so within one year of the date of the opt-out or its withdrawal as the case may be.

If rent plus balancing charge is over your limit for rent-a-room relief

18 If the rent plus any balancing charge in a basis period for the source is over your limit, you are entitled to:

(a) opt for the alternative computation; or

(b) ignore this schedule and calculate your taxable profit as normal (rent less actual expenses).

Defined terms
(see paragraph 24)
balancing charge
basis period
letting
rent
residence
tax year
you

Special Committee of Tax Law Consultative Bodies.
Redraft of Schedule 10, Finance (No. 2) Act 1992. Draft 9, 12/95

Opting for the alternative computation: effect on your tax

1996 c100
Finance Act 1995
Schedule 10
paragraph 23

19 If you opt for the alternative computation, then:

(a) if the rent, including any balancing charge, is treated for income tax purposes as coming from a single source in the basis period for the source, you are taxed on the rent less your limit;

(b) if the rent is treated for income tax purposes as coming from two or more separate sources (for example, where you both cater for lodgers and provide furnished letting) in the basis period for those sources, your limit is split between those sources. The result is that, for each source, the taxable amount is given by the formula

$$A - (B \times A)/C$$

where

A is the total amount coming from that source in the relevant tax year;

B is the amount of your limit for the year;

C is the total of the sums coming from furnished letting for the relevant tax year;

(c) you may not make a deduction for expenses, capital allowances or anything else.

Opting for the alternative computation: procedure

20 To opt for the alternative computation, you must notify your tax inspector in writing within a year of the end of the relevant tax year. You are entitled to withdraw your option for a particular tax year. To do so, you must notify your tax inspector in writing by the same deadline. In either case, late notice may be accepted at the discretion of the Board of Inland Revenue.

21 Withdrawal of your option will not prevent you from opting for the alternative computation in respect of a future tax year.

22 Your option for the alternative computation lasts until:

(a) you withdraw it; or

(b) the rent plus any balancing charge drops below your limit for any tax year. Paragraph 9 then applies.

23 When you opt for the alternative computation or withdraw that option for a tax year, the Board of Inland Revenue may assess you or adjust your existing tax assessment. The Board may do so within one year of the date of the option or its withdrawal.

Defined terms
(see paragraph 24)
balancing charge
basis period
letting
rent
residence
tax year
you

Special Committee of Tax Law Consultative Bodies.
Redraft of Schedule 10, Finance (No. 2) Act 1992. Draft 9, 12/95

3

1996 c100
**Finance Act
1995**
Schedule 10
paragraph 24

Definitions

24 (a) 'Balancing charge' is any amount assessable on an individual under section 24(5) of the Capital Allowances Act 1990[2].

(b) 'Basis period' means the accounting period or year of assessment, your income from which is assessed for a tax year.

(c) 'Letting' includes a room occupied under licence or at will.

(d) 'Rent' means amounts receivable from furnished letting. It includes amounts receivable from any provision of goods and services related to the letting (whether provided under a separate agreement or not) such as meals, laundry, cleaning, caring and other similar services. It excludes any adjustments for expenses, allowances or charges.

(e) 'Residence' means a building, or part of a building, occupied or intended to be occupied as a separate residence; a caravan; or a houseboat. A building or part of a building, designed for permanent use as a single residence but temporarily divided into multiple residences is to be treated as a single residence.

(f) 'Tax year' means a year of assessment from 6 April in a year to the following 5 April inclusive.

(g) 'You' means an individual.

Defined terms
(see paragraph 24)
balancing charge
basis period
letting
rent
residence
tax year
you

Footnote
[2] 1990c1

Special Committee of Tax Law Consultative Bodies.
Redraft of Schedule 10, Finance (No. 2) Act 1992. Draft 9, 12/95

Appendix 8
Example of flow chart, for legislation

After

(Proposed by a task force committee to the Alberta government but which did not appear in the final *Municipal Act*)

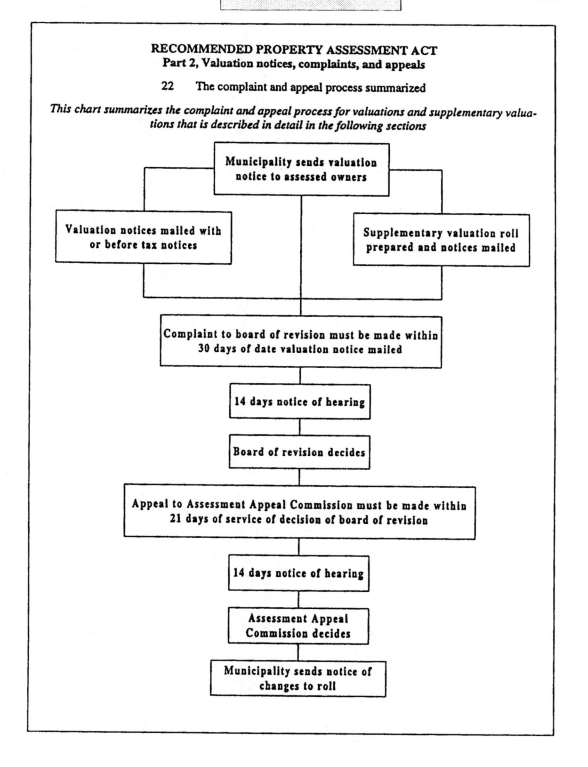

Example of flow chart in legislation

AFTER

RECOMMENDED PROPERTY ASSESSMENT ACT
Part 2, Valuation notices, complaints, and appeals

22   The complaint and appeal process summarized

This chart summarizes the complaint and appeal process for valuations and supplementary valuations that is described in detail in the following sections

Municipality sends valuation notice to assessed owners

Valuation notices mailed with or before tax notices

Supplementary valuation roll prepared and notices mailed

Complaint to board of revision must be made within 30 days of date valuation notice mailed

14 days notice of hearing

Board of revision decides

Appeal to Assessment Appeal Commission must be made within 21 days of service of decision of board of revision

14 days notice of hearing

Assessment Appeal Commission decides

Municipality sends notice of changes to roll

Appendix 8

Appendix 9
Examples from Income Tax Assessment Act 1997 (Australia)

After

Selected pages from an
outstanding plain language
Australian Act 1997

Income Tax Assessment Act 1997

No. 38, 1997

An Act about income tax and related matters

PLAIN LANGUAGE FEATURE

• a simple title for an Act

Three pages of Executive Summary contents

PLAIN LANGUAGE FEATURES

- Contents - not even "table of . . ."
- Clear descriptive titles for chapters, parts, divisions. Note the Dictionary is at the end, Chapter 6, divided into concepts and topics and definitions

Contents

Section 4-15

4-15 How to work out your taxable income

(1) Work out your *taxable income* for the income year like this:

taxable income = assessable income – deductions

> *Method statement*
>
> *Step 1.* Add up all your assessable income for the income year.
>
> > To find out about your assessable income, see Division 6.
>
> *Step 2.* Add up your deductions for the income year.
>
> > To find out what you can deduct, see Division 8.
>
> *Step 3.* Subtract your deductions from your assessable income (unless they exceed it). The result is your taxable income. (If the deductions equal or exceed the assessable income, you don't have a taxable income.)

Note: If the deductions exceed the assessable income, you may have a tax loss which you may be able to deduct in a later income year: see Division 36.

> **PLAIN LANGUAGE FEATURES**
>
> * descriptive heading formula (*How to work out your taxable income . . .*)
> * simple steps in command format
> * contrastive font to direct reader to where information on assessable income and deductions are
> * second person singular
> * boxed procedures

---

*To find definitions of asterisked terms, see the Dictionary, starting at section 995-1.

Income Tax Assessment Act 1997   No. 38, 1997   15

Appendix 9
Page 5 of 16

Part 1-3 Core provisions
Division 4 How to work out the income tax payable on your taxable income

Section 4-15

(2) There are cases where taxable income is worked out in a special way:

Item	For this case ...	See:
1.	A company does not maintain continuity of ownership and control during the income year and does not continue to carry on the same business	Subdivision 165-B
2.	A company becomes a PDF (pooled development fund) during the income year, and the PDF component for the income year is a nil amount	section 124ZTA of the *Income Tax Assessment Act 1936*
3.	A shipowner or charterer: • has its principal place of business outside Australia; and • carries passengers, freight or mail shipped in Australia	section 129 of the *Income Tax Assessment Act 1936*
4.	An insurer who is not an Australian resident enters into insurance contracts connected with Australia	sections 142 and 143 of the *Income Tax Assessment Act 1936*
5.	The Commissioner makes a default or special assessment of taxable income	sections 167 and 168 of the *Income Tax Assessment Act 1936*

*To find definitions of asterisked terms, see the Dictionary, starting at section 995-1.

Part 3-5 Corporate taxpayers and corporate distributions
Division 165 Income tax consequences of changing ownership or control of a company
Subdivision 165-B Working out the taxable income and tax loss for the income year of
the change

Section 165-20
_____

(2) However, that person's control of the voting power, or ability to
control it, does not prevent the company from deducting the *tax
loss if the company satisfies the *same business test for the income
year (the *same business test period*).

(3) Apply the *same business test to the *business that the company
carried on immediately before the time (the *test time*) when the
person began to control that voting power, or became able to
control it.

For the same business test: see Subdivision 165-E.

165-20 When company can deduct *part* of a tax loss

(1) If section 165-10 (which is about deducting a tax loss) prevents a
company from deducting a *tax loss, the company can deduct the
part of the tax loss that was incurred during a *part of the loss year*.

(2) However, the company can do this only if, assuming that *part* of
the *loss year had been treated as the *whole* of the loss year for the
purposes of section 165-10, the company would have been entitled
to deduct the tax loss.

Subdivision 165-B—Working out the taxable income and tax loss for the income year of the change

Guide to Subdivision 165-B

165-23 What this Subdivision is about

> A company that has not had the same ownership and control
> during the income year, and has not satisfied the same business
> test, works out its taxable income and tax loss under this
> Subdivision.

_____

*To find definitions of asterisked terms, see the Dictionary, starting at section 995-1.
_____

192   Income Tax Assessment Act 1997   No. 38, 1997

Corporate taxpayers and corporate distributions Part 3-5
Income tax consequences of changing ownership or control of a company Division 165
Working out the taxable income and tax loss for the income year of the change
Subdivision 165-B

Section

Table of sections

> ### PLAIN LANGUAGE FEATURES
>
> Note how well organized this 396-page Act is. Here is a table of sections just for this subdivision 165-B. Note the clean tabular format and all the "How to" segments. This is accessible tax law.

When a company must work out its taxable income and tax loss under this Subdivision

Working out the company's taxable income

Working out the company's tax loss

Special rules that apply if the company is in partnership

*To find definitions of asterisked terms, see the Dictionary, starting at section 995-1.

Income Tax Assessment Act 1997   No. 38, 1997   193

Part 3-5 Corporate taxpayers and corporate distributions
Division 165 Income tax consequences of changing ownership or control of a company
Subdivision 165-B Working out the taxable income and tax loss for the income year of the change

Section 165-25

165-25 Summary of this Subdivision

(1) The company calculates its taxable income for the income year in this way:

Method statement

Step 1. Divide the income year into periods: each change in ownership or control is a dividing point between periods.

Step 2. Treat each period as if it were an income year and work out the notional loss or notional taxable income for that period.

Step 3. Work out the taxable income for the year of the change by adding up:

- each notional taxable income; and

- any full year amounts (amounts of assessable income not taken into account at Step 2);

and then subtracting any full year deductions (deductions not taken into account at Step 2).

Note: Do *not* take into account any notional loss.

---

(2) As well as a taxable income, the company will have a *tax loss. It is the total of:

- each notional loss; and

- excess *full year deductions of particular kinds.

(3) Special rules apply if the company was in partnership at some time during the income year.

---

*To find definitions of asterisked terms, see the Dictionary, starting at section 995-1.

---

194   *Income Tax Assessment Act 1997   No. 38, 1997*

Corporate taxpayers and corporate distributions Part 3-5
Income tax consequences of changing ownership or control of a company Division 165
Working out the taxable income and tax loss for the income year of the change
Subdivision 165-B

Section 165-30

For the special rules that apply if the company was in partnership: see sections 165-75 to 165-90.

165-30 Flow chart showing the application of this Subdivision

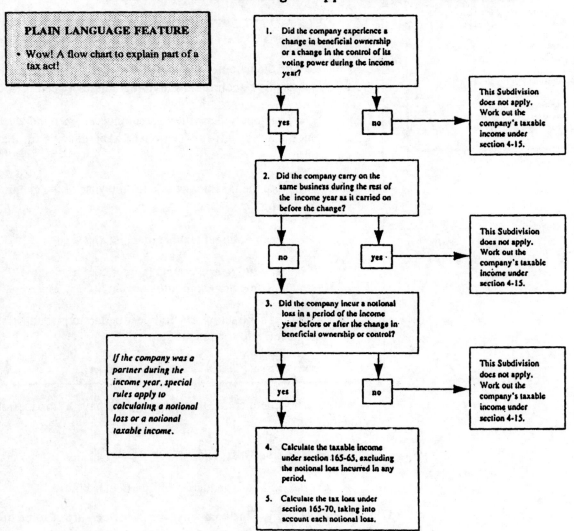

*To find definitions of asterisked terms, see the Dictionary, starting at section 995-1.

Income Tax Assessment Act 1997 *No. 38, 1997* 195

Part 3-5 Corporate taxpayers and corporate distributions
Division 165 Income tax consequences of changing ownership or control of a company
Subdivision 165-B Working out the taxable income and tax loss for the income year of the change

Section 165-35

When a company must work out its taxable income and tax loss under this Subdivision

> PLAIN LANGUAGE FEATURE
> • *must* is here instead of *shall*

165-35 On a change of ownership, unless the company carries on the same business

A company must calculate its taxable income and tax loss under this Subdivision unless:

(a) there are persons who had *more than a 50% stake in the company during the whole of the income year; or

(b) there is only *part* of the income year (a part that started at the start of the income year) during which the same persons had *more than a 50% stake in the company, but the company satisfies the *same business test for the *rest* of the income year (the *same business test period*).

For the purposes of paragraph (b), apply the *same business test to the *business that the company carried on immediately before the time (the *test time*) when that part ended.

For the same business test: see Subdivision 165-E.

> PLAIN LANGUAGE FEATURE
> • internal navigator

Note: In the case of a listed public company or its 100% subsidiary, Subdivision 166-B modifies how this Subdivision applies, unless the company chooses otherwise.

165-37 Who has more than a 50% stake in the company during a period

> PLAIN LANGUAGE FEATURE
> • substitute "when", "who", "what" headings

(1) If:

(a) there are persons who had *more than 50% of the voting power in the company during the whole of a period (the *ownership test period*) consisting of the income year or a part of it; and

---

*To find definitions of asterisked terms, see the Dictionary, starting at section 995-1.

> Appendix 9
> Page 11 of 16

Part 6-1 Concepts and topics
Division 950 Rules for interpreting this Act

Section 950-105

fact in deciding whether or not to apply to that term a definition or other interpretation provision.

PLAIN LANGUAGE FEATURE

• very specific guidelines for the courts

950-105 What does *not* form part of this Act

These do *not* form part of this Act:

- footnotes and endnotes;
- Tables of Subdivisions;
- Tables of sections.

950-150 Guides, and their role in interpreting this Act

(1) A *Guide* consists of sections under a heading indicating that what follows is a Guide to a particular Subdivision, Division etc.

(2) Guides form part of this Act, but they are kept separate from the operative provisions. In interpreting an operative provision, a Guide may only be considered:
  (a) in determining the purpose or object underlying the provision; or
  (b) to confirm that the provision's meaning is the ordinary meaning conveyed by its text, taking into account its context in the Act and the purpose or object underlying the provision; or
  (c) in determining the provision's meaning if the provision is ambiguous or obscure; or
  (d) in determining the provision's meaning if the ordinary meaning conveyed by its text, taking into account its context in the Act and the purpose or object underlying the provision, leads to a result that is manifestly absurd or is unreasonable.

[The next heading is the heading to Division 960.]

---

*To find definitions of asterisked terms, see the Dictionary, starting at section 995-1.

Appendix 9
Page 12 of 16

Section 950-100

Chapter 6—The Dictionary

Part 6-1—Concepts and topics

[The next Division is Division 950.]

Division 950—Rules for interpreting this Act

Table of sections

> **PLAIN LANGUAGE FEATURE**
>
> There will be no court interpretations of what does and does not form part of the Act. Sections 950-100 and 950-105 make those issues very clear.

950-100 What forms part of this Act

(1) These all form part of this Act:

- the headings of the Chapters, Parts, Divisions and Subdivisions of this Act;

- *Guides;

- the headings of the sections and subsections of this Act;

- the headings for groups of sections of this Act (*group headings*);

- the notes and examples (however described) that follow provisions of this Act.

(2) The asterisks used to identify defined terms form part of this Act. However, if a term is *not* identified by an asterisk, disregard that

---

*To find definitions of asterisked terms, see the Dictionary; starting at section 995-1.

Division 960—General

Subdivision 960-E—Entities

Table of sections

960-100   Entities

960-100 Entities

(1) *Entity* means any of the following:

(a) an individual;

(b) a body corporate;

(c) a body politic;

(d) a partnership;

(e) any other unincorporated association or body of persons;

(f) a trust;

(g) a superannuation fund.

Note: The term *entity* is used in a number of different but related senses. It covers all kinds of legal person. It also covers groups of legal persons, and other things, that in practice are treated as having a separate identity in the same way as a legal person does.

PLAIN LANGUAGE FEATURE
• This kind of detailed definition is extremely helpful to a lay reader.

(2) The trustee of a trust or of a superannuation fund is taken to be an *entity* consisting of the person who is the trustee, or the persons who are the trustees, at any given time.

Note: This is because a right or obligation cannot be conferred or imposed on an entity that is not a legal person.

(3) A legal person can have a number of different capacities in which the person does things. In each of those capacities, the person is taken to be a different *entity*.

Example: In addition to his or her personal capacity, an individual may be:

• sole trustee of one or more trusts; and

PLAIN LANGUAGE FEATURE
• Examples make the definition clear.

*To find definitions of asterisked terms, see the Dictionary, starting at section 995-1.

Concepts and topics **Part 6-1**
Concepts about companies **Division 975**
Wholly-owned groups of companies **Subdivision 975-W**

Section 975-505

975-505 What is a 100% subsidiary?

(1) A company (the *subsidiary company*) is a *100% subsidiary* of another company (the *holding company*) if all the *shares in the subsidiary company are beneficially owned by:

    (a) the holding company; or

    (b) one or more 100% subsidiaries of the holding company; or

    (c) the holding company and one or more 100% subsidiaries of the holding company.

(2) However, the subsidiary company is *not* a *100% subsidiary* of the holding company if a person is *in a position to affect rights, in relation to the subsidiary company, of:

    (a) the holding company; or

    (b) a 100% subsidiary of the holding company.

(3) The subsidiary company is also not a *100% subsidiary* of the holding company if at some future time a person will be *in a position to affect rights as described in subsection (2).

(4) A company (other than the subsidiary company) is a *100% subsidiary* of the holding company if, and only if:

    (a) it is a 100% subsidiary of the holding company; or

    (b) it is a 100% subsidiary of a 100% subsidiary of the holding company;

because of any other application or applications of this section.

[The next Part is Part 6-5.]

> **PLAIN LANGUAGE FEATURES**
>
> • Note the care taken to ensure the reader is aware of the transition from the last Subdivision in 975-W (with numbers left for amendments) to the beginning of Part 6-5 (see bottom of page).
> • clear plain language and parallel segments

*To find definitions of asterisked terms, see the Dictionary, starting at section 995-1.

Part 6-5 Dictionary definitions
Division 995 Definitions

Section 995-1

Part 6-5—Dictionary definitions

Division 995—Definitions

995-1 Definitions

(1) In this Act, except so far as the contrary intention appears:

4% manner has the meaning given by section 43-145.

100% subsidiary has the meaning given by section 975-505.

abnormal trading has the meaning given by Subdivision 960-H.

adopted child of a person means someone the person has adopted:
(a) under the law of a State or Territory about adoption of children; or
(b) under a *foreign law about adoption of children, if the adoption would be recognised as valid under the law of a State or Territory.

allowable capital expenditure has the meaning given by sections 330-85, 330-90 and 330-95.

amount includes a nil amount.

ancillary activities has the meaning given by section 330-445.

apartment building has the meaning given by section 43-95.

approved deposit fund has the meaning given by section 10 of the *Superannuation Industry (Supervision) Act 1993*.

approved stock exchange has the meaning given by section 470 of the *Income Tax Assessment Act 1936*.

*To find definitions of asterisked terms, see the Dictionary, starting at section 995-1.

Appendix 10
Separation Agreement

After

(from Wordsmith Associates files)

Sample separation agreement

AFTER

The following agreement shows the kinds of issues to consider but it shouldn't be used as a model for writing your own agreement. Each case is unique. The agreement is between a man and a woman who have been married nearly 11 years and who have an eight-year-old son. They've agreed that the wife will have custody of the son and that the husband will contribute $_____ a year for the son's support. The husband will also pay for the son's college education and will record the son as a dependent for tax purposes. The wife will receive $_____ a year for three years for maintenance while she goes back to college. They've agreed to sell their house and split the proceeds equally.

We, Ann Jones and Paul Jones made this agreement on March 30, 1998.

We were married on June 1, 1987 and our only child, Robert, was born September 27, 1990. Because our marriage has ended, we have separated and intend to live apart for the rest of our lives. We want to divide our property and make whatever legal and financial arrangements are necessary under the circumstances. This document is a record of the terms we have agreed on:

1. **Independence.** Except as noted below, each of us will live completely independent of the other. We will not interfere with each other in any way.

2. **Custody of our child.** Ann will have sole custody of our child as long as he is a minor and he will live with her.

3. **Robert's visits.** Robert will visit Paul at these times:
   * every other weekend, from 6 p.m. Friday to 6 p.m. Sunday
   * during the Christmas and Easter school holidays, from 6 p.m. the last day of school before the holiday to 6 p.m. the day before school starts again
   * at least 30 days during the summer recess

Paul will pick Robert up at home at the beginning of the visiting period and take him home at the end of the period. If we agree to do so, this schedule may be changed for any particular visit.

During Robert's visits, Paul will pay for his child's food, transportation, housing, and any other expenses connected with the visit. If Paul and Ann ever live permanently or temporarily at places more than 75 km apart, the schedule for Robert's visits with his father will be rearranged so it is equivalent to the present schedule.

4. **Payments for child support.** As basic child support, Paul will pay Ann $_____ a year in $_____ installments payable on the first day of each month. The first installment will be due on the first month after the date of this agreement. These payments will end if:
   * Robert becomes fully self-supporting
   * Robert reaches his 21st birthday
   * Robert stops living permanently with his mother (excluding periods away at school or college)
   * the father assumes custody by written agreement or by court order.

5. **Payments for education.** If Robert attends a post-secondary institution and if he remains a student in good standing, Paul will pay for room and board, textbooks, tuition, and any other charges billed by the institution. These payments will be in addition to the support payments described in section 4. Paul's obligation to make these payments will end under any of these conditions if:
   * either parent dies
   * Robert receives his bachelor's degree
   * Robert reaches his 23rd birthday.

6. **Payments for maintenance.** Paul will pay Ann $_____ a year in $_____ installments payable on the first day of each month. The first installment will be due the first month after the date of this agreement. These payments will end under any of these conditions:
   * after the 36th monthly payment
   * if either Paul or Ann dies
   * if Ann remarries
   * if Ann chooses to live with another male not related by blood or marriage.

Appendix 10
Page 1 of 2

7. **Personal property.** We have divided all the property acquired during our marriage. The list appended to this agreement shows the items each of us will own separately from now on. We are satisfied with this division, and neither will later ask the other for any of the property divided according to this agreement.

8. **Real estate.** We jointly own the house and land at 100 Maple Street, Peterborough, Ontario. We will try to sell this property as soon as possible. After the sale, we will pay off the mortgage and divide the net proceeds equally. In the interim, Paul will pay 70 percent of the carrying costs (mortgage payments, property taxes, and homeowners insurance premiums) and Ann will pay 30 percent.

9. **Taxes.** The maintenance payments described in section 6 will be considered part of Ann's taxable income and will be deducted from Paul's taxable income. If those payments are affected by a subsequent change in the tax laws, the payments will be adjusted so Ann will end up with an after-tax maintenance income equal to the amount resulting from the present arrangement.

   As in the past, we will file a joint income-tax return this year. If there are any refunds, we will share them equally. If there are any taxes, assessments, or penalties due, each of us will pay half.

   Next year, Robert will be listed as a dependent on Paul's tax returns.

10. **Debts.** A list of debts is attached to this agreement, indicating which debts will be paid by Paul and which by Ann. Our understanding is that there are no other debts for which we are jointly liable and we agree not to incur any such debts in the future.

11. **Cooperation in handling documents.** We will promptly sign and deliver any papers necessary to carry out the terms of this agreement.

12. **Entire agreement.** We have made no agreements about separation other than those detailed in this document. If we choose to make any changes later, the changes must be in writing and signed and dated by both of us.

13. **Governing laws.** This agreement is covered by the laws of Ontario.

14. **Partial invalidity.** If we find that part of this agreement isn't valid for some reason, the rest of the agreement will remain in effect.

15. **Subsequent divorce.** If we are divorced later, we will ask the court to append this agreement to the divorce decree.

16. **Waiver of estate claims.** Except for the terms already stated in this agreement, each of us agrees not to make any claims against the other's estate. We also waive all such rights that exist now or may exist in the future.

17. **Release from other obligations.** Except as noted in this agreement, and except for any obligations in connection with a subsequent divorce decree, each of us releases the other from all past, present, and future obligations.

18. **Change of status or address.** If one of us remarries, he or she will notify the other of the date and the name of the new spouse. Also, each will notify the other of any change of address.

19. **Binding effect.** This agreement will bind our heirs, representatives, and assignees.

Signed: _____ Signed: _____
    Ann Jones   Paul Jones
    100 Maple Street   4 Valley Road
    Peterborough, ON   Peterborough, ON

Notarized _____, 1998.

Ann and Paul Jones signed this document in my presence.

Signed: _____
    Notary Public

Appendix 11
Feeder Agreement

Before and After

(Reprinted with the permission of Alberta Agriculture, Food and Rural Development, an Alberta government department)

BEFORE

FEEDER AGREEMENT

FORM 3

MEMORANDUM OF AGREEMENT made this .... day of .... A.D. 19 ....
BETWEEN:

....
body corporate having its registered office at .... **G 26155**
in the Province of Alberta
(hereinafter called "the Association")

OF THE FIRST PART

- and -

....
of .... in the Province of Alberta
(hereinafter called "the Feeder")

OF THE SECOND PART

The Association is the owner of certain livestock specifically described as follows:

No.	Kind	Brand	Location of Brand	Cost

(hereinafter called "the livestock")   (Not to exceed $100,000)

RECITALS:

The Feeder is a member of the Association and has been an active member for .... years.
The Feeder has agreed to accept the said livestock for growing and finishing or either of them in accordance with the by-laws of the Association and the Regulation made pursuant to The Feeder Associations Guarantee Act.

The Parties agree as follows:

1   The Feeder hereby Covenants and Agrees:
   (a)   that ownership of the said livestock shall remain with the Association until the said livestock are sold;
   (b)   to feed the said livestock and make the same ready for market under the supervision of the local supervisor of the Association or of the Feeder Associations Supervisor appointed by the Minister of Agriculture of the Province of Alberta;
   (c)   to maintain the health of the said livestock and in this regard to provide proper veterinary services at his own expense;
   (d)   to ensure that all of the said livestock are branded with the Association brand and to pay for such branding if required or reimburse the Association for all branding done by it;
   (e)   to deliver the said livestock on or before the .... day of .... A.D. 19 .... or such other date as may be authorized in writing by the Association;
   (f)   to make all arrangements to ensure that the entire proceeds from the sale of the said livestock will be paid directly to the Association;
   (g)   to save and keep harmless and fully indemnify the Association from and against all manner of actions, claims and demands which the Association may at any time hereafter suffer, sustain or be put to, for or by any reason whatever or on account of anything in any matter relating to the said livestock or as a result of the sale thereof;
   (h)   to locate said livestock at .... section .... township .... range
   .... of the .... meridian in the Province of Alberta or in a commercial feedlot
   commonly known as .... ;
   (i)   that when cattle are custom fed, to provide the supervisor a feeding agreement signed by the member feeder and the commercial feeder;
   (j)   to give to the Association security by way of a promissory note in the form attached to this Agreement.

2   The Association Covenants and Agrees to pay to the Feeder that part of the net amount received by the Association from the sale of the said livestock which exceeds the aggregate of any amounts owing to the Association pursuant to this Agreement.

3   The Association and the Feeder Covenant and Agree:
   (a)   If in the opinion of the local supervisor of the Association, proper care and feeding of the said livestock is not being provided by the Feeder, or in the event the Feeder has not delivered the said livestock for marketing in accordance with this Agreement or in the event of any other breach or non-observance of any of the provisions of the Agreement or of The Feeder Associations Guarantee Act or Regulation thereunder, the Association may enter on the Feeder's land to take possession of the said livestock and may remove and sell the same;
   (b)   there are no representations, conditions or terms of the agreement between the Parties other than those expressed herein in writing.

4   This Agreement is subject to the Regulation established pursuant to The Feeder Associations Guarantee Act.

5   This Agreement shall enure to the benefit of and be binding on the Parties hereto and their respective heirs, successors and assigns.

IN WITNESS WHEREOF the Association has hereunto caused its corporate seal to be affixed, attested to by the hands of its duly authorized officers in that behalf and the Feeder has set his hand and seal both as of the day and year first above written.

PER: ....
Association
PER: ....

(feeder association seal)
SIGNED, SEALED AND DELIVERED BY

Feeder ....

Co-signor ....
(When applicable)

PROMISSORY NOTE

Date: ....

On Demand, I/we promise to pay to the order of ....

Association Ltd. the principal sum of ....dollars

together with interest thereon on all amounts of the said principal sum remaining unpaid from the date hereof until paid, both before and after judgment at the

rate of .... percent per annum.

Feeder ....   Witness, ...

Co-signor (When applicable) ....

"Prime" if used in this Promissory Note means the floating annual rate of interest established from time to time by ....
as the base rate it will use to determine rates of interest on Canadian dollar loans to customers in Canada and announced from time to time by the Bank as its prime rate.

PROBLEMS INDEX

- archaic language: *body corporate, hereinafter, Recitals, said, pursuant to, hereby, shall, thereof*
- unnecessary legalese: *to save and keep harmless and fully indemnify, in witness thereof, attested to by the hands of*
- triplets: *suffer, sustain, or be put to* and *signed, sealed and delivered*
- tiny font, justified right text

Alberta
AGRICULTURE, FOOD AND RURAL DEVELOPMENT

DRAFT

Feeder Agreement and Promissory Note

AFTER

Date of agreement		New member ☐	Member more than one year ☐

Name of feeder association		Name of feeder member

Address of feeder association	**and**	Address of feeder member

agree to the terms outlined below for the growing or finishing of the following livestock owned and held in trust by the Feeder Association for the purposes of this agreement.

Number	Kind	Brand	Location of brand	Cost

Contract Due Date		Administration	
		Insurance	
		Total	

PLAIN LANGUAGE FEATURES

- easy-to-fill-in boxes
- no legalese or clumsy syntax
- short, parallel items as key terms
- clarification of ability of the Feeder Association to retake possession of the livestock. Readers had misunderstood this key term.

(This version was reduced 164% from the original form size.)

The Feeder Member agrees:

- To accept the livestock listed above for growing or finishing according to the bylaws of the Association and the Feeder Guarantee Act and regulations.
- To feed the livestock and prepare them for market under the supervision of the Association.
- To keep the livestock healthy and to pay for proper veterinary service.
- To make sure the livestock are branded with the Association brand.
- To ensure that all livestock sale proceeds are paid to the Association.
- To deliver the livestock for sale (on behalf of the Association) by the contract due date.
- To indemnify the Association from any legal claims arising in connection with the livestock.
- To give the Association, as security for performance of the Feeder Member's obligations under this agreement, a Promissory Note in the form and amount below.
- To keep the livestock in Alberta at:

Qtr	Sec	Twp	Rge	W of	**or**	at a custom feedlot named

- If the livestock will be custom-fed, to give the Association a copy of the contract for feeding signed with the custom feedlot.

The Feeder Association agrees:

- To hold the livestock, and all proceeds received from sale of the livestock by the Association, in trust for the Feeder Member and the Association, as their respective interests appear from this agreement.
- To apply the net sale proceeds from the livestock first against the amount owing under the Promissory Note, and second, to pay the Feeder Member any remaining balance of the sale proceeds.

The Feeder Association can retake possession of the livestock and sell the livestock:

If the Feeder Member does not:
- on the contract due date, pay any remaining balance on the Promissory Note
- properly feed or care for the livestock
- follow the bylaws of the Association
- follow the Feeder Association Guarantee Act and regulations.

The Feeder Member agrees that, if the Association judges that the Feeder Member is in breach of this agreement, the Association may enter the land where the livestock are located and retake possession of, remove, and sell them.

Signature for Association	Signature of Feeder Member
Signature for Association	Signature of co-signer (when applicable)

Promissory Note

I (we, if co-signed) promise to pay, on demand, to the Feeder Association the principal amount of $ _____
plus interest on the principal amount, from today, at the rate of _____ % per year, both before and after demand.

"Prime," if used in this Promissory Note, means the rate from time to time announced by _Name of bank_ _____
as its prime rate to customers in Canada.

Signature of witness	Signature of Feeder Member
Date	Signature of co-signer (when applicable)

AC0044 Rev. 91/08

Appendix 11
Page 2 of 2

Appendix 12
Notice of Annual Meeting

Before and *After*

(from Wordsmith Associates files)

BEFORE

NOTICE OF ANNUAL MEETING

Take notice that the Annual Meeting of the Institute will be held at 2:00 p.m. on June 8, 1998, at Palliser Hotel, 9th Avenue and First Street S.W., Calgary, Alberta.

Below is a form of proxy which may be filled out and returned to the Head Office of the Institute prior to the meeting.

- -

PROXY

KNOWN ALL MEN BY THESE PRESENTS that I hereby make, constitute and appoint:

B. Jones	L. Ferguson
J. Palmer	T. Smith
J. Sears	C. Kartz
J.C. Thompson	

or any of them, my attorney or agent for me and in my name, place and stead to attend and vote as my proxy at the Annual General Meeting of members of the Institute, to be held the 8th day of Jun 1998 and at any adjournment thereof, as fully and will the same effects as I might or could were I personally present at such meeting: and I hereby revoke any proxy or proxies heretofore given by me to any person or persons whatsoever.

DATED _____ 1998

Name: _____
(Please Print)

_____
(Signature)

PROBLEMS INDEX

- antiquated language: *Take notice . . ., Know all men by these presents . . ., hereby, thereof, heretofore*
- triplets: *make, constitute and appoint* and *name, place and stead*
- awkward syntax: *as I might or could were I . . .*
- capitalization
- passive voice / third person
- repetitions

Appendix 12
Page 1 of 2

AFTER

Notice of Annual Meeting of the Institute

Date: June 8, 1998
Time: 2:00 p.m.
Place: Palliser Hotel
9th Avenue & 1st Street S.W.
Calgary, Alberta

If you are unable to attend, you may wish to fill out the proxy form below and return it to the Head Office of the Institute before the meeting.

Proxy

I appoint _____, or any of the following:

B. Jones   L.Ferguson
J. Palmer   T. Smith
J. Sears   C. Kartz
J.C. Thompson

to attend and vote as my proxy at the Annual General Meeting of the Institute, June 8, 1998.

Date   _____

Name   _____
                    (*Please print*)

            _____
                    (*Signature*)

PLAIN LANGUAGE FEATURES

- key date/time/place data clearly laid out at top
- active voice "you" and "I" point of view
- straightforward, natural language

Appendix 12
Page 2 of 2

Appendix 13
Grievance Mediation Forms
- **Memorandum of Understanding**
- **Agreement to Mediate Form**
- **Mediator Appointment Agreement**

Before and After

(These plain language forms appear in *Grievance Mediation: Why and How it Works* (Aurora, ON: Canada Law Book, 1994), co-authored by David Elliott and Joanne H. Goss. The documents reprinted here are done so under a special caveat granted to readers who are "invited to use all or parts of the documents, as they consider appropriate, without breaking copyright.")

100 GRIEVANCE MEDIATION

MEMORANDUM OF UNDERSTANDING[1]

AFTER

This *Memorandum of Understanding* is made between

_____ and _____
       (Union)   (Employer)

and is intended to provide an option for the parties to resolve grievances through a grievance mediation process.

The parties agree that:

Proposal to mediate

1 Either party may suggest to the other that a grievance filed under the collective agreement be referred to mediation.[2] The party to whom the suggestion is made is free to accept or reject the suggestion. The parties will use the attached *Agreement to Mediate Form*, or one substantially similar to it, to suggest grievance mediation.

Both parties must agree to mediate

2 Grievances will only be referred to mediation if both parties so agree.[3]

Authority to agree to a mediation process

3 The person or persons with authority to agree to refer a particular grievance to mediation are:

- for the Union: _____
                         (name of individual or title)

- for the Employer: _____
                         (name of individual or title)

Authority and training of representatives

4 (1) The representatives[4] attending mediation sessions will have authority to settle the grievance.

   (2) Representatives from each party will take at least one-half day of training in the process and procedure of grievance mediation *before* they participate in grievance mediation processes.

Mediator's appointment

5 (1) When both parties agree to mediate a grievance, the *Agreement to Mediate Form* will be completed.[5]

---

[1] The alternative to a *Memorandum of Understanding* is to amend the collective agreement.

[2] If only certain types of grievances are to be referred to mediation or "all grievances *except* for specified types", then this clause will need to be modified accordingly.

[3] This may need to be modified if only certain grievances are eligible for mediation.

[4] If necessary, make it clear that this includes legal counsel.

[5] If more than one mediator is named, this clause will need to make clear who is appointed, unless some alternative arrangement is made.

254 ■ Appendices

(2) _____ will mediate grievances,
(name of Mediator(s))

unless both parties agree to appoint another person.[6] A *Mediator Appointment Agreement* will be entered into in the attached form, or one substantially similar to it.

Sharing the cost of mediation

6 The parties agree to share equally the fees and expenses of the Mediator, unless the parties and Mediator otherwise agree.

Payment of wages and benefits

7 [Include appropriate provision for employees attending mediation sessions, if required.]

Time limits suspended

8 (1) If an *Agreement to Mediate Form* is signed by both parties, the period of time from the date the form is completed by the parties until

(a) one party revokes, in writing, the reference to mediate, or
(b) the mediation ends (whether successfully or not),

is to be excluded from the computation time under the steps of the grievance process.

(2) A mediation ends in accordance with clause 10 of the *Mediator Appointment Agreement*.

Results of the mediation

9 (1) If the mediation resolves the grievance, the Mediator will provide the parties with a report outlining the basis for settlement.

(2) If mediation does not resolve a grievance, either party is free to start proceedings or to continue proceedings to resolve the grievance.

Review of Memorandum of Understanding

10 The operation of this *Memorandum of Understanding* will be reviewed (on or before _____[7]) (after _____ mediations), at which time this *Memorandum* can be continued, modified, or terminated.

Termination date

11 This *Memorandum of Understanding* terminates on _____.[8]

Dated in _____, _____ on _____ 199__.
    (Municipality)   (Province)

SIGNED _____   SIGNED _____
    For the Union   For the Employer

---

[6] If a panel of mediators is agreed on, or an organization is to be named to appoint the mediator, this clause will require modification.
[7] The review should take place far enough in advance of the specific review date or termination date that it does not unduly affect mediations started close to the review date.
[8] Some parties may want a fixed termination date so that a review of the process is guaranteed. A termination date is not essential.

Appendix 13
Page 2 of 6

——————————————————————————— DRAFT FORMS   103

AGREEMENT TO MEDIATE FORM

The _____ and _____ agree:
         (Union)   (Employer)

> **PLAIN LANGUAGE FEATURES**
>
> Excellent plain language form

1 To refer to mediation grievance #_____ (*add Grievor's name*). The grievance submitted to mediation is attached to this form.[1]

2 To appoint _____[Mediator]_____[2] to mediate the grievance in accordance with the *Memorandum of Understanding* between the parties dated _____,[3] and a completed *Mediator Appointment Agreement*.[4]

3 The parties request the Mediator to schedule a mediation meeting.[5] The anticipated time required is _____ hours.

4 The persons to contact for the mediation meeting are:

   (a) for the Employer:

   • name   _____

   • telephone _____

   • fax   _____

   • address   _____

   (b) for the Union:

   • name   _____

   • telephone _____

   • fax   _____

   • address   _____

Dated _____ 199__ .

(To be dated when both parties have signed the form)

SIGNED _____   SIGNED _____
         (For the Union)   (For the Employer)

———————————

[1] The amount of information provided before a mediation should be discussed by the parties and the mediator in joint session, while the mediation process is being designed.

[2] Modify this if an organization is to appoint the mediator.

[3] This assumes a *Memorandum of Agreement* has been signed rather than an amendment to the collective agreement.

[4] If there is a standard arrangement with a mediator, this can be referred to. If not, this point will need modification to deal with the mediator's appointment.

[5] If location of the mediation is an important issue, this should be mentioned in the form, otherwise the mediator will make the arrangements.

———————————————————————————————— DRAFT FORMS 103

MEDIATOR APPOINTMENT AGREEMENT

This Agreement is made between _____

(Mediator)

_____ and _____ .

(Employer)   (Union)

Purpose

1 This agreement governs the terms and conditions of mediation and describes the process of mediation to be used by the Employer, the Union and the Mediator, in attempting to resolve grievance #_____ .

What the Mediator will do

2 (1) The Mediator agrees to help the Employer and the Union discuss the matters in dispute between them, assist the parties in communicating and negotiating as effectively as possible, and assist the parties in effecting a settlement of the matters in dispute.

> **PLAIN LANGUAGE FEATURES**
>
> • clear layout and good use of white space and bulleted sub-items
> • very specific information to help the process
> • information in square brackets allows tailoring to specific circumstances
> • clear, direct language

(2) The mediator also agrees to keep confidential:

• discussions in the mediation proceedings; and
• all documents generated for the purpose of effecting a settlement of the grievance or other matters in dispute

(3) The Mediator's agreement to keep matters confidential does not apply if the Mediator is required by law to disclose the discussions or documents, or if the Employer and the Union both agree in writing that the Mediator can disclose all or part of the discussions or documents.

What the Mediator will not do

3 Mediation is a process of facilitated negotiations and accordingly the Mediator will not make decisions for the Employer or the Union, nor will the Mediator provide legal advice to either the Employer or the Union.

Fees and expenses

4 (1) The Mediator's fees will be charged at the rate of $_____ per hour for telephone discussions, preparation, meetings, mediation sessions and follow-up work.

(2) All expenses incurred by the Mediator will be paid by the parties. Expenses could include fax messages, messenger costs, long distance telephone calls, travel, accommodation, meal costs and word processing.

(3)   The Employer and the Union agree to each pay half of the Mediator's fees and expenses, plus G.S.T.

Full disclosure   5   The Employer and the Union agree to fully disclose all material information relating to the issues in dispute.

Mediator privilege   6   The Employer and the Union each agree that:

- neither of them will subpoena or otherwise request or require the Mediator to be a witness in any legal, arbitration, or other proceedings relating to the matters in dispute, or dealt with under this agreement, nor subpoena any document or other information in the possession of the Mediator; and
- they each waive any right they may individually or jointly have to call the Mediator as witness in any legal, arbitration, or other proceedings

Without prejudice proceedings   7   The Employer and the Union agree that the proceedings, the subject of this agreement, will be conducted with a view to settling their dispute and as such, everything said, prepared, generated or proposed is for that purpose and is privileged and will not be used for any other purpose.

Comment to media, public and employees   8   [Include if required.]

Representatives   9   The Employer and the Union agree that the persons attending the mediation on their behalf have authority to negotiate and settle the grievance.

Termination   10   [Add circumstances under which the mediation is terminated — usually:

- by either party
- by the mediator
- by joint agreement of the Union and the Employer to terminate
- by settling the grievance.]

[Note: The parties may wish to consider saying that if there is doubt about when a mediation ends, the Mediator may state the date, which is then a binding determination on both parties. This could be useful to determine when grievance process time limits are no longer suspended.]

> **Appendix 13**
> **Page 5 of 6**

258 ■ Appendices

Advisory opinion¹   11 [Add if required.]

Dated in _____ , _____ on _____ 199__ .
         (Municipality)   (Province)

SIGNED _____   SIGNED _____
         For the Union   For the Employer

SIGNED _____
                    Mediator

PLAIN LANGUAGE FEATURES

Stellar signature segment

---

¹ Add if need be, but this can be dealt with separately at the conclusion of an unsuccessful mediation. Usually the agreement is (if the opinion is desired at all) that one opinion will be provided in writing to the parties if they jointly request it. Some arrangements in the United States allow for an oral opinion given by the mediator privately to each party.

Plain Language Toolbox

- CLARITY exercises
- Legal Wordskills

CLARITY

C - Conciseness

L - Lean Language

A - Active Voice

R - Regular and Reasonable Language

I - Image-evoking and Specific

T - Tight Organization

Y - You and Your Audience

C - Conciseness

Make the following sentences more concise.

1. The Fudgit Company agrees to purchase from the Consultant, and the Consultant agrees to furnish to Fudgit Company, professional services of the type, and under the terms and conditions, described below:

2. The services of the consultant and its personnel are that of an independent contractor. Neither the Consultant nor its personnel shall be considered to be employees, agents, servants or representatives of The Fudgit Company.

3. If Council attempted to pass a bylaw dealing specifically with circuses there may be an argument that such a bylaw is discriminatory on the basis that other keepers of wild animals, such as West Edmonton Mall, are not affected by the bylaw.

4. The undersigned, being all of the shareholders of Fudgit Law (the "Corporation"), including those not otherwise entitled to vote, hereby consent to dispensing with the requirement to appoint an auditor of the Corporation.

5. The undersigned hereby subscribes for ____ Fudgit shares in the capital of the corporation, and tenders herewith the price of $X per share.

6. The deep street flooding (1.5 metres or greater) from storm events renders the road impassable for vehicular traffic for a short period of time during the storm event.

7. The process of dispute resolution can be complicated even when negotiations are informal.

8. The parties have expressed their entire understanding and agreement concerning the subject matter of this agreement and no implied covenant, condition, term, or reservation shall be read into this Agreement relating to or concerning such subject matter, nor shall any oral or written understanding heretofore entered into modify or compromise any of the terms and conditions herein.

9. My will is governed by and must be construed in accordance with the laws of the province of Ontario and any trustees must administer my estate under the laws of Ontario.

10. If any vacancy occurs in the office of Executor and Trustee of my Will by reason of the death, either before or after me, or the renunciation, resignation or incapacity of any of my three children appointed in clause 2.1 as Co-executors and Co-trustees of my will, the surviving or remaining of them may act or continue to act as the case may be.

11. **DEFINITIONS**

The following words when used in *The Right to Information Bylaw* mean:

12. The learned trial judge misdirected himself/herself as to the law applicable to the evidence.

Answers to Conciseness

1. The Fudgit Company will purchase from the Consultant professional services as described below: (This version combines the consultant's services and conditions in the descriptions.)
   (31 to 13 words)

2. As an independent contractor, the Consultant and its personnel are not employees or agents of the Fudgit Company. **(34 to 18 words)**

3. A bylaw which only governs circuses may be criticized as discriminatory. This is because other keepers of wild animals, such as West Edmonton Mall, are not affected by the bylaw.
   (2 sentences / from 42 to 30 words)

4. We, all the shareholders of Fudgit, including those not otherwise entitled to vote, agree not to appoint an auditor for Fudgit Law. **(33 to 22 words)**

5. We agree to purchase, and now pay for, ____ Fudgit shares at $X a share. **(23 to 15 words)**

6. During storms, deep street flooding (1.5 metres or greater) impedes vehicle movement for a short time. **(29 to 17 words)**

7. Even informal negotiations may result in complicated dispute resolution. **(13 to 9 words)**

8. This document is the entire agreement between the parties. **(57 to 9 words)**

9. The laws of Ontario govern my will. **(31 to 7 words)**

10. (Define executor and trustee in both singular and plural forms at the beginning of the will. Then use the singular throughout.)

    If any of my trustees dies, does not wish to be or is incapable of being, an executor and trustee of my will, whoever remains will be the trustee. **(64 to 29 words)**

11. **Definitions** **(3 lines to 1 title line; 13 to 1 word)**

12. "Avoid standard clauses that say nothing".*

---

* This example and the advice to dispense with such clauses is given in "Supreme Court of Canada—Process and Advocacy—A Practical Guide for Practitioners", *The Canadian Bar Review*, March, 1996, p. 102. (Yet the article goes on to inconsistently advise ending a leave to appeal with this unplain standard phrase: "And **upon** such further and other grounds as the court may **entertain** and counsel may advise." The phrase may be translated as "and on further and other grounds acceptable to the court and advised by counsel".)

L - Lean Language

Rewrite the following sentences with lean language.

1.	We seek to address the time poverty of our readers (through better labelling, news decks, summaries, indexes, and cross-references.)	**(10 words)**

2.	An Act respecting the Sovereignty of Québec.	**(7 words)**

3.	The Government shall, in accordance with the procedure determined by the National Assembly, see to the drafting of a constitution for Québec and to its adoption.	**(26 words)**

4.	If an armoured car crew member employed by an armoured car company has in effect a license issued by the appropriate provincial agency (in the province in which **such** member is primarily employed by **such** company) to carry a weapon while acting in the service of **such** company in that province, and **such** provincial agency meets the minimum provincial requirements under subsection (b), then **such** crew member shall be entitled to lawfully carry any weapon to which such licence relates in any province while **such** crew member is acting in the service of **such** company.	(Document this example)	**(96 words)**

5.	This organization shall be known as the United Nurses of Alberta (hereinafter referred to as U.N.A.) [from bylaws]

6.	Further to your letter, we enclose a copy of the relevant bylaw.

7.	As an articling student, I may be assigned to draft a Statement of Claim or make a motion in Chambers Court, but would not have carriage of the entire file.

8.	This alternative would not minimize endangerment to human life.

9.	I trust the foregoing is satisfactory and should you have any questions, please do not hesitate to contact the undersigned.

10.	The *Hospitals Amendment Act, 1995* amends parts of section 40 by **providing that** a board of an approved hospital may disclose information **respecting** diagnostic and treatment services **with respect to** a patient if it is needed for a preliminary investigation . . . **provided that** . . . the patient or the patient's legal representative consents to a disclosure . . . (specific problems for EASL readers)

11.	No person shall be entitled to any remuneration by reason of being a director of the Society provided that the directors may, by resolution, award special remuneration to any director in undertaking any special services on the Society's behalf other than the routine work ordinarily required of a director of the Society. The confirmation of any such resolution by the members shall not be required.

12.	In support of the quantum of $42,000, I indicated the relevant factors considered.

L - Lean Language (continued)

13. I, Carol Jean Douglas, am of sound mind and my intentions for the distribution and administration of my estate are set out in my Will, written upon this and the __ preceding pages of paper, signed by me at the City of Ottawa, in the province of Ontario this ___ day of _____, 1998.

     SIGNED, PUBLISHED, AND)
     DECLARED by Carol Jean)
     Douglas in the presence of us)
     both at the same time who at her)   _____
     request, in her presence and in)   Carol Jean Douglas
     the presence of each other have)
     hereunto subscribed our names)
     as witnesses.)

     [witnesses segment not included here]

14. Any trustee who, or whose spouse or issue, may be interested pecuniarily . . .

15. 2. In all other respects I confirm my said Will. IN WITNESS whereof I have hereunto set my hand this first day of February, One thousand nine hundred and ninety-six.

     SIGNED by HER ROYAL HIGHNESS   )
     in our joint presence and then   )   (This was signed by Diana)
     by us in her presence   )

     (witnesses segments omitted)

Answers to Lean Language

1. To save our readers' time, we use better labelling, news decks, summaries, indexes, and cross-references. **(10 to 5 words)**

2. The Sovereignty of Québec Act **(7 to 5 words)**

   or The Québec Sovereignty Act **(7 to 4 words)**

3. Using a procedure the National Assembly determines, the Government will draft and adopt a constitution. **(26 to 15 words)**

4. *The rewrite starts with the main point, and segments the conditions. Instead of one long paragraph, four shorter units are created. The relationship between the main term and conditions are visually and conceptually clearer. "Such" is gone.*

   An employed member of an armoured car crew is lawfully entitled to carry a weapon if:

   (i) the member is licensed to carry that weapon by the appropriate provincial agency in the province where the member is primarily employed,

   (ii) the member carries the weapon while acting in the service of the company in the province, and

   (iii) the licensing agency meets the minimum provincial requirements under subsection (b) when the member is acting for the company in any other province. **(96 to 81words)**

5. The name of the organization is United Nurses of Alberta (U.N.A.) **(16 to 11 words)**

6. As you requested, I have enclosed a copy of the ABC Bylaw.

7. . . . but would not be responsible for the entire file.

8. This alternative would not reduce the danger to human life.

9. I hope this is satisfactory. If you have any questions, please call me .

10. Section 40 amendments in the *Hospitals Amendment Act,* 1995 allow the board of an approved hospital to disclose information about the diagnosis and treatment of a patient if (i) it is needed for a preliminary investigation and, (ii) the patient or the patients' legal representative consents to the disclosure. **(52 to 47 words but note that segmentation lowers the readability level)**

11. **Payment of Directors**
    The Society does not pay its directors for their services. However, by resolution, the directors may pay a director for special services beyond the routine work for the Society. This resolution does not require member confirmation. **(73 to 41 words; 2 to 3 sentences)**

12. I indicated my reasons for the $42,000 settlement. **(15 to 8 words)**

Answers to Lean Language - continued

13.   On _____, 1998, I signed my will and initialled the previous pages in the presence of two witnesses who each signed my will in my presence and in the presence of each other.

_____
Carol Jean Douglas

(Attach affidavits of the witnesses to the will.)

(92 to 33 words)

14.   Any trustee who, or whose spouse or descendants, may be interested financially . . .

15.   *Does the rewrite lose the royal elegance? Perhaps simplicity carries its own elegance.*

2.   In all other respects I confirm my will and sign below on February 1, 1996.

SIGNED by HER ROYAL HIGHNESS   )
in our joint presence and then   )   (This was signed by Diana)
by us in her presence   )

(witnesses segments omitted)

A - Active Voice

Rewrite the following sentences to the passive verb active. You may wish to make some sentences more concise as well. The passive forms may reveal imbiguities.

1. The Government is authorized to conclude with the Government of Canada, an agreement the purpose of which is to maintain an economic association between Québec and Canada.

2. Such an agreement must be approved by the National Assembly before being ratified.

3. He is denied his rights by the new law.

4. Because of the urgency of the matter, a reply would be appreciated by November 1.

5. If City employees are uncertain about what information should be released or disclosed, their supervisors must be consulted with.

6. *Exempted information* is information that the City cannot release because it is prevented from releasing the information by statute.

7. High suicide rates have been observed in the north-east part of the city that have been determined to have particularly high population densities.

8. If a representative plaintiff is successful at trial on common issues, notice to individual class members must be given.

9. Any notice or written communication which either party desires or is required to give the other may be delivered or mailed by prepaid post to _____.

10. The use of mail hereunder shall be suspended during postal strikes.

11. Processing of your contract will begin once all relevant papers are received by myself and submitted to our financial department.

12. The duplicate copy should be returned for your records, and for presentation upon entry into Canada if you are not a Canadian citizen.

Answers to Active Voice

These are not the only solutions but they are good plain language rewrites using the active voice.

1.   The Government has authority to develop an agreement with the Government of Canada for an economic association between Québec and Canada.

     ["Conclude" sounds as though the process has already started. "An agreement the purpose of which" is clumsy, difficult-to-read syntax.]

2.   The National Assembly must approve the agreement before it is ratified (by the Government of Canada? by the Québec government?).

     . . . before the Government of Canada **or** Québec government ratifies it.

3.   The new law denies him of his rights.

4.   Because of the urgency of the matter, we, (our committee, Forbes & Co., I, etc.) would appreciate (request?) a reply by November 1.

     or

     Because of the urgency of this matter, may we have your reply by November 1?

5.   If City employees are uncertain whether they should release or disclose information, they must consult with their supervisors.

6.   *Exempted information* is information that the City cannot release because a statute forbids it.

7.   [Passive voice here creates a kind of anonymous hedging because the writer does not specify who the observor is.]
     Recent department statistics show that high suicide rates occur in the north-east part of the city where the population density is particularly high.

8.   If a representative plaintiff is successful at trial on common issues, the Court must give notice to individual class members.

9.   The parties may deliver, or mail by prepaid post, any written material to _____.
     (26 to 13 words)

10. The parties must not use mail during postal strikes.   **(11 to 9 words)**

11. Processing of your contract will begin once I have received all relevant papers and submitted them to our financial department.

12. Please keep the duplicate copy for your records.

R - Regular and Reasonable Language

In the following sentences correct mistakes in grammar, spelling, punctuation or capitalization.

1. The Publisher will pay the Author a royalty based on the actual cash received on the sale of the work (excluding shipping and handling charges) by the Publisher of 15%.

2. The location of the buildings and other improvements on the property complies with all municipal bylaws.

3. This form should be signed by yourself and returned as a director of Devilsticks Inc.

4. We appreciate you reviewing this with your senior counsel.

5. The instructor for the mediation course called for a committment to a new dispute resolution paradym.

6. The Board needs to keep itself appraised of current developments in government.

7. First Nations fears the Parti Queb cois government is based on a narrow colonial paradigm.

8. Any restraint on the level of taxation which the separate board may choose to impose should be unconstitutional.

9. The Administration Branch consists of eight employees, including myself.

10. Payments are to be divided as follows: 1/2 to Elizabeth Gunter and 1/2 to Pauline Jackal.

11. All three districts report that H_2S signs are on the sites that require them, and those sites that have signs and don't require them have been removed.

12. Billionaire businessman Ross Perot said the chances of him re-entering the presidential race are about as likely as him "leaping over a tall building in a single bound."

13. In the House of Commons on Monday, Chretien scornfully mocked the re-election chances of maverick Toronto MP John Nunziata, who hours earlier the prime minister had banished from the government benches for opposing a budget bill on the grounds the Liberals had failed to meet an election promise to kill the GST.

14. The judge alluded to three specific violations of the Canadian Constitution.

15. Such share or the amount remaining will be held by my Trustee, in trust, for the children of such child who survive him or her in equal shares.

    [How do they survive in equal shares?]

16. My trustees must pay and deliver one such equal share of the residue of my estate to each of my children, Carol, Alex, and Vicki, who survives me for 30 clear days and for each such child of mine who predeceases me and leaves issue surviving me, as soon after my death as is practical and convenient . . .

Answers to Regular and Reasonable Language

1. The publisher will pay the *author* a 15% royalty based on the actual cash the *publisher* receives for the sale of the work (minus the shipping and handling charges).

    Misplaced modifier

2. The location of the buildings and other improvements on the property comply with all municipal bylaws.

    Subject/verb agreement

3. You as director of Devilsticks Inc. must sign and return this form.

    Ungrammatical use of *myself*

4. We appreciate your reviewing this with your senior counsel.

    Possessives

5. The instructor for the mediation course called for a commitment to a new dispute resolution paradigm

    Spelling

6. The Board needs to keep itself apprised of current developments in government.

    Commonly confused words

7. First Nations fear the Parti Québécois government is based on a narrow colonial paradigm. (First Nations stands for a plural- *members of the First Nations* in Quebec.)

    Subject /verb agreement

8. It is unconstitutional for another authority (the provincial government, for example) to place any restraint on the level of taxation which the separate board may choose to impose.

    Misplaced modifier

9. I am one of eight employees in the Administration Branch.

    Ungrammatical use of *myself*

10. Payments are to be divided as follows: half to Elizabeth Gunter and half to Pauline Jackal.

    Numbers guidelines

11. All three districts report that H_2S signs are now only on the sites that require them.

    or

    The three districts report that H_2S signs which were on improper sites have been removed; only sites which require signs now have them.

    Pronouns and their references

12. . . . the chances of his re-entering . . . about as likely as his . . .

    or

    . . . said that his chances for re-entering the presidential race are about as likely as his . . .

    Possessives

Answers to Regular and Reasonable Language - continued

13.   In the House of Commons on Monday, Chretien scornfully mocked the re-election chances of maverick Toronto MP John Nunziata, **whom** hours earlier the prime minister had banished from the government benches for opposing a budget bill on the grounds the Liberals had failed to meet an election promise to kill the GST.

Objective, not subjective case

14.   The judge referred to three specific violations of the Canadian Constitution.

Commonly confused words

15.   Such share or the amount remaining will be held in equal shares by my Trustee, in trust, for the children of such child.

Misplaced modifier

16.   As soon as is practical and convenient after my death, my trustees must pay and deliver one such equal share of the residue of my estate to each of my children, Carol, Alex, and Vicki, who survives me for 30 clear days and for each such child of mine who predeceases me and leaves issue surviving me.

Misplaced modifier

I - Image-evoking and Specific

Since the birth of the Charter of Rights and Freedoms, the Supreme Court of Canada, in a series of decisions, has used a "void for vagueness" interpretation. In other words, it has held that penal law should be declared unconstitutional if it is too vague. A vague law thus runs the anger of being unenforceable. However, the best reason for writing succinctly and specifically is to respect the reader's need to understand.

Rewrite the following sentences with image-evoking or specific language.

1.   Slowly he became cognizant of the fact that he was being terminated.

2.   It was a good meeting.

3.   An annual report is required of educational institutions and corporations making charitable donations.

4.   A release agreement should make clear that the releasing party is not to be regarded as prevailing for any purpose such as awarding attorney's fees.

5.   This paper provides an analysis of over 85% of the Data Processing Service Department staff's interpretation of the mission statement. [Is it 85% of the staff or 85% of their interpretations?]

6.   Gushing Oil makes no representations or warrantees as to the accuracy or completeness of the data.

7.   The hearsay rule is an exclusionary rule which renders certain kinds of evidence inadmissible unless they are covered by one of a number of exceptions. The rule is a creature of the adversarial system, and arises out of suspicion of the reliability of out-of-court statements which afford no opportunity for cross-examination.

8.   In an earlier *Employment Standards Code*, drafters defined *entitlements* as "vacation pay, general holiday pay, and pay in place of notice of termination of employment". The result was that *entitlements* was used extensively in the code without a definitions' identifier in the text. [Consider a drafting solution to replace *entitlements*.]

Answers to Image-evoking and Specific

1. He gradually realized he was being fired.

2. It was a productive meeting: we set up two committees and settled on the zero-based budget.

3. The original is ambiguous. Either:

   An annual report is required of these organizations which make charitable donations:
   (i) educational institutions, and (ii) corporations

   or

   An annual report is required of (i) educational institutions and (ii) corporations making charitable donations.

4. A release agreement should clearly state that the releasing party will not pay for such costs as the attorney's fees of the released party.

5. This paper analyses differing interpretations of the mission statement submitted by 85% of the Data Process Service Department staff.

6. Gushing Oil takes no responsibility for (**does not guarantee?**) the accuracy or completeness of the data.

7. (No changes are required."The rule is a creature of the adversarial system" creates a pleasing image.)

8. In the new plain language code, the drafter eliminated "entitlements" from the definitions and substituted *earnings* and then defined one of the examples, *termination pay*:

(a) *earnings* means wages, overtime pay, vacation pay, and termination pay, and

(b) *termination pay* means pay given to an employee instead of a termination notice.

[**Note:** The common terms are easier for readers to recognize.]

T - Tight Organization:
Star/Chain/Hook

> The traditional organizing formula of introduction, body, and conclusion focuses writers only on chronology. Yet choosing the best order for material depends on the function of each part. A more helpful formula based on the respective functions of the three parts is the **star** (what attracts the reader's attention and clarifies the purpose of the document), the **chain** (the logical and visual links which develop this purpose), and the **hook** (what completes or ties up the material, and creates any required action).
>
> Improve the **stars**, **chains**, and **hooks** on the passages reproduced below.

Star

Before

1994 Employment Standards Code

1. Preamble   WHEREAS it is recognized that a mutually effective relationship between employees and employers is critical to the capacity of Albertans to prosper in the competitive world-wide market economy of which Alberta is a part; and

WHEREAS it is fitting that the worth and dignity of all Albertans be recognized by the legislature of Alberta through legislation that encourages fair and equitable resolution of matters arising in respect of terms and conditions of employment; and

WHEREAS the employee-employer relationship is based on a common interest in the success of the employing organization, best recognized through open and honest communication between affected parties; and

WHEREAS employers and employees are best able to manage their affairs where statutory rights and responsibilities are clearly established and understood; and

WHEREAS it is recognized that legislation establishing general employment standards is an appropriate mechanism through which terms and conditions of employment may be established;

THEREFORE HER MAJESTY, by and with the advice and consent of the Legislative Assembly of Alberta, enacts as follows:

Tight Organization: Star/Chain/Hook - continued

Star

After

(Suggestions for the 1996 Employment Standards Code, Bill 29)

1. **Background*** * A mutually effective relationship between employees and employers is critical to the capacity of Albertans to prosper in the competitive world-wide market economy of which Alberta is a part.

    It is fitting that the worth and dignity of all Albertans be recognized by the legislature of Alberta through legislation that encourages fair and equitable resolution of matters arising in respect of terms and conditions of employment.

    The employee-employer relationship is based on a common interest in the success of the employing organization, best recognized through open and honest communication between affected parties.

    Employers and employees are best able to manage their affairs when statutory rights and responsibilities are clearly established and understood.

    Legislation is an appropriate means of establishing minimum standards for terms and conditions of employment.

    Her Majesty, by and with the advice and consent of the Legislative Assembly of Alberta, enacts as follows:

    Note: Rather than five single sentence paragraphs, this opening segment could also be re-organized. One paragraph could combine sentences #2 and 5; another, sentences #3 and 4.

* Or, **A context for the Code**

Tight Organization: Star/Chain/Hook - continued

Chain

Before (from an association's bylaws)

NOTICE

A printed, written or typewritten notice stating the day, hour and place of meeting and, if special business is to be transacted thereat, stating (i) the nature of that business in sufficient detail to permit a member of the Society to form a reasoned judgment on that business and (ii) the text of any special resolution to be submitted to the meeting, shall be sent to each member entitled to vote at the meeting, who on the record date for notice is registered on the records of the Society as a member in good standing; to each director of the Society; and to the auditor of the Society not less than 15 days and not more than 50 days (exclusive of the day of mailing and of the day for which notice is given) before the date of every meeting of the members of the Society; provided that meeting of members of the Society may be held for any purpose on many day and at any time and, at any place without notice if all the members and all other persons entitled to attend such meetings are present in person or represented by proxy at the meeting (except where a member or other person attend the meeting for the express purpose of objecting to the transaction of any business on the grounds that the meeting is not lawfully called) or if all the members and all other persons entitled to attend such meetings and not present in person nor represented by proxy thereat waive notice of the meeting.

A director of the Society is entitled to receive notice of and to attend and be heard at every meeting of members of the Society.

The auditor of the Society is entitled to receive notice of every meeting of members of the Society and, at the expense of the Society, to attend and be heard at every meeting on matters relating to his duties as auditor.

WAIVER OF NOTICE

Notice of any meeting of members of the Society or the time for the giving of any such notice or any irregularity in any meeting or in the notice thereof may be waived by any member, any director or the auditor of the Society in writing or by telegram, cable or telex addressed to the Society or in any other manner, any such waiver may be validly given either before or after the meeting to which such waiver relates. Attendance of a member or any other person entitled to attend at a meeting of members of the Society is a waiver of notice of the meeting, except when he attends a meeting for the express purpose of objecting to the transaction of any business on the grounds that the meeting is not lawfully called.

OMISSION OF NOTICE

The accidental omission to give notice of any meeting of members of the Society to or the non-receipt of any notice by, any person shall not invalidate any resolution passed or any proceeding taken at any such meeting.

Tight Organization: Star/Chain/Hook - continued

Chain

After

Notices

- *Who receives notices?*
Meeting notices must be sent to all voting members (those registered), to Directors, and to the Society's Auditor.

- *When are notices due?*
Notices must be mailed not less than 15 days or more than 50 days (exclusive of the mailing day and the notice date before each Society meeting).

- *What is the notice's content?*
A meeting notice must state

  (a)   the date, time, and place of the meeting, and

  (b)   if special business is on the agenda, the nature of the business in sufficient detail to allow recipients to form a measured judgement about it, and

  (c)   any special resolution for the meeting.

- *May the society meet without notice?*
If Society members wish to meet without notice to the members, they may do so if all members or others entitled to attend

  (a)   are present or

  (b)   are represented by proxy,

  unless a member or other person entitled to attend the meeting attends expressly to object to the transaction of business on the grounds that the meeting is not lawfully called.

- *What is a waiver of notice?*
Any member, director or the auditor of the society may in writing waive:

  (a)   the notice of a member meeting of the Society

  (b)   the time required to give such notice, or

  (c)   any irregularity in any meeting or its notice by giving the written waiver before or after the related meeting.

- *What if the notice is omitted?*
A meeting notice that

  (a)   is accidentally omitted, or

  (b)   is not received by a member or other entitled person

  does not invalidate a passed resolution or agreement made at the meeting.

Tight Organization: Star/Chain/Hook - continued

Hook

Before

(from letters to clients)

1. I trust the foregoing is satisfactory and should you have any questions or concerns, please do not hesitate to contact the undersigned. **(21 words)**

2. In future, however, this language could be negotiated and clarified with the insurer prior to issuance of a policy.

3. Upon reviewing the brief and flow sheets, we would appreciate any feedback you can provide us with.

Tight Organization: Star/Chain/Hook - continued

Hook
(an ending that is action-oriented, friendly, specific, and grammmatically correct)

After

(from letters to clients)

1.	If you have any questions, please call me at 555-4545.	**(10 words)**

2.	Finally, if you wish, you could negotiate clearer language for your policy with your insurer before the next renewal.

3.	Please review the brief and flow sheets. We would appreciate any feedback you can give us.

Y - You and Your Audience

Rewrite the following sentences to show sensitivity to clients, the public, or specific audiences.

1. *The following example contains specific problems for English-as-a-second-language readers. Rewrite for a multicultural public.*

   The *Hospitals Amendment Act,* 1995 amends parts of the old Act's section 40 by **providing that** a board of an approved hospital may disclose information **respecting** diagnostic and treatment services **with respect to** a patient if it is needed for a preliminary investigation . . . **provided that** . . . the patient or the patient's legal representative consents to a disclosure . . .

2. *Rewrite this clause from a lease for a community organization that is renting a building from a municipality.*

   Provided that the Organization shall not then be in default of any of the terms, covenants and conditions of this Lease to be kept, observed and performed by the Organization upon the expiry of the Term, the Organization may, no later than six (6) months prior to the expiration of the Term, apply in writing to the City to renew this Lease for a further period of five (5) years upon the term, covenants and conditions herein contained excepting any further right to renew the Term of this Lease and subject to the then current policies of the city governing the terms and conditions of social recreation organization leases and the City hereby agrees that approval of such a written request for renewal will not be unreasonably withheld.

Answers to You and Your Audience

1. In amending parts of section 40 of the old Act, the *Hospitals Amendment Act, 1995* **permits** the board of an approved hospital to disclose information **about** a patient's diagnosis and treatment **if**:

    (i)   it is needed for a preliminary investigation . . .

    (ii) the patient or the patient's legal representative consents to a disclosure, etc.

2. To be eligible to renew this lease for five years, the Organization must:

    a)   apply in writing to the City no later than six months prior to expiry of the term,

    b)   agree to the city policies governing the terms and conditions of social recreation organization leases in the year 2000,

    c)   not be in default of any part of this lease, and

    d)   accept that the right to renew this lease will occur only once.

    The City agrees not to unreasonably withhold approval of the Organization's written request for renewal.

Legal Wordskills

Ancient Language

Cover the right-hand column and create plain language translations for the bolded words in the left-hand column below. These are just a few of many examples. But thinking about these will help develop a mindset for clear and accurate translations for non-legal readers.

Ancient Language

Plain Language Substitutes

Ancient Language	Plain Language Substitutes
at page 233	Legal publishers and writers will probably not give this (**at**) up. But for non-legal readers, **on** is an easy choice.
The judge **did not attach liability** to the insurance broker.	The judge decided that the insurance broker was not liable.
The redemption price held in trust would not **escheat** to the Crown.	Because the redemption price is held in trust, the Crown has no right to take the money or property.
The article **addresses the issue** of whether Québec has the right to secede from Canada, and claim international recognition at international law.	The article **examines whether** Québec . . . **under** international law.
The authors argue that, **absent** recognition by the Government of Canada, the answer to both questions is in the negative.	The authors argue that, **without** recognition by . .
The authors review conventional and customary international law **respecting** the right to self-determination, and conclude that that right is only applicable **where** the sucessionist movement meets certain subjective criteria.	The authors review conventional and customary international law **about** the right to . . . applicable **if** the . . .
First, the seceding unit **shall be comprised** of "people" meeting both subjective and objective international law standards.	First, the seceding unit **must consist of** . . .
stare decisis	**principles of precedent: to stand by things decided** (literal Latin translation)

Ancient Language (cont'd)	
The Securities Act is not clear **as to** when the **election** must be made by a purchaser between **rescission and damages**.	The Securities Act is not clear on when a purchaser must **choose** beween: 1.　rescission (*undoing,* **different from** *ending* **or** *cancelling*)**, or** 2.　damages **(compensation or money awarded in law for harm suffered)**
The plaintiffs have **framed their action** on the basis that Dr. Douglas and Dr. Campbell **breached** their standard of care and that their conduct was **negligent**.	The basis of the **plaintiffs' legal action (or lawsuit)** was that Doctors Douglas and Campbell violated their standard of care and that their conduct was **negligent (failed to meet the care of a reasonable person)**.
The material I write is prepared for a variety of readers **including but not limited to** individual and corporate clients, expert and lay witnesses, other lawyers and judges.	The material I write is prepared for a variety of readers **such as** individual and corporate clients, expert and lay witnesses, other lawyers and judges.
provided that	The circuitous history of legal language which began with the Latin *Provisum est,* and the Norman French *purveu est,* brought us to today's common and widely misused *provided that* phrase.[1] Driedger describes it as a "legal incantation . . . , an all-purpose conjunction . . ." and continues "[b]ut what it is supposed to be in any particular case is largely a matter of speculation."[2] He chastises drafters for using provisos to tack on words that are grammatically incapable of being added. Here are substitutes for *provided that*: • **and** • **or** • **but** • **except that** • **with the exception of** • **nevertheless, moreover** • **if** • **as long as**

---

[1] E. Driedger, *The Composition of Legislation,* 2nd ed. (Ottawa: The Department of Justice, 1976), pp. 93-103.
[2] As above, p. 96.

Capitalization Rules

1. *Capitalize the titles of acts, laws, bylaws, bills, government papers, and treaties, but use lower case for their common-noun forms (as in this sentence).*

    Freedom of Information and Protection of Privacy Act
    > Bill 19: Financial Consumers Act
    > Alberta Regulation 448/83

2. *Choose either the traditional or contemporary style for capitalizing headings or titles.* The traditional heading is more difficult to read:

    Reclaiming the Imagination in Legal Writing

    The more contemporary heading uses only one opening capital:

    Reclaiming the imagination in legal writing

    Plain language writers more often use the latter.

3. *Capitalize the first word of every sentence.*

    No North American city has ever seriously followed the philosophy of E. F. Schumacher: Small is beautiful.

4. *Capitalize the first word of quotations that function as a sentence.*

    "Be patient," said Clinton's lawyer.

5. *Capitalize proper nouns and adjectives.*

    The House of Commons is the centre of Canada's political activity. (proper noun)

    The baby was delivered by Caesarian section.
    (proper adjective derived from Julius Caesar)

6. *Capitalize all proper geographical names.*

    A flight connects Calgary and Edmonton in Alberta with Hay River, Fort Smith, and Yellowknife in the Northwest Territories.

7. *Capitalize streets, buildings, parks, public places, companies, and other organizations.*

    The University of Toronto graduate waited at Portage and Main for the representative from the City of Winnipeg to arrive.

Capitalization Rules (cont'd)

8.   *Capitalize events, eras, prizes, documents.*

In 1976, Saul Bellow won the Nobel Prize for Literature.

Those who lived through the Great Depression will never recover from its effects.

9.   *Capitalize military and civil titles when they precede a name, indicate high rank, or are used as substitutes for the names of individuals.*

The press watched Mayors Bennett and Lemire very carefully.

Do not use capitals in descriptive terms, position-words, or identifiers separated from the person's name by a comma: "the president, Conrad Black", or "Carolyn Magellan, deputy minister" or "president-elect, Carol Boudreau".

8.   *Capitalize all academic degrees and their abbreviations.* For example:

She decided that a Masters of Arts was not enough; she went on to get a Ph.D.

9.   *Capitalize the first word and all important words in the title of a book, play, story, article, poem, musical work, journal, magazine, or newspaper. (Unimportant words are words such as* the, and, of, for, in, to, but, *etc. If they are five letters or more, the words are considered important. Some publications now use the contemporary style described in rule two above for papers or articles in bibliographies and footnotes. Even publishers are using lower case for book titles.) Yet for the most part:*

        Alice in Wonderland   The Satanic Verses

10.   *Avoid the bureaucratic habit of capitalizing to impress the public or other readers, or to make concepts or people look more official.*

11.   *Use capitals with all true proper names, but usually not with generic terms.*

Judi Gunter, Public Relations Consultant (at the top of a page)

Judi Gunter, a public relations consultant at the conference . . .

On board was a renowned photographer who had sailed extensively in the Arctic Ocean. His assistant had spent much time in the arctic as well.

12.   *Do not capitalize direction words such as "east" or "southern" unless part of a proper name such as the "North Saskatchewan River".*

13.   *Capitalize the names of months and the days of the week, but not the four seasons ("September" and "Sunday" but "autumn".)*

14.   *Consider italics and lower case to replace the traditional capitals for defined terms in legal agreements. See examples in this book.*

Capitalization Test

Capitalize words that warrant capitalizing in the sentences below.

1. When does a sentence begin with a lower case letter?

2. A significant number of Examinations for Discovery have been held to date.

3. Although my practice involves going to or avoiding Court, depending whether I am acting for a Plaintiff or a Defendant, much of my time is spent on correspondence to and from clients and other lawyers.

4. The Infant Plaintiff has also worn protective braces.

5. Well known to those in the development field, the Canadian International Development Agency spawned Cross-Cultural Centres across the country in the seventies. As a result, the Agency became well known.

6. In literature about North American natives, many terms are used: *Indigenous people*, *Aboriginals*, *Native People*, *Inuit*, *Métis*, *First Nations People*, and *Status* and *Non-Status Indian population*.

7. Last year, the plaintiffs conducted business in the prairie provinces and the maritime provinces.

8. The 13 compatibility groups are listed in Table 4.1 of the United Nations recommendations on the transport of dangerous goods, called the "Orange Book".

Answers to Capitalization Test

1.   No capital is required when a name with a lower case spelling begins a sentence. For example:

> **de**Beurs, an accounting analyst with Imperial Oil Resources,
> moved to Calgary from Holland in 1982.

cmowat@ccinet.ab.ca was the E-mail address given.

If the lower case opening does not begin a paragraph, recast the sentence without the lower case at the beginning.

2.   A significant number of **e**xaminations for **d**iscovery have been held to date.

3.   Although my practice involves going to, or avoiding, court, depending whether I am acting for a **p**laintiff or a **d**efendant, much of my time is spent on correspondence to and from clients and other lawyers.

4.   Even the **i**nfant Jesus is not capitalized! The infant plaintiff has also . . .

5.   Well known to those in the development field, the Canadian International Development Agency spawned **c**ross-cultural **c**entres across the country in the seventies. As a result, the **a**gency became well known.

6.   In literature about North American natives, many terms are used: *indigenous people*, *aboriginals*, *native people*, *Inuit*, *Métis*, *First Nations people*, and *status* and *non-status Indian population*.

7.   Last year the plaintiffs conducted business in the **p**rairie provinces and the **M**aritime provinces.

[**Note**: *Maritime* could mean all provinces bordering the sea and include British Columbia and Newfoundland. The capitalized *Maritime* refers to the provinces of New Brunswick, Nova Scotia, and Prince Edward Island, and so is more than a descriptive term.]

8.   The 13 compatibility groups are listed in Table 4.1 of the United Nations **R**ecommendations on the **T**ransport of **D**angerous **G**oods, called the "Orange Book".

Colons Rules

1. *Use the colon to introduce enumerations and lists. Note that before the colon there must be a general word or umbrella phrase that describes the list.*

    Remember to bring *the following items*: a pen, paper, and good ideas. (The phrase *the following items* describes in general the list that follows.)

    The LRT offers *three advantages*: speed, efficiency, and convenience. (The phrase *three advantages* describes in general the list of specific advantages that follows.)

    Incorrect: Before leaving, she was required to: lock the cabinets and desks, hide the copy machine key, and tidy her desk. (No general phrase describes the duties that follow.)

    Correct: Before leaving, she was required to lock the cabinets and desks, hide the copy machine key, and tidy her desk.

2. *Use the colon to introduce explanatory material, i.e., to show that the second part of the sentence further explains the first.*

    The common causes of failure are many: laziness and lack of self-discipline usually top the list.

    (Since the explanatory material here is a complete sentence, a semicolon could be used; the colon provides more emphasis.)

3. *Use the colon for emphasis.*

    The debate will be lively if they choose a certain topic: politics.

4. *Use the colon to set off expressions that introduce formal statements, quotations, and questions.*

    Mr. Spark was firm on the issue: "We have not engaged in any price-fixing or collusion and no grounds have been found during the nearly eight years of investigation to make any such charges."

Colons Test

Punctuate the following sentences correctly.

1. The plain language instruction focused on eliminating such legalese as: *shall, in respect of,* and *includes but is not limited to.*

2. Many statutes have similar limitations on liability. Some examples are: the *Architects Act, Chartered Accountants Act, Engineering and Geological Act, Environmental Protection Act, Freedom of Information Act, Labour Relations Act,* and the *Nursing Profession Act.*

3. So what should you look for? A lawyer who: will keep you informed; shows a genuine personal interest in your transaction; gives clear explanations; is prompt and responsive; charges a fair and reasonable fee; writes well-organized plain language documents.

4. These requirements include: obtaining a National Energy Board license, and gaining approval to construct pipeline facilities to deliver gas.

5. In some countries, copyright protection lasts forever; in Canada, if the product has not been marketed or presented to the public; in the United Kingdom, if the work is James Barrie's *Peter Pan* and . . .

6. Additionally, a sound understanding of: current equality theory and practice; adult learning principles; relevant provincial and equity legislation; best practices concerning human resources management; and the changes required to achieve equality are essential.

Answers to Colons Test

1. The plain language instruction focused on eliminating such legalese as *shall*, *in respect of*, and *includes but is not limited to*.

2. Many statutes have similar limitations on liability. Some examples are the *Architects Act*, *Chartered Accountants Act*, *Engineering and Geological Act*, *Environmental Protection Act*, *Freedom of Information Act*, *Labour Relations Act*, and the *Nursing Profession Act*.

3. So what should you look for? Look for a lawyer who will keep you informed, shows a genuine personal interest in your transaction, gives clear explanations, is prompt and responsive, charges a fair and reasonable fee, and writes well-organized plain language documents.

4. These requirements include obtaining a National Energy Board license and gaining approval to construct pipeline facilities to deliver gas.   **[No comma between only two items]**

5. In some countries, copyright protection lasts forever: in Canada, if the product has not been marketed or presented to the public; in the United Kingdom, if the work is James Barrie's *Peter Pan* and . . .

6. Additionally, a sound understanding of current equality theory and practice, adult learning principles, relevant provincial and equity legislation, best practices concerning human resources management, and the changes required to achieve equality are essential.

Comma Rules

Use commas:

1. *To separate introductory elements (dependent clauses, phrases, transitional expressions, and interjections) from the rest of the sentence.*

   If you have any further questions or comments, please do not hesitate to contact me.

   In addition, several homes along 87 Avenue have an unobstructed view of the total lot.

2. *To separate items in a series.*

   A "Council/Commissioner Report" is defined as a report which could be submitted as an item on the Agenda of Council, Committees of Council, or Commission Board, or to an individual Commissioner.

3. *To set off clauses and phrases which give extra but not essential information. Compare the two examples below:*

   Medical science has placed in their hands an instrument that can determine the whole future of heredity. (Essential)

   Major famines, which were frequent in the early 1900s, have ceased. (Non-essential)

4. *To separate adjectives which are reversible (or can have "and" placed between them).*

   The tangled, confusing language of legal contracts is slowly being improved.

5. *To separate the two parts of a compound sentence when "and", "but", "or", "for," or "yet" is used between two complete thoughts.*

   Katrina Foster is in charge of training, but she also coordinates the benefits program.

6. *To substitute for words deleted in the second part of a sentence with parallel structure.*

   Legalese is preferred by 20% of the respondents; plain English, by 80%.

7. *To separate names from designations or titles, or to set off words in direct address.*

   Janice, we need your president, Mr. Topper, to meet with us next week.

Commas Test

Correct the comma usage in the following sentences.
(Note the obvious plain language substitutes as well.)

1. If the Buyer fails to perform this contract then the deposit monies and any interest will be forfeited to the Seller as liquidated damages; this contract will be terminated; and the Buyer will have no further liability to the Seller.

2. Matrimonial law practitioners are frequently asked if a divorce can be obtained with a joint application; that is, so neither party assumes the role of Petitioner in commencing a divorce action.

3. As a result on October 24 1995 the James Bay Cree voted in their own referendum.

4. If French Quebecers can be considered the founders of a homeland with an alleged occupation of 400 years, then First Nations who have lived in what is now known as Quebec since the Ice Age have a stronger claim to the homeland.

5. Although the judgment awarded damages to the appellants it was a meagre contribution to the area of consumer protection.

6. During unannounced spot checks investigators may review mandatory reporting information related to contravention reports and take samples for substances regulated by legislation.

7. How many people were arrested?
The police arrested two thugs, a pimp and a drug dealer.

Answers to Commas Test

1.   If the Buyer does not carry out the terms of the contract, the deposit money and any interest will be given to the Seller as liquidated damages (financial compensation), this contract will be ended, and the Buyer will have no further liability (obligations) to the Seller.

2.   Matrimonial law practitioners are frequently asked if a divorce can be obtained with a joint application, that is, so neither party assumes the role of Petitioner in commencing a divorce action.

3.   As a result, on October 24, 1995, the James Bay Cree voted in their own referendum.

4.   If French Quebecers can be considered the founders of a homeland with an alleged occupation of 400 years, then First Nations, who have lived in what is now known as Quebec since the Ice Age, have a stronger claim to the homeland.

5.   Although the judgment awarded damages to the appellants, it was a meagre contribution to the area of consumer protection.

6.   During unannounced spot checks, investigators may review mandatory reporting information related to contravention reports and take samples for substances regulated by legislation.

7.   We don't know.
      If two were arrested:
      The police arrested two thugs: a pimp and a drug dealer.

      or

      The police arrested two thugs—a pimp and a drug dealer.

      If four were arrested:
      The police arrested two thugs, a pimp, and a drug dealer.

Commonly Confused Words

With a sheet of paper, cover the answers on the right side of the page. Distinguish between meanings of each set of words on the left side of the page either by giving definitions or by writing sentences to illustrate differences.

Word	Explanation	Example
affect / effect	affect: **verb** meaning *to influence* or *to produce an effect on* effect: **verb** meaning *to bring about, accomplish* **noun** meaning *result*, or *consequence*	The new ruling will **affect** all employees. She wants to **effect** a change in the by-laws. The **effect** of the drownings was devastating.
aggravate / irritate	aggravate: to make (a situation) worse irritate: to annoy, provoke, exasperate:	In Alberta's view, the minister's behaviour only **aggravated** the impasse. Reports of increased absenteeism usually **irritate** supervisors.
allusion *illusion* *elusion*	allusion: indirect reference illusion: a false idea or perception elusion: the act of eluding or evasion especially of a problem or order	The judgment contained an **allusion** to former injustices by the government. (Better to say **alluded to**) Is the idea of a social safety net for all an **illusion**? Better to use the more familiar **evasion** than the more difficult **elusion**.

	Commonly Confused Words (cont'd)	

Word	Explanation	Example
*between / among** * Bill Bryson, in *The Mother Tongue*, refers to "the clearly nonsensical belief that *between* can apply only to two things and *among* to more than two" (p. 141)	Three rules are needed: (i) **The General Rule** Use *between* as a relationship word between two and *among* for three or more. (ii) **The Couple Rule** Use *between* with three or more when the relational references are only between the coupled sets, not spread among all items. (A more lawyerly explanation is found in *The New York Times Stylebook: Between* is correct when referring to more than two when the items are related both individually and severally.) (iii) **The Crossroads Rule** Use *between* when the the first of several items is in the midst of several pairs.	This information should be kept between the two of us. The dispute occurred among hospital administrators, doctors and nurses, and government health officials. What's the difference between *between, among* and *amidst*? Let's keep this information between you and me and the lamp post. The economic battle between Japan, Europe, and America was documented in the early nineties. Calgary is between Regina and Vancouver and between Edmonton and Fort Macleod.

Commonly Confused Words (cont'd)

Word	Explanation	Example
comprises / consists	Think of *comprising* as "containing" or "embracing" elements in a unit. The whole comprises the parts, so *comprise* must never be used in the passive voice: *is comprised of* is a misnomer. This mistake also happens because writers think of *includes* as a synonym for *comprises*, which it is not. **Recommendation** Because its misuse is so widespread, and because the word is stuffy-sounding, use words such as *consists of* or *have* instead.	**Wrong**: Canada is comprised of ten provinces and two territories. **Right**: Canada comprises ten provinces and two territories (in 1998 anyway!) **Better**: Canada consists of ten provinces and two territories.
credible / creditable	credible: believable creditable: worthy of praise; that brings credit or honour	The defendant was a **credible** witness. The executor did a **creditable** job winding up the estate.
deprecate / depreciate	deprecate: to express mild or regretful disapproval depreciate: represent as of little value or less than usually assigned	Most Canadians **deprecate** any risk to our healthcare safety net. Yet government commitment to funding healthcare **depreciates** the equal treatment principle. (Use **devalues** as a plain language substitute.)
discreet / discrete	discreet: diplomatic; not obvious discrete: separate	Though emotionally involved, her behavior was **discreet**. Don't bundle these ideas together, they are three **discrete** points.

Commonly Confused Words (cont'd)

Word	Explanation	Example
disinterested / uninterested	disinterested: impartial	In spite of his contract, he claimed to be a **disinterested** person in the Council's proceedings.
	uninterested: not interested	Her young son was certainly **uninterested** in the Council's proceedings.
e.g. / i.e.	e.g.: for example (Latin *exempli gratia*)	Writing the English words out in full is preferable. Commas enclose both the abbreviation and the long forms.
	i.e.: that is (Latin *id est*)	
eminent *imminent* *immanent*	eminent: distinguished	She is an **eminent** physician.
	imminent: soon to happen	A decision on the new policy is **imminent**.
	immanent: inherent, present throughout the universe	The spirit of life is **immanent**.
fewer / less	fewer: countables	Vivian Clark writes **fewer** reports than William Meyers.
	less: amount	In the long run, writing several drafts costs the company **less** time.
flaunt / flout	flaunt: to display arrogantly	He **flaunted** his new clothes.
	flout: to defy contemptuously	She instinctively **flouts** regulations.
fortuitous / auspicious	fortuitous: by chance	The meeting was **fortuitous**, but it led to a job.
	auspicious: favourable, promising success	All the signs were **auspicious**.

Commonly Confused Words (cont'd)		
Word	**Explanation**	**Example**
levied / levelled *(or leveled)*	levied: impose or collect by legal authority levelled: aimed or directed	**Wrong** He **levied a change of slander** against his colleague. **Right** He **levelled a charge of slander** against his colleague. Although the taxes **levied** in Denmark are higher, the social safety net is strong.
refer / allude	refer: to point specifically to something allude: to mention something indirectly or in passing	The article **refers** to three essential sources. Do not ask him about his failure; do not even **allude** to it.
tortuous / torturous	tortuous: winding, twisting torturous: involving or causing torture	The **tortuous** trail through the bush left us disoriented. The investigation of the murder was a **torturous** experience for the family of the deceased.

Rules to Eliminate Dangling Participles

*A participle is a verbal adjective (a word or group of words) which modifies (or describes) a noun. For example, in the sentence below, **not wishing to be bothered** is the participal phrase which grammatically must describe the noun **telephone**:*

> Not wishing to be bothered, the telephone was left with the answer message on.

To correct the dangling participle, described as *dangling* as it is not linked to the correct word, write:

> Not wishing to be bothered, the lawyer left the telephone with the answer message on.

As you can see, the results of dangling participles can range from awkward to ridiculous. An *ing* word or *ed* word at the beginning of a sentence always modifies the subject of the main clause. So in *Improving keyboarding skills, practice is needed*, grammatically, the noun practice is improving!

Rule: To eliminate a dangling participle, write the sentence so the action is correctly connected to the subject-agent. *To improve your keyboarding skills, practise regularly.* (You, the agent, is understood here.)

Dangling Participles Test

Eliminate the dangling participles in the following sentences.

1. On Saturday, while driving on a trail between pumpjacks, the left rear wheel hit a marker post that was buried in the snow.

2. By entering into an agreement with a shorter term, it may give the club an incentive to work on eliminating their budget deficit.

3. After reviewing the damage, an estimate was prepared by Fudgit Law, which is attached.

4. Speaking in terms of its private law system, Quebec certainly is distinct from the rest of Canada.

5. Illustrating the evolution of trade mark law, Harley Davidson is seeking to register this sound as a U.S. trademark.

6. In advising people on the preparation of their wills or estate planning, it is critical to remember that a plan may meet the Income Tax Act requirements but not the clients' personal requirements.

7. Reading those provisions together, the constitutional protection provided for Alberta is as follows:

8. Divisional staff who disagree with a supervisor's decision have the right to appeal the decision utilizing Departmental conflict resolution process guidelines in Appendix 2.

9. Based on the results of the field testing, we used gender-neutral language in the new legislation.

Answers to Dangling Participles Test

1. On Saturday, while driving on a trail between pumpjacks, the driver hit his left rear wheel on a marker post buried in the snow.

2. An agreement with a shorter term may give the club an incentive . . .

3. Fudgit Law prepared the attached estimate after they had reviewed the damage.

4. Quebec's private law system exemplifies how it is distinct from the rest of Canada.

5. Harley-Davidson's quest to register this sound as a U.S. trademark illustrates how far trade mark law has evolved.

6. If you advise people on the preparation of their wills or estate planning, remember that a plan may meet the Income Tax Act requirements but not the clients' personal requirements.

7. The constitutional protection provided for Alberta in all these provisions is as follows:

8. Divisional staff who disagree with a supervisor's decision have the right to appeal the decision. To do so, staff (or you) should use Departmental conflict resolution process guidelines in Appendix 2.

9. Because of the field testing, we used gender-neutral language in the new legislation.

Dashes and Parentheses Rules

Use the dash for the following:

1.   *to mark an abrupt change or break in the continuity of a sentence:*

When in 1950 the stockpile was sold off—indeed, dumped as surplus—natural rubber sales were hard hit.

2.   *in place of other punctuation (like the comma) when special emphasis is needed:*

The companies who have agreed to the merger—Petrodome, Canarctic and Oil Inc.—are united in their philosophy.

3.   *to introduce a summary statement that follows a series of words or phrases:*

Oil, steel and wheat—these are the sinews of industrialization.

Remember   Use dashes carefully in formal writing. Do not use them as awkward substitutes for end marks or when unsure whether to use commas, semicolons, or colons.

Note: A dash is different from a hyphen. In most computer software, you can find the em dash (-) in the 'symbols' chart. The old typewriter style of using two hyphens for a dash (—) is no longer acceptable.

Use parentheses:

1.   *To minimize the importance of material which, however, you want to include.*

Analysis of that pedestrian crossing showed it rated 38th out of 300 crossings (listed in descending order according to the index).

Note that, if the parenthetical material is not a complete sentence, it is inserted in parentheses inside the sentence, and the period follows the closing parenthesis. (If, however, the material to be enclosed is in a complete sentence, it is placed outside the sentence within the parentheses with the period before the closing parenthesis.)

2.   *For supplementary or illustrative matter.*

We wish to lease Block J and the 102 Street right-of-way between 86 and 87 Avenues (see Enclosure I).

3.   *To enclose numbers within a sentence.*

Each entry will be judged on the basis of (1) its artistic value, (2) its technical competence, and (3) its originality.

Dashes and Parentheses Test

1. The National Native Women's Association of Canada, NWAC, — which represents about 120,000 aboriginal women — asked the Federal Court of Canada to block constitutional participation grants of about $10 million to four native organizations.

2. The products of copyright are protected from copying or other forms of exploitation, public performance, broadcasting, casting, translation, and other spin-offs, for the lifetime of the producer plus another 50 years.

3. The Supreme Court of Canada tends to refuse to hear cases of relevance only to the parties, whether criminal or civil, unless serious legal error (one of public importance) can be identified.

4. A general rule is to make a pronoun refer to the immediately preceding matching noun singular or plural.

5. If the reference for the pronoun is not exact and clear, or if the antecedent is omitted, confusion (or unintended humour) may result.

Answers to Dashes and Parentheses Test

1. The National Native Women's Association of Canada, NWAC—which represents about 120,000 aboriginal women—asked the Federal Court of Canada to block constitutional participation grants of about $10 million to four native organizations.

    [**Note:** Use the em dash, not double hyphens (a typing, not word processing style) for the dash function. The words between dashes are more emphasized by dashes than by commas, though commas are also correct.]

2. The products of copyright are protected from copying or other forms of exploitation—public performance, broadcasting, casting, translation, and other spin-offs—for the lifetime of the producer plus another 50 years.

    [**Note:** The two dashes more precisely partition and subordinate the examples.]

3. Correct.

4. . . . matching noun (singular or plural).

5. Correct.

Gender-neutral Language Test

Correct the following sentences.

1. A person who dies without a will may leave his family to face unfortunate circumstances.

2. The doctrine of the reasonable man (See Mellinkoff's Dictionary)

3. Any party who fails to comply with a request given to him pursuant to subsection (1) within 10 days from the receipt thereof shall not thereafter be at liberty to put the requested document in evidence on his behalf in the proceeding, unless he satisfies the Board that he had sufficient excuse for his default.

4. The Alberta Court of Queen's Bench in *Royal Bank v. Aleman* (1988), 3 W.W.R. 461 suggested four factors for fiduciary obligations to arise between a banker and a client. They are:

   a. that he relied on the advice

   b. that the defendant was aware of this reliance etc.

5. Criminal Libel is a matter published without lawful justification or excuse, that is likely to injure the reputation of any person by exposing him to hatred, contempt or ridicule, or that is designed to insult the person of or concerning whom it is published. Truth is not necessarily a defence.

6. It is well settled, indeed it is hornbook law, that the reasonable expenses incurred by an indemnitee in defending a claim against him may be recovered of his indemnitor.

7. One interpretation is that the Charter gives no right to anyone to enter a public place to express his views.

8. The agent has a duty to provide coverage that would be sufficient to adequately insure against these specific risks. If he cannot and does not provide such coverage, he has a duty to inform the insured of a lack of coverage.

9. The careful draftsman should follow the rules of English usage.

Answers to Gender-neutral Language Test

1. Those (or A person) who die(s) without a will may leave their (his or her) families (family) . . .

2. The doctrine of the reasonable person

3. Unless there is sufficient excuse to satisfy the Board for defaulting, a party who does not comply within 10 days of receiving a request governed by subsection (1) loses the right to provide the requested document as evidence on his or her behalf in the proceeding.

4. a. that the client relied on the advice

5. . . . by exposing that person to hatred, contempt or ridicule, or that is designed to insult the person about whom it is published.

6. . . . the reasonable expenses incurred by an indemnitee in defending a claim may be recovered from the indemnitor.

7. . . . that the Charter does not give people (us) the right to enter a public place to express their (our) views.

8. The agent has a duty to provide coverage that would be sufficient to adequately insure against these specific risks. An agent who cannot cannot and does not provide such coverage has a duty to inform the insured of a lack of coverage.

9. The careful drafter (or writer) should follow the rules of English usage.

Hyphen Rules

Use the hyphen:

1. *to express the idea of a unit and avoid ambiguity.*

    a do-it-yourself scheme
    right-of-way

2. *to join two or more words serving as a single adjective before a noun.*

    conservationist-oriented participants
    easy-to-follow steps

3. *with compound numbers from twenty-one to ninety-nine and with fractions.*

    two-thirds

4. *with prefixes like **ex-** ("former"), **self-**, **all-**, and **great-**; between a prefix and a proper name; and with the suffix **-elect**.*

    mayor-elect, all-purpose, great-uncle, president-elect, pro-native people, self-made, ex-priest

5. *to avoid ambiguity or an awkward combination of letters or syllables.*

    semi-independent, shell-like

    His re-creation of the old City Hall was excellent.
    (But: Hiking is good recreation.)

Hyphens Test

Rewrite the following sentences, adding hyphens when necessary.

1. The administration of the estate is entrusted to a Court appointed administrator rather than an Executor who has been carefully selected.

2. What's the difference between extra-marital sex and extra marital sex?

   Or between 100 odd people or 100-odd people in a CBA Plenary?

3. The errors are mostly slave and printer related.

4. The virtue of a laser method of tattoo removal is that it is a non scarring procedure.

5 Each month, we write and distribute twenty 30 and 60 second radio scripts on legal issues.

6. Oil spills are problems for state owned institutions and private companies.

7. The bacteria is not related to flesh-eating disease, a fast acting bacteria that can kill if not treated immediately.

8. An employer of independent contractors is no longer responsible for employment related deductions like UIC, CPP and tax remittances.

9. Spousal support is not a gender based entitlement, but an entitlement flowing from economic decisions made during marriage.

10. a) TSE plummets on prereferendum jitters. (news headline)
     b) Many students require assistance in a pre-employment stage.
     c) Community services took on more responsibility for pre- and postnatal care.

Answers to Hyphens Test

1.   . . . Court-appointed administrator . . .

2.   Plenty.

3.   The errors are mostly slave- and printer-related.

4.   The virtue of a laser method of tattoo removal is that it is a non-scarring procedure.

5.   Each month, we write and distribute twenty 30- and 60-second radio scripts on legal issues.

6.   . . . state-owned institutions

7.   . . . flesh-eating . . . fast-acting

8.   An employer of independent contractors is no longer responsible for employment-related deductions like UIC, CPP and tax remittances.

9.   . . . is not a gender-based entitlement . . .

10.   a) Correct
            (Note: Do not use a hyphen to set off a prefix at the beginning, or a suffix at the end, of a word.)

        b) Correct
            (Exception: If the prefix ends with "e" or "o", and the base word begins with the same letter, add the hyphen.)

        c) Correct
            (When two or more prefixes have a common element and the unit appears only with the final prefix, insert a suspending hyphen after each unattached prefix to show the connection to the common unit. See also #5 above.)

Illegal Twinning

The twinning of synonyms springs from either long-outdated legal clichés or an attempt to cover all possible contingencies. Mellinkoff says writing becomes more precise by deciding on what one word best matches your meaning, and dropping the other.

authorize and empower
construed and interpreted
covenant and agree
due and payable
duties and obligations
each and all
each and every
encumbrances or burdens of any nature
express and constitute
fit and proper
force and effect
free and clear
goods and chattels
including but not limited to*
just and reasonable
last will and testament
maintenance and upkeep
null and void
place and stead
represent and warrant
save and except
seized and possessed
set forth and described
supersedes and replaces
terms and expressions
to have and to hold
void and of no effect
warrantee or representation
will and testament

---

*Garner's *Dictionary of Modern Legal Usage* says it is hornbook law that the use of the word *including* indicates that the specified list is illustrative, not exclusive.

Misplaced Modifiers Test

Correct the misplaced modifiers in the following sentences.

1. The publisher will pay the author a royalty based on actual cash received on the sale of the work (excluding shipping and handling) by the Publisher of 15%.

2. In the settlement offer, they are **only** considering the gas sales issues with producers and not the transportation aspects.

3. As promised, we have reviewed the proposed settlement details contained in our letter of 1996 07 16 with Fudgit Law partners.

4. We recommend that you provide all new employees including articling students with the package.

5. After reviewing the damage, an estimate was prepared by Fudgit Law, which   is attached.

6. This paper provides an analysis of over 85% of the Data Processing Service Department staff's interpretation of the mission statement.

7. As promised, we have reviewed the proposed settlement details contained in our June 20, 1996 letter with the Gushing Oil working interest owners.

8. If there are payments under the contract, it is important not only to specify when and where they are to be paid but to whom payments are delivered.

9. Though we are now consulting the public, we originally intended to have Draft One only reviewed within Transport Canada and by provincial regulators.

10. The review of ecomonic developments examines the actions of the Conservative government to reduce the deficit in more detail.

Answers to Misplaced Modifiers Test

1. The publisher will pay the author a 15% royalty based on . . .

2. In the settlement offer, they are considering **only** the gas sales issues with producers, not the transportation aspects.

3. As promised, we have reviewed with Fudgit Law partners the proposed settlement details contained in our letter of 1996 07 16.

4. We recommend that you provide the package to all employees and articling students.

5. Fudgit Law reviewed the damage and prepared the attached estimate.

6. [Does the writer mean 85% of the staff or 85% of their interpretations? If it were the second, *interpretation* should be plural.]

   This paper provides an analysis of over 85% of the Data Processing Service Department staff's interpretations of the mission statement.

7. As promised, we have reviewed with the Gushing Oil working interest owners the proposed settlement described in our June 20, 1996 letter.

8. If there are payments under the contract, it is important to specify not only when and where they are to be paid but to whom payments are delivered.

9. Though we are now consulting the public, we originally intended to have Draft One reviewed **only** within Transport Canada and by provincial regulators.

10. The review of ecomonic developments to reduce the deficit examines in more detail the actions of the Conservative government.

Numbers Rules

1. **Words or figures: over and under 10**
   In running text, generally write out numbers from one to nine in words; use figures for numbers 10 or greater.

2. **Figures don't begin sentences**
   Never begin a sentence with a figure: place the number elsewhere in the sentence, or spell it out.

3. *In technical writing (see box on numbers in legislation below) and especially in tables and charts, figures are almost always preferable. In general business writing, use them when needed for greater emphasis and clarity.*

4. **Spelling out numbers** *When writing out numbers in words, hyphenate all compound numbers (cardinal and ordinal) between 21 and 99, even within larger numbers. Do not hyphenate other numbers.*	twenty-one; thirty-six hundred; ninety-nine
5. **Adjacent numbers** *When two adjacent numbers are not separated by punctuation, spell one out and write the other in figures. (Write out the shorter number.)*	two 7-drawer files 20 ten-drawer files
6. **Series of numbers** *When a number beginning a sentence is followed by another related number, spell out both.* *When a series of three or more numbers appears in a sentence, express all in figures (even though some are under 10).* *When two series of numbers referring to different things appear in a single sentence, avoid confusion by writing one series in words and the other in figures.*	Thirty or forty new jobs will be created. We had 12 applicants from Edmonton, 14 from Calgary, and 3 from Regina. Two applicants scored 80 points, thirteen scored 75 points, and four scored 60.

Numbers Rules (cont'd)	
7. **Measurements** *Use figures before symbols or abbreviations for units of measurements*	15 cu. ft. (or 15 cu ft)
Repeat the unit symbol in a range or a series.	20% - 40%; discounts of 5%, 10% and 15%
If the unit is written out, you may write out the numbers as well; in a range or series, write the unit only once.	fifteen cubic feet; thirty miles from 20 to 50 percent
8. **Percentages** *You may write out "percent" in non-technical text.*	Only 55 percent agreed
Do not hyphenate a percentage used as an adjective.	a 55 percent increase
Use the % sign in technical materials or in tables.	a 55% increase
9. **Fractions and decimals** *Use words for common fractions in running text; use figures for mixed numbers (whole number plus a fraction).*	One-half of the employees; 7 3/4
Use figures in tables or series. Do not add "th".	1/2"; 6/32; 1/25; (**not** 1/25th)
Use decimals (not fractions) in technical and statistical writing and with metric and SI (International System) units.	1.75
Insert a zero before the decimal point in numbers less than one.	0.25; 0.0037
10. **Time** *Use words for numbers with "o'clock" or when "o'clock" is understood.*	four o'clock; They left before six.
Use figures with "a.m." or "p.m." and with the hour clock.	4:30 a.m.; 6 p.m.; 24-13:00; 23:30

Numbers Rules (cont'd)	
11. **Dates** *Day, month and year (preferred for clarity)*	May 15, 1991 (**not** May 15th, 1991)
Year - month - day	1991 03 26 (or 1991-03-26) 1991 May 20

Numbers in Legislation

Legislation is a form of technical writing. Yet numbers and numbering are distinctive from other documents. For example:

1. ***Numbering of items changes***
   Numbers appear without periods and in two different fonts if there is a duplication of numbers.

   1(1)(a) "collective agreement" has the same meaning that it has in the *Labour Relations Code*;

2. *Rule about under 10 is ignored:*

   Days of rest   19. (1) Every employer must allow each employee at least

        (a) One day of rest in each work week,

        (b) 2 consecutive days of rest in each period of 2 consecutive work weeks,

        (d) 4 consecutive days of rest in each period of 4 consecutive work weeks.

       (2) Every employer must allow each employee at least 4 consecutive days of rest after each 24 consecutive work days.

Numbers Test

1. A public hearing will be held in council chambers, Municipal Building, Calgary, Alberta on 1996 November 19th at 1:30 o'clock in the afternoon.

2. The proposed By-law twenty nine M ninety establishes a revised City of Calgary transportation system.

3. In describing the quality of service in London magistrates' courts, *The Times* legal correspondent said, "So many young barristers seemed incapable of forming a grammatically correct English sentence." (*New Law Journal*, 15 Nov. 79, p. 1117)

4. Insurance benefits will be extended for up to 6 months to terminated employees not going to another employer.

5. 8 of the twelve companies surveyed had no policy on this item.

6. The Vice President reported that three applicants were from Ontario, 18 from Alberta, and one from the Northwest Territories.

7. Under the bid, corporations would pay a few hundred million dollars towards Olympic costs— estimated to be at least $2 1/2 billion.

8. The computerized system calculates the working interest % we are to receive from each property.

9. The 2 main cities in Newfoundland are St John's with one hundred thousand and Corner Brook with twenty thousand.

10. 99% of DNA is identical in humans; 1% of DNA is unique to each human.

11. The encyclopedia has a 1824-page COLORPEDIA section illuminating the great themes of knowledge, a 885-page quick-reference ALPHAPEDIA, and a 51-page time chart of human history.

12. Before 2000, UNICEF wishes to reduce mortality rates for children under five in all countries by 1/3 or to between 50 and 70 per one thousand live births respectively, whichever is less.

13. 44 bills were introduced, and 43 were passed, including one private member's bill.

14. The community chicken supper has been the largest annual event in Maple Leaf, the tiny hamlet, population 155, 45 km northeast of the city.

Answers to Numbers Test

1.   . . . on 1996 November 19 (or November 19, 1996) at 1:30 p.m.

2.   . . . By-law 29M90

3.   Correct

4.   . . . six months

5.   Eight of the twelve

6.   3 . . . , 18 . . . , and 1 . . .

7.   . . . $2.5 billion

8.   . . . working interest percentage

9.   The two main cities . . . 100,000 . . . 20,000

10.   Ninety-nine percent of DNA is identical in humans; one percent of DNA is unique to each human.

         Or, recast to avoid starting with a number:

         Scientists tell us that though 99% of DNA in humans is identical, 1% is unique to each human. (Digits are quicker to read.)

11.   Correct

12.   . . . children under 5 in all countries by one-third or to between 50 and 70 per 1000 live births . . .

13.   Of the 44 bills introduced, 43 were passed, including 1 private member's bill.

14.   The community chicken supper has been the largest annual event in the tiny hamlet of Maple Leaf, 45 km northeast of the city. The population is a mere 155.

Opening Sentences / Segments Test

Study the examples below and rewrite them in plain language.

1.   Further to our attendance before Justice Douglas on April 2, 1996, as I mentioned after that meeting, I was going to meet with my client on the following day. I have received instructions to provide you with a settlement offer of $55,000, which includes general and specific damages, and interest, and will further include your reasonable taxable costs.   **(59 words)**

2.   Please find attached my trust cheque in the amount of $9,000 which I provide on the express trust condition that you will not use these funds in any way, but for depositing them in your trust account, until you provide me with the following documentation: **(46 words)**

3.   Further to your correspondence dated February 28, 1996 and our subsequent discussions, we confirm your client's proposal to resolve matters on the basis described in your letter of January 14, 1996 is totally unacceptable to my client.   **(37 words)**

4.   We have been retained by Mrs. Fiona Redmonds to act on her behalf in the matter of her recent termination from your employ. It is our opinion that our client was wrongfully dismissed, without just cause, and without sufficient notice or payment in lieu thereof. Furthermore, it is our opinion that Mrs Redmonds has quite clearly been the target of discrimination, by you and your firm, contrary to section 7(1)(b) of the *Individual Rights Protection Act*, R.S.A. 1980 c. 1-2.
     (80 words)

5.   In rendering the opinion contained herein, documents in respect of A, B, and C have been reviewed.   **(17 words)**

6.   Thank you for your correspondence of September 22, 1998.

     As I understand the issue raised by our discussions and your correspondence, the Association's Registration Committee wishes to fine a member who let his membership lapse and, prior to obtaining readmission, continued to use his professional designation of Registered XXX YYY.

     The *Act* indicates . . .   **(56 words)**

7.   The tenderer guarantees that the Commission may

     (1) keep the tender deposit for the Commission's use, and
     (2) accept any tender, advertise for new tenders, negotiate a contract, or not accept any contract,

     if the tenderer withdraws the tender

     (1) before the Commission has considered the tenders, or
     (2) before or after the tenderer has been notified that the tender has been recommended to the Commission for acceptance,

     or if, within seven days, the Commission does not receive the following:

     (1) the Agreement executed by the tenderer,
     (2) the Performance Bond and the Payment Bond executed by the tenderer and the surety company, and
     (3) other documents described in clauses x and y.   **(113 words)**

Answers to Opening Sentences / Segments Test

1. My client has asked me to offer you a settlement of $55,000. This offer includes general and specific damages, interest, and your reasonable taxable costs.   **(26 words)**

2. Attached is my trust cheque for $9, 000 for you to deposit and keep in your trust account until I have received the following from you: **(25 words)**

3. My client and I have carefully considered your client's proposal in your January 14, 1996 letter and your February 28, 1996 letter and our subsequent discussions. The proposal is totally unacceptable to my client.   **(34 words)**

4. We are (or I am) acting for Mrs. Fiona Redmonds in the case of her recent termination from your company. We believe that our client

    (i) was wrongfully dismissed without just cause and without sufficient notice or payment in place of notice, and

    (ii) has been the target of discrimination by you and your firm, contrary. . .   **(58 words)**

5. This opinion is based on a review of A, B, and C.   **(12 words)**

6. As you requested, I have researched whether your Association's Registration Committee has the legal right under the *Health Discipline Act* to fine a member who used his professional designation after his membership had lapsed.

    The *Act* indicates . . .   **(37 words)**

7. The Commission may

    (i) keep the tenderer's deposit, and

    (ii) accept any other tender, advertise for new tenders, negotiate a contract, or not accept any contract

    if the tenderer withdraws the tender.   **(32 words)**

Parallelism Rules

1. *When you write a series of sentence elements that serve the same function, put them into the same grammatical form. For example:*

    Poor: Consider the following factors: distance of viewers from exhibit, average viewing time, and what material should be used.

    Good: Consider the following factors: distance of viewers from exhibit, average viewing time, and material to be used.

2. *The same principle applies in the example below:*

    Poor: Design your exhibit for a technically skilled audience or to please the general public.

    Good: Design your exhibit either for a technically skilled audience or for the general public.

3. *To emphasize parallelism between two elements, you may use the following paired expressions:*

    both . . . and   either . . . or   neither . . . nor

    not . . . but   not only . . . but also

4. *A sentence which has two complete thoughts joined by a semicolon or a colon is awkward if you slip from the active into the passive voice. For example, the rewrites of the following examples keep the same voice to create parallelism:*

    Poor: People want to grow and succeed; challenge and security are needed by them.

    Good: People want to grow and succeed; they need challenge and security.

    Poor: They met over lunch; by 5 p.m., the contract was signed by both parties.

    Good: They met over lunch; by 5 p.m., both parties had signed the contract.

Parallelism Test

Correct the parallelism in the following sentences.

1. Poorly managed facilities will eventually result in excessive downtime for equipment repair, costly remediation, the potential for long-term liabilities, as well as contravene government regulations.

2. Section 164 of our *Municipal Government Act* states that for the purpose of regulating and controlling animals a council may pass bylaws:

   (c) regulating the keeping by any person of wild or domestic animals or poultry within the limits of the municipality;

   (d) prohibiting the keeping by any person of wild or domestic animals or poultry in any specified part or parts of the municipality when, in the opinion of council, that keeping is likely to cause a nuisance;

   (e) for the prevention of cruelty to animals.

3. As long as we Canadians are committed to equality, so also will the country and its institutions.

4. The powers of the Committee essentially relate to deciding whether or not applicants should or should not be admitted for registration and thus the use of the professional designation.

5. The consignor must:

   1) Ensure that all employees handling, offering for transport or transporting dangerous goods are qualified persons and issue Certificates of Training to these people.

   2) As the manufacturer of the dangerous goods or the importer, classify the dangerous goods by following the procedures set out in Part III of the Regulations.

   3) Check List II of the Regulations for a shipping name.

   4) Check special provisions in Schedule III of the Regulations.

   5) Check exemptions and prohibitions in Part II of the Regulations, and according to the mode.

   6) If the goods are regulated but no shipping name is found in the Lists of the Regulations, obtain complete information related to the classification from the manufacturer.

Parallelism Test (cont'd)

6.   (from a provincial act)

Notice to   16.1 Before refusing to register or renew the registration of a charitable
the applicant   organization or imposing a term or condition on the registration, the
Minister must

(a) notify the charitable organization of the reasons why the organization
may be refused or the proposed terms and conditions and the reasons
why they may be imposed, and

(b) provide the charitable organization with an opportunity to make
representations to the Minister . . .

7.   If an action goes ahead years later, evidence may have been lost (witnesses dead or unavailable);
memories faded; documents lost or inadvertently destroyed.

Answers to Parallelism Test

1.   . . . liabilities, and the contravening of government regulations.

2.   (This part is rewritten more concisely, too)
        . . . *Municipal Government Act* states that to regulate and control animals, a council may pass bylaws:

        (e) preventing cruelty to animals.

3.   As long as we Canadians are committed to equality, so also will the country and its institutions be so committed.

4.   The powers of the Committee essentially relate to deciding whether applicants should be allowed to register and thus use the professional designation.

5.   Correct

        [**Note:** The parallel structures using the command format (imperative verbs) may begin with a phrase modifying the subject, "consignor" (as in #2), or with a subordinate clause (as in #6).]

6.   Correct
        Yet, to ensure readers do not regress in their reading, add **before** and **of** as in

        16.1 **Before** refusing to register or renew the registration of a charitable organization or **before** imposing a term or condition on the registration, the Minister must

              (a) notify the charitable organization of the reasons why the organization may be refused or **of** the proposed terms and conditions and the reasons why they may be imposed, and . . .

              (b) use a plain language substitute for **to make representations to** in (b).

7.   If an action goes ahead years later, evidence may have been lost (witnesses dead or unavailable), memories **may have** faded, and documents **may have been** lost or inadvertently destroyed.

        [**Note:** Because the verbs are not exactly parallel, the extra words must be added. The punctuation needed corrections as well.]

Possessives Rules

Stamp your work with the mark of an expert by learning to use the apostrophe correctly.

1.   *The apostrophe is used:*

        a)   to show possession or ownership
        b)   to indicate a contraction, e.g., *can't* = cannot
        c)   to make a plural form in rare cases: She has too many *a*'s in that word.

2.   **Singular Forms** - *Possessive forms of singular nouns are formed by adding the apostrophe and s ('s).*

    the attorney's office

3.   *When the singular noun already ends in -s, use this rule: if the noun contains one syllable, add an apostrophe and an s ('s).*

    If the noun (that ends in an s) is more than one syllable long, use the apostrophe alone to form the possessive (').

    Cross's contribution   **but:**   Purves' folly
    Hoss's horse   Erasmus' decision

4.   **Plural Forms** - *When the plural noun does not end in -s, add the apostrophe and the s ('s).*

    women's rights   salesmen's supplies

    When the plural noun ends with an -s, add only the apostrophe:

    boys' clothing   employees' benefits

5.   **Special Rules**

    i)   *To show joint ownership, add the apostrophe to the last word only.*

        Clark and Fisher's store (one store only)

    ii)   *To show separate ownership, add the apostrophe to both words.*

        Clark's and Fisher's stores (two stores — separate owners)

    iii)   *In compound expressions, the apostrophe appears at the end of the last word only.*

        editor-in-chief's desk   a mother-in-law's prerogative

    iv)   *The noun or pronoun before a verbal noun must have an apostrophe.*

        White's campaigning has been well received (whose campaigning? White's)

        My supervisor's nagging is driving me crazy (whose nagging? my supervisor's)

Possessives Test

Add apostrophes to any words which require them.

1. With a few notable exceptions, Canada did not experience in the 1980's the insolvencies of large, widely traded public companies.

2. Mr. Charles will was read after several relatives requests.

3. You will be charged a months interest for the delay.

4. St. Johns Cathedral will be completed in five years.

5. You need your attorneys signature on this form.

6. Ten years experience makes you a strong candidate for this position.

7. A childrens home was built in Edmonton.

8. One vital feature of the *Privacy Act* is its' prohibition against the government disclosure of clients and employees personal information without their consent.

Answers to Possessives Test

1.   . . . 1980s

2.   Mr. Charles' will was read after several relatives' requests.

3.   You will be charged a month's interest for the delay.

4.   St. John's Cathedral will be completed in five years.

5.   You need your attorney's signature on this form.

6.   Ten years' experience makes you a strong candidate for this position.

7.   A children's home was built in Edmonton.

8.   One vital feature of the *Privacy Act* is its prohibition against the government's disclosure of clients' and employees' personal information without their consent.

Rules for Pronouns and their References

1. *A pronoun has no specific meaning. It usually takes its meaning from an antecedent—the word or words for which it stands.*

   Examples of pronouns: he, she, it, they, we, you, one, him
   her, them, us, which, this, that

2. *If the reference for a pronoun is not exact and clear, or if the antecedent is omitted, confusion (or unintended humour) may result. A general rule is to make the pronoun refer to the immediately preceding matching noun (singular or plural).*

3. ***Ambiguous Reference*** *occurs when a sentence has two or more words which could act as the antecedent. Avoid ambiguity by:*

   i)   replacing the pronoun with a noun
   ii) moving the pronoun closer to the intended antecedent
   iii) rephrasing the sentence

   Before: Alex passed Brian on the way to the meeting but he didn't speak to him.

   After: Alex passed Brian on the way to the meeting but Brian didn't speak to him.

4. ***Vague Reference*** *occurs when the intended antecedent is implied instead of explicit. The reference, one (below), has no grammatical antecedent (**a fish**).*

   Example: Fishing isn't any fun for me unless I catch one.

5. ***Indefinite Reference*** *occurs when an antecedent is omitted. This is sometimes acceptable in conversation, but writing should be more specific.*

   Before: Since office automation has become such a time saver, they need personal computers more than ever.

   After: Since office automation has become such a time saver, businesses (or office personnel) need personal computers more than ever.

6. **Reflexive Pronouns:**   myself, yourself, himself, herself, itself,
   ourselves, yourselves, themselves

   Use these pronouns only:

   i)   *When the subject does something to itself.*
   They separated themselves from the crowd.

   ii) *For emphasis.*
   The president himself greeted the visiting delegation.

   iii) *When the pronoun is reflexive in a literal sense, that is, refers back to the antecedent.*
   Let me do it myself.

Test on Pronouns and their References

Rewrite the following sentences so the pronouns and their references are properly positioned and match.

1. The members of the legislature are not necessarily charged with a knowledge of the grammatical rules of the English language, and in the interpretation of their acts, such construction is given the language as will best effectuate **their intent** without reference to the accurate grammatical construction of words, phrases, and sentences.[1]
   (Section 251, *McKinney's Codes*, the guide to interpret New York statutes)

2. All of the cases impose liability because the defendant has failed to procure the requested coverage and has failed to advise **their** client of the deficiency.

3. One idea we used was first raised for discussion by the Department of Justice. **It** concerns allowing regulations to contain explanatory material. Although **this** is still under review by Justice, we've used **it** and find **it** is a significant initiative for presenting our regulations in an understandable form.

4. I expect this workshop will reinforce my good writing habits and remind me of **the ones** I need to eliminate.

5. Fires resulted and Advocates Inc. indicated they were ignited by static electricity rather than the exhaust system.

6. The technical challenge was to design a recovery facility that would recover DMT from an aqueous stream, so that it might be recycled to the new synthetic fibres plant.

7. I understand you are looking for a receptionist or typist, male or female. Being both, I am applying for the job.

8. Angus wrote and edited the report, which everyone on the committee thought was remarkable.

9. John told Gerry that he had given Dan the wrong advice.

---

[1] "Grammar Scandal" in the *New York Times Magazine*, March 29, 1992 provides a quashing of this section's contempt for the fundamental tool of the law, of its lazy approach to interpreting "by divining rod", and of its "laid-back laxity and wanton permissiveness as the basis for adjudication of disputes." In a final impatient statement, the writer hypothesizes about what the drafters were trying to say: "Judge us not by what we say in cold print, but by what you can read of our minds."

Answers to Test on Pronouns and their References

1. Members of the legislature are not required to be English grammar specialists in writing legislation. Thus, judicial interpretation should be guided by the intent of the members, not by the grammatical construction of the legislation.

2. All of the cases impose liability because the defendants failed to procure the requested coverage and failed to advise **their** clients of the deficiencies.

3. One idea we used was first raised for discussion by the Department of Justice—**allowing regulations to contain explanatory material**. Although Justice is still reviewing **the idea**, our use of **it** (or **of explanatory material**) represents a significant initiative in making our regulations more understandable.

4. I expect this workshop will reinforce my good writing habits and remind me of **the poor habits** I need to eliminate.

5. Advocates Inc. indicated the resulting fires were ignited by static electricity rather than the exhaust system.

6. The technical challenge was to design a facility to recover DMT from an aqueous stream, so that the DMT might be recycled to the new synthetic fibres plant.

7. I understand you are looking for a receptionist or typist. As I have experience in both positions, I am applying for the job.

8. Everyone on the committee thought it was remarkable that Angus wrote and edited the report.

   or

   Everyone on the committee thought the report, which Angus wrote and edited, was remarkable.

9. John told Gerry that he (or John) had given Dan the wrong advice.

Punctuation Test

Correct the punctuation in the following sentences.

1. Each month, we write and distribute 20 thirty second and sixty second radio scripts on legal issues.

2. If the buyer fails to perform this contract then the deposit monies and any interest will be forfeited to the seller as liquidated damages; this contract will be terminated; and the buyer will have no further liability to the seller.

3. Matrimonial law practitioners are frequently asked if a divorce can be obtained by way of a joint application; that is, where neither party must assume the role of Petitioner in commencing a divorce action.

4. Further it should be noted that news reports have indicated that the Federal Justice Minister is appealing to the Texas Governor to commute Mr. Faulder's sentence to life imprisonment.

5. As a private citizen I have disagreed with some of your positions on national and economic issues, but I do know, you are a compassionate person who does not like injustice.

6. The *Firearms Act* sets out the criteria to possess the various categories of firearm e.g. ordinary, restricted, or prohibited.

Answers to Punctuation Test

1. Each month, we write and distribute twenty 30-second and 60-second radio scripts on legal issues.

2. If the buyer fails to perform this contract, then (i) the deposit monies and any interest will be forfeited to the seller as liquidated damages, (ii) this contract will be terminated, and (iii) the buyer will have no further liability to the seller. **numbers optional**

3. Matrimonial law practitioners are frequently asked if a divorce can be obtained by way of **(with)** a joint application, that is, with neither party assuming the role of Petitioner in the divorce action.

4. Further, it should be noted that ...

5. As a private citizen, I have disagreed with some of your positions on national and economic issues, but I do know you are a compassionate person who does not like injustice.

6. The *Firearms Act* sets out the criteria to possess the various categories of firearm, e.g., the ordinary, restricted, or prohibited categories.

Test on *with respect to, in respect of,* and *respecting*

Eliminate the doggedly persistent *with respect to, in respect of,* and *respecting* and substitute clear connectors instead—*on, about, for,* etc.

1. Colour has been registered as a trademark in Canada **with respect to** pharmaceutical tablets.

2. According to Dr. Hall's report dated March 20, 1996, as of February 3, 1996, your client had a normal range of motion **with respect to** his cervical and lumbar spine.

3. **With respect to** Mr. Morrow's Affidavit, I note that the Affidavit does not refer to all the documents listed in my December 14, 1995 letter to you.

4. The target corporation is required to claim its maximum available deduction **in respect of** doubtful debts against income for the same year-end.

5. My calculations are based on information **with respect to** John Douglas's tenure.

6. **With respect to** Alberta, the rights of separate school supporters were considered at length in cases X and Y.

7. The majority of the Court clarified that the right of the trustees of dissenting schools to levy taxes was a right **with respect to** denominational schools, and protected under the Constitution.

8. **In respect of** Dr Boudreau, there have been no allegations of negligent treatment beyond those contained in the Statement of Claim.

9. Does the proposed legislation have a prejudicial effect **with respect to** those rights or privileges?

10. A warranty under subsection (1) does not apply **in respect of**
    (a) defects in materials, design and work supplied by the owner
    (b) normal wear and tear
    (c) damage resulting from improper maintenance
    (d) damage resulting from an act of God

11. The Minister may make regulations
    (a) **respecting** the conversion to this Act of anything from the former Act;
    (b) to deal with any difficulty or impossibility resulting from this Act or the transition to this Act from the former Act.

Answers to Test on *with respect to, in respect of,* and *respecting*

1.   A colour **for** pharmaceutical tablets has been registered as a trademark in Canada.

2.   Dr. Hall's March 20, 1996 report states that, as of February 3, 1996, your client had a normal range of motion in his cervical and lumbar spine area.

3.   I note that Mr. Morrow's Affidavit does not refer to all the documents listed in my December 14, 1995 letter to you.

4.   The target corporation is required to claim its maximum available deduction for doubtful debts against income for the same year-end.

5.   My calculations are based on information **about** John Douglas's tenure.

6.   In Alberta, the rights of separate school supporters were considered at length in cases X and Y.

7.   The majority of the Court clarified that the right of the trustees of dissenting schools to levy taxes was a right **referring to** denominational schools, and protected under the Constitution.

8.   There have been no allegations of negligent treatment **by** Dr. Boudreau beyond those contained in the Statement of Claim.

9.   Does the proposed legislation have a prejudicial effect **on** those rights or privileges?

10.   . . . does not apply to

11.   The Minister may make regulations

  (a) **related to** converting anything in the former Act to this Act.

or

  (a) **covering** the conversion of anything in the former Act to this Act.

[**Note:** The drafter of this Act felt there was a slightly different meaning with "(a) to convert anything from the former Act to this Act", and so, even though the phrase is more parallel with (b), I have avoided it.]

Semicolons Rules

1. *Use a semicolon when the two independent clauses (sentences) you are joining are closely connected in meaning or when there is a cause-and-effect relationship between them.*

   I am too tired; I can't stay awake any longer.

   While there is a lower class, I am in it; while there is a criminal element, I am of it; while there is a soul in prison, I am not free.

2. *Use a semicolon before certain transition words when these are used to link two separate but closely related* **sentences**. *The transition word is always followed by a comma. Use this rule with these "glue words":*

besides	however
consequently	in fact
for example	moreover
furthermore	nevertheless
therefore	thus

   Right: Not all properties are reviewed every year; consequently, ownership changes may not occur.

   Wrong: Officials abruptly terminated many worthwhile projects; for example, day care centres and senior citizens' homes.

   *(The section after **for example** is not a complete sentence. A colon or a comma should replace the semicolon.)*

   [**Note:** The most common words which can connect two complete sentences **without** a semicolon are these: *and, but, for, or, nor, so, yet.*]

3. *Use a semicolon to make a lengthy, complex list easier to read and understand (especially when any of the elements have internal commas).*

   My favourite small cities in Canada are Peterborough, Ontario; Victoria, British Columbia; Kingston, Ontario; and Saskatoon, Saskatchewan.

Semicolons Test

Correctly punctuate the following sentences.

1. Simply put, civil litigation involves disputes between private parties; either individuals or corporations.

2. The Solicitor General's department thanks all applicants for their interest, however only those under consideration will be contacted.

3. Many statutes have similar limitations on liability. Some examples are the *Architects Act*; *Chartered Accountants Act*; *Engineering and Geological Act*; *Environmental Protection Act*; *Freedom of Information Act*; *Labour Relations Act*; and the *Nursing Profession Act*.

4. (Eliminate the ancient language as well.)
   Default by the Contractor hereunder shall occur if the Contractor fails to fufil any term or condition of this Agreement; in which case all monies unpaid cease to become owed by the Minister to the Contractor.

5. There is some improvement in your total performance, however in certain major areas, your performance still falls far short of that expected.

6. The committee members were Judith Sherrington, 38, from Airdre, John Douglas, 50, from Ottawa, Kristan Boudreau, 42, from Quebec, and Timothy Palmer, 33, from Vancouver.

Answers to Semicolons Test

1. Simply put, civil litigation involves disputes between private parties—either individuals or corporations. (Or, use a comma in place of a dash.)

2. The Solicitor General's department thanks all applicants for their interest; however only those under consideration will be contacted.

3. Many statutes have similar limitations on liability. Some examples are the *Architects Act*, *Chartered Accountants Act*, *Engineering and Geological Act*, *Environmental Protection Act*, *Freedom of Information Act*, *Labour Relations Act*, and the *Nursing Profession Act*.

4. If the Contractor fails to fufill any term or condition of this Agreement, then the Minister will not pay any money owed to the contractor.

   [**Note:** The semicolon in the original should be a comma.]

5. There is some improvement in your total performance; however, in certain major areas, your performance still falls far short of that expected.

6. The committee members were Judith Sherrington, 38, from Airdre; John Douglas, 50, from Ottawa; Kristan Boudreau, 42, from Quebec; and Timothy Palmer, 33, from Vancouver.

Sentence Fragments Rules

1. Most sentence fragments fall into two categories: the suspense-builders, and the danglers. You can learn to make all your sentences complete simply by listening closely to the sound of the fragment as you read it aloud.

2. Fragments which are suspense-builders usually begin with one of the following words:

after	so that
although	that
as, as if	though
as soon as	unless
as long as	until
because	what, whatever
before	when, whenever
even if	where, wherever
even though	whether
if	which, whichever
in order that	while
since	who, whom, whose

3. Listen to the following examples closely as you read them aloud:

   i)   As soon as I am able to find your invoice . . .
   ii) Before I can process your license renewal . . .
   iii) Whenever a tag notice is issued . . .

4. The fragments above build suspense; they leave the reader wondering what will happen next. Kill the suspense and provide the information.

   i)   As soon as I am able to find your invoice, I will mail it to you.
   ii) Before I can process your license renewal, you must sign it.
   iii) Whenever a tag notice is issued, the recipient must pay promptly.

5. Fragments which are danglers often include a verb with an -ing ending. Listen to the following examples as you read them aloud:

   i)   Having recently completed a computer training program . . .
   ii) Informing the public about bylaws . . .
   iii) Transferring twice and missing one connection . . .

6. The fragments above leave the information (and the reader) dangling. Having recently completed—who has recently completed the program, and what of it? Informing the public—what about it?

   i)   Having recently completed a computer training program, I got the job.
   ii) Informing the public about bylaws, the councillor hoped to arouse discussion.

   Informing the public about bylaws is a necessary procedure.

   iii) Transferring twice and missing one connection, Freddy finally arrived at the coliseum at the beginning of the third quarter.

Sentence Fragments Test

Except for titles, headings, margin notes, bulletted lists, or tabular information, all business and legal writing must be in complete sentence format.

Change the sentence fragments below into complete sentences (and use plain language, too).

1. The Short Title, the *Transportation of Dangerous Goods Act, 1992*, has been changed to distinguish it from the previous Act by adding the date 1992. When referenced the date must appear. For example: *Transportation of Dangerous Goods Act, 1992*; *TDG Act, 1992*, or *TEGA, 1992*.

2. Whereas the Minister desires the performance of services respecting the development and delivery of **"Written Communication - Two Day Workshop"** training for Ontario X Department as set out in Schedule "A", attached hereto.

3. AND whereas the Contractor has agreed to perform the services as specifically stated herein.

Answers to Sentence Fragments Test

1.   . . . When referenced, the date must appear, for example, *Transportation of* . . .

2.   The Minister requests and the Contractor agrees to develop and deliver a two-day *Written Communications* training workshop as described in Schedule "A".

3.   The Contractor agrees to perform the services specifically stated in this agreement.

Shall Test

Rewrite the following sentences to eliminate the ambiguity of the archaic *shall*.

1. The judges **shall hold** office during good behaviour, but **shall be removable** by the Governor General on address of the Senate and House of Commons: Provided that[1] each judge, whether heretofore appointed or hereafter to be appointed, **shall cease** to hold office upon attaining the age of seventy-five years, or immediately, if he has already attained that age.[2]

2. Here are several clauses from The United Nurses of Alberta Constitution with differing uses of *shall*:

   BYLAW IV
   There **shall be** a Grievance Committee. The Local is to decide the composition of this Committee. One of the members of the Committee **shall act** as Chair. The members of the Grievance Committee **shall be elected** at an annual or Special Meeting of the chartered Local.

3. District Committee Meetings **shall be** held at least quarterly.

4. The objectives of such meetings **shall be**:

5. The regular terms of Directors **shall be** for two (2) years.

6. The directors **shall** not transact business at a meeting of directors unless a quorum is present.

7. Questions arising **shall be** decided by a majority of votes.

---

[1] See discussion on *provided that* in "Ancient Language", p. 288. Here *provided that* means *and*.
[2] In 1976, Driedger wrote, "Incidentally, the *shalls* could be dropped in favour of *are removable* and *cease to hold*", p. 101. See also the *Handbook* section, "Kicking *shall* out of the court", p. 146, in the chapter "The Future of Plain Language".

Answers to Shall Test

1. The judges **hold** office during good behavior, but (i) **are removable** by the Governor General on address of the Senate and House of Commons and (ii) **cease to** hold office at age 75. These conditions apply to present and future judges.

2. BYLAW IV
   The Local **must** set up, and decide on the composition of, a Grievance Committee. One Committee member **will be** the Chair. Members of the chartered Local **will elect** the members of the Grievance Committee at an annual or a special Meeting.

3. District Committee Meetings **must be** held at least quarterly.

4. The objectives of such meetings **are** :

5. Directors serve a two-year term.

   or

   A Director's term **is** two years.

6. Directors must not transact business at a directors' meeting unless there is a quorum.

7. Questions are decided by majority votes.

Standard English Test

In the following sentences, correct mistakes in grammar, spelling, punctuation or capitalization.

1. The Publisher will pay the Author a royalty based on the actual cash received on the sale of the work (excluding shipping and handling charges) by the Publisher of 15%.

2. The location of the buildings and other improvements on the property complies with all municipal bylaws.

3. This form should be signed by yourself and returned as a director of Devilsticks Inc.

4. We appreciate you reviewing this with your senior counsel.

5. The instructor for the mediation course called for a committment to a new dispute resolution paradym.

6. The Board needs to keep itself appraised of current developments in government.

7. First Nations fears the Parti Quebécois government is based on a narrow colonial paradigm.

8. Any restraint on the level of taxation which the separate board may choose to impose should be unconstitutional.

9. The Administration Branch consists of eight employees, including myself.

10. Payments are to be divided as follows: 1/2 to Elizabeth Gunter and 1/2 to Pauline Jackal.

11. All three districts report that H_2S signs are on the sites that require them, and those sites that have signs and don't require them have been removed.

12. Billionaire businessman Ross Perot said the chances of him re-entering the presidential race are about as likely as him "leaping over a tall building in a single bound."

13. In the House of Commons on Monday, Chretien scornfully mocked the re-elections chances of maverick Toronto MP John Nunziata, who hours earlier the prime minister had banished from the government benches for opposing a budget bill on the grounds the Liberals had failed to meet an election promise to kill the GST.

Answers to Standard English Test
Corrections are bolded

1.   The publisher will pay the **author a 15% royalty based** on the actual cash the **publisher** receives for the sale of the work (minus the shipping and handling charges).

     Misplaced modifier

2.   The location of the buildings and other improvements on the property **comply** with all municipal bylaws.

     Subject/verb agreement

3.   **You** as director of Devilsticks Inc. **must** sign and return this form.

     Ungrammatical use of *myself*

4.   We appreciate **your** reviewing this with your senior counsel.

     Possessives

5.   The instructor for the mediation course called for a commitment to a new dispute resolution **paradigm**.

     Spelling

6.   The Board needs to keep itself **apprised** of current developments in government.

     Commonly Confused Words

7.   First Nations fear the Parti Québécois government is based on a narrow colonial paradigm. (First Nations stands for a plural—*members of the First Nations* in Quebec.)

     Subject /verb agreement

8.   It is unconstitutional for another authority (the provincial government, for example) to place any restraint on the level of taxation which the separate board may choose to impose.

     Misplaced modifier

9.   I am one of eight employees in the Administration Branch.

     Ungrammatical use of *myself*

10. Payments are to be divided as follows: half to Elizabeth Gunter and half to Pauline Jackal.

     Numbers guidelines

11. All three districts report that H$_2$S signs are now only on the sites that require them.

     or

     The three districts report that H$_2$S signs which were on improper sites have been removed; only sites which require signs now have them.

     Pronouns and their references

Answers to Standard English Test (cont'd)

12.   . . . the chances of his re-entering . . . about as likely as his . . .

     or

     . . . said that his chances for re-entering the presidential race are about as likely as his . . .

Possessives

13.   In the House of Commons on Monday, Chretien scornfully mocked the re-elections chances of maverick Toronto MP John Nunziata, **whom**, hours earlier, the Prime Minister had banished from the government benches for opposing a budget bill on the grounds the Liberals had failed to meet an election promise to kill the GST. (But better to break this into two sentences: " . . . John Nunziata. Hours earlier, the Prime Minister had banished him from . . .".)

Subjects and Verbs: Agreement Test

Make subjects and verbs match.

1. Persistent beliefs about individual genius and single authors has detracted from the status of collaborative writing. Hidden and repressed elements of collaboration inhabits most academic writing.

2. The Document Management System Project will provide an integrated electronic solution for all the agendas, minutes, referrals and correspondance which is now distributed, piled, and archived in entirely paper form.

3. The location of the buildings and other improvements on the Property complies with all municipal by-laws.

4. Quick thinking and team effort limits effects of floods.

5. Babson's Reports, founded in 1904, appears to be the first investment advisory newsletter.

6. Maintaining partnerships also fall under management of regional issues.

7. Since its 1991 inception, an inter-industry task force representing railways, shippers, tank-car fleet owners and manufacturers have been working to reduce . . .

8. Safety marks communicates by colour and symbol the degree and nature of the hazard of dangerous goods.

Answers to Subject/Verb Agreement Test

1. Persistent beliefs about individual genius and single authors **have** detracted from the status of collaborative writing. Hidden and repressed elements of collaboration **inhabit** most academic writing.

2. . . . which **are** now distributed. . .

3. . . . Property **comply** with . . .

4. . . . team effort **limit** effects . . .

5. Correct: Babson's Reports is the name of a publication.

6. . . . also **falls** . . .

7. . . . manufacturers **has** been working . . .

8. Safety marks **communicate** . . .

Subjects and Verbs: Placement Test

Rewrite the following sentences with the subject and verb together. Note that the plain language rewrites illustrate that plain language is not always a matter of length, but may be a matter of layout, better structured syntax, segmentation, or active voice.

1. Similarly, in *Weaver*, the D.C. Court of Appeals held that the **qualifying word "estimate"** used in conjunction with the stipulations and qualifications that the quantities were "to be used to canvass bids" and not to be the basis for any payment by the ultimate consumer of the products" and that payments would be made "only for actual quantities of work completed" transformed the contract into a requirements contract.

   (68 words)

2. Since frequently these contracts are not in writing, **the courts**, when presented with a dispute over the termination of a contract of employment, **have held** that certain terms concerning termination of an employee are implied in the agreement.

   (38 words)

3. But **attacks**—by groups purporting to work in the public interest—that verge on censorship while at the same time insidiously impugning the ability of so-called average individuals to manage their own affairs, **must be rebuffed**.

   (36 words)

Answers to Subject/Verb Placement Test

1. Similarly, in *Weaver*, the D.C. Court of Appeals **held** that the qualifying word "estimate" **transformed** the contract into a requirements contract when the word was used in conjunction with the following stipulations and conditions:

    (i)   that the quantities were "to be used to canvass bids";
    (ii) that the quantities were "not to be the basis for any payment by the ultimate consumer of the products"; and
    (iii) that payments would be made "only for actual quantities of work completed".[1]

    [75 words]

2. Frequently these contracts are not in writing. When ruling on disputes over termination of employment contracts, **the Courts have held** that the agreement implies certain terms about terminating an employee.
    [Two sentences, subject and verb together, active voice verb, 30 words]

3. But groups who purport to work in the public interest yet verge on censorship must be rebuffed. They insidiously impugn the ability of so-called average individuals to manage their own affairs.
    [Two sentences, subject with qualifier and verb joined, active voice, 37 words]

---

[1] This example from George D. Gopen, Department of English, Duke University, in his paper "Real Plain English: Not a Matter of Length or Jargon", presented to The Legal Writing Institute, University of Puget Sound Law School, Summer, 1992.

Typical Problems in Legal Writing

Problems

Examples

Problems	Examples
Awkward, unnatural language (Legal writers often mimic the language of legislation, the bulk of which is still not in plain language.)	Section 21(2) of the Public Health Act provided that no liability would attach to a community health nurse by reason of any act done or omitted by the nurse in good faith in performing services permitted by the regulations. Section 21(2) of the Public Health Act prohibits liability (being held responsible by law) for community health nurses' services: (i) which are permitted by the regulations, and (ii) which the nurses carry out (or do not carry out) in good faith.
Overly formal language	**Before:** I trust you will find this of some assistance. **After:** I hope this helps. **Before:** Upon reviewing case law on this matter . . . **After:** My review of relevant case law . . .
Confusing vocabulary	**WITHOUT PREJUDICE** (usually at the top of a letter) Mellinkoff says this expression is "confusing nonsense" and should never be used in the presence of non-lawyers (pp. 689-90, Mellinkoff's *Dictionary of American Legal Usage*). Instead, the writer could state at the beginning of the letter that the position promoted in the letter is tentative, not definitive, and thus cannot be raised subsequently in legal proceedings. Or, the expression could be used and asterisked with a definition at the foot of the page.
Incorrect word usage	opined Writers misuse it to mean giving an opinion. Yet the word means forming a judgment on insufficient grounds.

Typical Problems in Legal Writing (cont'd)	
Problems	**Examples**
Redundant coupled synonyms In other words . . .	authorize and empower covenant and agree each and every last will and testament goods and chattels Mellinkoff lists **77** coupled synonyms which he says are "simply redundancies" (*Dictionary of American Legal Usage*, p.129). He refers to the "misplaced reliance on the precision of what has endured".
Legal jargon: verbifying nouns	Additional examinations for discovery were held in 1996. Both Dr. Jane Welch and Dr. Susan Stratt **have also been discovered**. (under a rock?)

Verbose Verbs

Replace the bolded words in the following sentences with a clear, direct verb.

1. The Purchasing Department **performs the ordering function for** office supplies.

2. Harvey **raised the question about** citizens' rights at the meeting.

3. The new administration **placed a limit on** available computer time.

4. The committee **made a decision** to postpone the appropriation of houses.

5. This community project must be **brought to a conclusion** by May 15.

6. One alderman's work **exhibits a tendency** to be sloppy.

7. This LRT accident report **gives an indication** of what went wrong with the rail switching.

8. Poor quality steel **was a contributing factor in** the collapse of the tower.

9. Our department has always **performed the maintenance of** the bicycle and foot bridge.

10. The new staff training binders **were found to meet** the department's needs.

11. We will **conduct a survey of** our clerks to find out their opinions.

12. This report **constitutes a list of** all our past transactions.

13. We will **make the selection of** a candidate as soon as we can.

14. We would like you to **provide an explanation of** your behavior.

15. After you have talked to the drivers, **carry out an inspection of** the equipment.

16. Our lost employee days last year **were in excess of** 300.

17. Her decision **is dependent upon** the findings in your report.

18. This change **amounts to a simplification of** the procedure.

Answers to Verbose Verbs

1. orders

2. Correct. "questioned citizens' rights" changes the meaning.

3. limited

4. decided

5. concluded

6. tends

7. indicates

8. contributed to

9. maintained

10. met

11. survey

12. lists

13. select

14. explain

15. inspect

16. exceeded

17. depends on

18. simplifies

Visual Layout

Improve the visual impact of the following examples by changing the layout.

1. **Before**
    Please credit the Reservoir Engineering travel account #666 434 1111 for two (2) Air BC quick tickets for Edmonton-Calgary, (2 tickets x $102.60) for the total amount of $205.20. Please charge the above mentioned amount to the Production Department Travel Account #012.

    After
    Please transfer a charge for Air BC quick tickets (for Edmonton-Calgary) as follows:

Action Amount	Details	
Credit for two tickets	Reservoir Engineering Travel Account # 666 434 1111 ($102.60 x 2)	$205.20
Debit for two tickets	Production Travel Account # 012 ($102.60 x 2)	$205.20

2. **Before**
    Accordingly, in order to identify whether or not provincial legislation proposed or enacted by the Newfoundland government violates those rights or privileges with respect to separate schools which have constitutional protection, one must examine the *School Ordinance and School Assessment Ordinance* to ascertain, firstly, what rights and privileges are protected, and, secondly, whether the proposed legislation has a "prejudicial effect" with respect to those rights or privileges.

    After
    Therefore, we need to determine whether Newfoundland legislation violates those rights or privileges of separate schools which have constitutional protection. To do so, we refer to the *School Ordinance and School Assessment Ordinance* to find out:

    (i)   what rights and privileges are protected, and,

    (ii) whether the proposed legislation has a "prejudicial effect" on those rights or privileges.

3. **Before**
    The following savings, totalling nearly $4 million, have been identified by the Capacity Expansion project team as contributing to the reduction in the overall costs of the project:

    *   Cost savings of $900,000 for Station piping design using smaller pipe size, which was selected based on the combination of trade-offs between capital and energy costs.
    *   Cost savings of $120,500 for redesign of building renovations to achieve lower capital costs.
    *   Cost savings of $110,000 for bulk purchase of cable and cutting to length, saving normal overage for estimated lengths.
    *   Estimated cost savings of between $1 million and $2 million by use of ice plugs for Line 13 hydro test.
    *   Cost savings of an estimated $1 million by use of sulphur hexafluoride for Line 13 hydro test as compared to other leak detection methods.

After

The Capacity Expansion project team reported the following savings of nearly $4 million in overall project costs:

Activities	Savings
Use of a smaller pipe size based on trade-offs between capital and energy costs	$900, 000
Redesign of building renovations to lower capital costs	$120, 000
Bulk purchase of cable and cutting to length saving overage for estimated lengths	$110, 000
Use of aniline dye for the Line 13 hydro test	$500, 000 (approx.)
Use of ice plugs for Line 13 hydro test	$1 - $2 million (estimated)
Use of sulphur hexaflouride for Line 13 hydro test as compared to other leak detection methods	$1 million (estimated)

4. **Before**

To arrive at the most realistic committed costs for a project, the following process is used: last month's total expended to date from Status Report plus spreadsheet total to the end of the month plus any open purchase orders and FPOs = total committed costs for the project to date.

After

To arrive at the most realistic committed costs for a project, we use the following process:

| Last month's total expended to date (from Status Report) | + | Spreadsheet total to the end of the month | + | Any open purchase orders and FPOs | = | Total committed costs for project to date |

5. **Before**

Since we are concerned with the *materiality* of these unrecorded costs, we set a limit to determine if the accrual will be recorded or not. For example:

If net unrecorded cost (gross accrual × company participation percentage) < materiality limit

the accrual is ignored.

If net unrecorded cost   >   materiality limit

the accrual is recorded.

After
Since we are concerned with the **materiality** of these unrecorded costs, we set a limit to determine whether the accrual will be recorded:

If net unrecorded cost   <   materiality limit, *the accrual is ignored.*

If net unrecorded cost   >   materiality limit, *the accrual is recorded.*
(gross accrual x company
participation percentage)

6.   **Before**
For example, if there are to be payments under the contract, it is important not only to specify when and where they are to be paid, but it may also be relevant to specify the form of payment such as cash, certified cheque, or rank draft; to whom payment is to be delivered; the consequences of failure to pay; the remedies for non-payment and the obligation, if any, to pay interest; at what rate and whether interest is payable both before and after judgment.

(85 words)

After
When relevant, specify the following payment details in a contract:

- when and where payment is to be paid
- whether payment is in cash, certified cheque or bankdraft
- who payment goes to
- what the consequences of not paying are
- what the penalties for non-payment are
- whether interest is to be paid as part of the penalty
- if so, what interest rate, and when interest is due

(66 words)

Bibliography

(This list is far from complete. But it provides seminal information over a broad range of plain language areas.)

Dictionaries
Black's Law Dictionary, 5th ed. (St. Paul, MN: West Publishing Company, 1979).

Garner, Bryan A., *A Dictionary of Modern Legal Usage* (New York: Oxford University Press, 1987).

Maggio, Rosalie, *The Nonsexist Word Finder: A Dictionary of Gender-Free Usage* (Boston: Beacon Press, 1988).

Mellinkoff, David, *Mellinkoff's Dictionary of American Legal Usage* (St. Paul, MN: West Publishing Company, 1992).

Oran, Daniel, *Law Dictionary for Nonlawyers*, 3rd ed. (St. Paul, MN: West Publishing Company, 1991).

Plain English Dictionary (London: Harper Collins Publishers Ltd., 1996).

The Canadian Oxford Dictionary (Toronto: Oxford University Press, 1998).

The New Oxford Dictionary of English (Oxford: Oxford University Press, 1998).

Yogis, John A., *Canadian Law Dictionary* (Woodbury, NY: Barron's Educational Series, Inc., 1983).

Texts
Asprey, Michele M., *Plain Language for Lawyers* (Annandale, Australia: The Federation Press, 1991).

Canadian Bar Association and the Canadian Bankers' Association, *The Decline and Fall of Gobbledygook: Report on Plain Language Documentation* (Ottawa: Canadian Bar Association and the Canadian Bankers' Association, 1990).

Charrow, Veda R. and Myra K. Erhardt, *Clear and Effective Legal Writing* (Toronto: Little, Brown and Company, 1986).

Child, Barbara, *Drafting Legal Documents: Principles and Practices*, 2nd ed., and *Teacher's Manual to Accompany Drafting Legal Documents*, American Casebook Series (St. Paul, MN: West Publishing Company, 1992).

Cutts, Martin, *The Plain English Guide: How to write clearly and communicate better* (New York: Oxford University Press, 1996).

Dick, Robert C., *Legal Drafting in Plain Language* (Toronto: Carswell Thomson Professional Publishing, 1995).

Texts (cont'd)

Felsenfeld, Carl and Alan Siegel, *Writing Contracts in Plain English* (St. Paul, MN: West Publishing Company, 1981).

Goldstein, Tom and Jethro K. Lieberman, *The Lawyer's Guide to Writing Well* (Toronto: McGraw-Hill Publishing Company, 1989).

Gowers, Sir Ernest, *The complete plain words* (Harmondsworth, Australia: Penguin Books Pty Ltd, 1963).

Language and Public Policy, Hugh Park, ed., NCTE Committee on Public Doublespeak (Urbana, IL: National Council of Teachers of English, 1974).

Law Words: 30 Essays on Legal Words and Phrases, Mark Duckworth and Arthur Spyrou, eds. (Sydney, Australia: Centre for Plain Legal Language, 1995).

McCrum, Robert, William Cran and Robert MacNeil, *The Story of English* (New York: Viking Penguin Inc., 1986).

Mellinkoff, David, *Legal Writing: Sense and Nonsense* (St. Paul, MN: West Publishing Company, 1982).

— *The Language of the Law* (Toronto: Little, Brown and Company, 1963).

Perrin, Timothy, *Better Writing for Lawyers* (Toronto: The Law Society of Upper Canada, 1990).

Smith, Robert B., *The Literate Lawyer: Legal Writing and Oral Advocacy* (Toronto: Butterworth & Co. (Canada), 1986).

Weihofen, Henry, *Legal Writing Style* (St. Paul, MN: West Publishing Company, 1980).

Williams, Joseph M., *Style: Ten Lessons in Clarity and Grace*, 3rd ed. (Glenview, IL: Scott, Foresman and Company, 1989).

Woolever, Kristin R., *Untangling the Law: Strategies for Legal Writers* (Belmont, CA: Wadsworth Publishing Company, 1987).

Wydick, Richard C., *Plain English for Lawyers*, 3rd ed. (Durham, NC: Carolina Academic Press, 1994).

Articles

Bell, John A., "Extremist Drafting of Federal Statutes", *The Scribes Journal of Legal Writing*, Vol. 1, 1990, pp. 31-44.

Benson, Robert W., "The End of Legalese: The Game is Over", *New York University Review of Law and Social Change*, Vol. XIII, No. 3, 1984-1985, pp. 519-573.

Cutts, Martin, "Clear writing for lawyers", *English Today: The International Review of the English Language* (New York: Cambridge University Press), Vol. 7, No. 1, January 1991, pp. 40-43.

Articles (cont'd)

Gopen, George D., "The State of Legal Writing: Res Ipsa Loquitur", *Writing in the Business Professions*, Myrna Kogen, ed. (Urbana, IL: National Council of Teachers of English and the Association for Business Communication, 1989), pp. 146-173.

Kimble, Joseph, "Answering the Critics of Plain Language", *The Scribes Journal of Legal Writing*, Vol. 5, 1994-1995, pp. 51-85.

— "Plain English: A Charter for Clear Writing", *Thomas M. Cooley Law Review*, Vol. 9, No. 1, 1992.

— "Writing for Dollars, Writing to Please", *The Scribes Journal of Legal Writing*, Vol. 6, 1996-1997.

Knight, Philip, "New Words and Old Meanings", *The Advocate*, Vol. 56, Part I, January 1998, pp. 27-33.

McArthur, Tom, "The pedigree of plain English", *English Today: The International Review of the English Language* (New York: Cambridge University Press), Vol. 7, No. 3, July 1991, pp. 13-19.

Mowat, Christine, "Buddhists, Running, and Plain Language in Calgary (Part One)", *Michigan Bar Journal* (Lansing, MI: The State Bar of Michigan), July 1994, pp. 696-697.

— "Buddhists, Running, and Plain Language in Calgary (Part Two)", *Michigan Bar Journal* (Lansing, MI: The State Bar of Michigan), August 1994, pp. 828-831.

Mowat, Christine M., "Alderman or Councillor — Is it a Tempest in a Teapot?", *LawNow* (Edmonton: Legal Studies Program, University of Alberta), December 1995/January 1996, p. 41.

— "A plain language writer considers consideration", *LawNow* (Edmonton: Legal Studies Program, University of Alberta), April/May 1995, p. 40.

— "Plain Language: Gone Underground?", *LawNow* (Edmonton: Legal Studies Program, University of Alberta), October/November 1995, p. 38.

— "With All Due Respect to Legalese", *LawNow* (Edmonton: Legal Studies Program, University of Alberta), August/September 1995, p. 45.

Mowat, Christine M. and Margaret James, "A Plain Language Audit on 'The Decline and Fall of Gobbledygook: Report on Plain Language Documentation'", *Papers from the Proceedings of the Canadian Corporate Counsel Association Third Annual Meeting* (Toronto: Emond Montgomery Publications Limited, 1991).

Stephens, Cheryl, "U.S. Pushing Forward with Plain Language", *LawNow* (Edmonton: Legal Studies Program, University of Alberta), October/November, 1998, p. 44.

Other Publications

A Plain Language Report - Language Issues for Service Agencies & Their Clients (Vancouver: The Plain Language Institute of British Columbia).

Other Publications (cont'd)

A Plain Language Report - Critical Opinions: The Public's View of Lawyers' Documents (Vancouver: The Plain Language Institute of British Columbia).

A Plain Language Report - Critical Opinions: The Public's View of Legal Documents (Vancouver: The Plain Language Institute of British Columbia).

A Plain Language Report - Editorial and Design Stylebook (Vancouver: The Plain Language Institute of British Columbia).

Bell, John A., *Dispatch*, League for Literate Laws, P.O. Box 2101, Fort Davis, TX 79734-2101, USA, e-mail: litlaw@overland.net (newsletter on legislative drafting).

Cutts, Martin, *Lucid Law*, Plain Language Commission (Stockport, UK: Spectrum Press, 1994).

Eagleson, Robert D., *Writing in Plain English* (Canberra, Australia: Australian Government Publishing Service Press, 1990).

Felker, Daniel B. ed., *Document Design: A Review of the Relevant Research* (Washington: Document Design Center - American Institutes for Research, 1989).

Felker, Daniel et al, *Guidelines for document designers*, Document Design Project (Washington: Document Design Center - American Institutes for Research, November 1981).

Fisher, David, *Legally Correct Fairy Tales: Bedtime Classics Translated into the Legalese* (New York: Warner Books, Inc., 1996).

Free Your Words: A Quick and Easy Guide to Clear Legal Writing (Vancouver: The Plain Language Institute of British Columbia).

Garner, Bryan A., *Guidelines for Drafting and Editing Court Rules* (Washington: Administrative Office of the United States Courts, 1996).

Just Language Conference (1992), *Proceedings: Just Language Conference 1992* (Vancouver: The Plain Language Institute of British Columbia, 1992).

Miles, John, *Design for Desktop Publishing* (San Francisco: Chronicle Books, 1987).

Murawski, Thomas A., *Writing Readable Regulations* (Colorado Springs, self-published, 1998).

Plain Language — Clear and Simple (Ottawa: Multiculturalism and Citizenship Canada). [Available through Associated Bookstores and other booksellers or by mail from Canada Communication Group - Publishing, Ottawa, ON K1A 0S9. Catalogue no. Ci53-3/3-1991E; ISBN 0-660-14185-X]

Plain Language Forms Guidelines: Creating user-friendly forms, published by the Government of Alberta, March 1993 ISBN: 0-7732-1075-X.

Plain Language Resource Centre Catalogue (Ottawa: Multiculturalism and Citizenship Canada, September 1992). [Available at: Departmental Library, Department of

Human Resources Development Canada, 140 Promenade du Portage, Phase IV, Level I, Hull, Quebec K1A 0J9 (819) 994-2604]

Plain Language Wills, The Continuing Legal Education Society of British Columbia Plain Language Project, #150, 900 Howes Street, Vancouver, BC V6Z 2M4.

Redish, Janice C., *How to Write Regulations and other Legal Documents in Clear English* (Washington: Document Design Center - American Institutes for Research, September 1991).

Tufte, Edward R., *The Visual Display of Quantitative Information* (Cheshire, CT: Graphics Press, 1983).

The *Michigan Bar Journal* has been running a plain language column since 1984. Here is a sampling of the subject coverage:
Aslanian-Bedikian, Mary, "Clear Expression in Labor Arbitration", *Michigan Bar Journal* (Lansing, MI: The State Bar of Michigan, November 1984), pp. 1068-1069.

Benson, Robert W., "Plain English Comes to Court", *Michigan Bar Journal* (Lansing, MI: The State Bar of Michigan, March 1989), pp. 302-303.

Bruno, J.C. and James S. Rosenfeld, "Wither Whereas — The Legal Implications of Recitals", *Michigan Bar Journal* (Lansing, MI: The State Bar of Michigan, July 1988), pp. 634-635.

Garner, Bryan A., "An Excerpt From *The Elements of Legal Style*: Rooting Out Sexism" *Michigan Bar Journal* (Lansing, MI: The State Bar of Michigan, September 1991), pp. 942-943.

Hathaway, George, H., "Plain English Acknowledgment Forms", *Michigan Bar Journal* (Lansing, MI: The State Bar of Michigan, March 1991), pp. 338-340.

— "Plain English in Michigan Insurance Policies", *Michigan Bar Journal* (Lansing, MI: The State Bar of Michigan, August 1986), pp. 813-815.

— "Plain English in Residential Real-Estate Listing Contracts", *Michigan Bar Journal* (Lansing, MI: The State Bar of Michigan, December 1991), pp. 1320-1322.

Grammar and Usage
Bryson, Bill, *The Mother Tongue: English and How It Got That Way* (New York: William Morrow & Company, Inc.), 1990.

Freeman, Morton S., *The Grammatical Lawyer* (Philadelphia: American Law Institute American Bar Association Committee on Continuing Professional Education, 1979).

Joseph, Albert, *Executive Guide to Grammar* (Cleveland: International Writing Institute, Inc., 1987).

Sabin, William A. et al, *The Gregg Reference Manual*, Fourth Canadian Edition (Toronto: McGraw-Hill Ryerson Limited, 1992).

The New Fowler's Modern English Usage, Third Edition (Oxford: Oxford University Press, 1996).

Readability
Carey, Robert F., *Reading - What can be measured?*, 2nd ed. (Newark, DE: International Reading Association Inc., 1986).

Fry, Edward B., "A Readability Formula for Short Passages", *Journal of Reading* (Newark, DE: International Reading Association Inc., May 1990), pp. 594-597.

Pearson, P. David, *Handbook of Reading Research* (New York: Longman Inc., 1984).

The Southam Literacy Report, *"Broken Words: Why Five Million Canadians are Illiterate"* (Toronto: Southam Communications, 1987).

Zakaluk, Beverley L. and S. Jay Samuels, *Readability: Its Past, Present and Future* (Newark, DE: International Reading Association Inc., 1988).

International Journal
CLARITY, a movement to simplify legal language (Patron: Rt. Hon. Sir Christopher Staughton). This is *the* journal to subscribe to. A quarterly, 50-page journal, it is excellent! Its members and authors span Australia, Canada, England, Hong Kong, India, Singapore, South Africa, USA and more. For information contact:

Mark Adler
74 South Street, Dorking RH4 2HD, Surrey, UK
Tel: 01306 [44 1306] 741055 Fax: 741066
e-mail: adler@adler.demon.co.uk

Internet Resources
Lawyers for Literacy
http://www.cle.bc.ca/literacy

Plain Language Action Network
A U.S. government plain language web site that provides supportive services and examples of clear regulations, letters, forms, and manuals
http://www.plainlanguage.gov

Plain Language Online Center
http://www.web.net/~raporter/

Plain Language Online Training
Canada's own online training for plain language produced by the National Literacy Secretariat
http://www.web.net/~plain/PlainTrain

Rapport Plain Language Resources
http://rapport.bc.ca

Index